The Religious and the Political

While the relationships between ethics and religion, and violence and politics, are of enduring interest, the interface between religion and violence is one of the most problematic features of the contemporary world. Following in the tradition of Max Weber's historical and comparative study of religions, this book explores the many ways in which religion and politics are both combined and separated across different world religions and societies. Through a variety of case studies including the monarchy, marriage, law and conversion, Bryan S. Turner explores different manifestations of secularization, and how the separation of church and state is either compromised or abandoned. He considers how different states manage religion in culturally and religiously diverse societies and concludes with a discussion of the contemporary problems facing the liberal theory of freedom of religion. The underlying theoretical issue is the conditions for legitimacy of rule in modern societies experiencing global changes.

BRYAN S. TURNER is the Presidential Professor of Sociology and the Director of the Committee on Religion at the Graduate Center, the City University of New York, and the Director of the Centre for Religion and Society at the University of Western Sydney. He is the author of *Religion and Modern Society* (Cambridge, 2011) and the editor of *The Cambridge Dictionary of Sociology* (Cambridge, 2006).

The Religious
and the Political

A Comparative Sociology of Religion

BRYAN S. TURNER

CAMBRIDGE
UNIVERSITY PRESS

CAMBRIDGE UNIVERSITY PRESS
Cambridge, New York, Melbourne, Madrid, Cape Town,
Singapore, São Paulo, Delhi, Mexico City

Cambridge University Press
The Edinburgh Building, Cambridge CB2 8RU, UK

Published in the United States of America by Cambridge University Press, New York

www.cambridge.org
Information on this title: www.cambridge.org/9780521675314

First published 2013

Printed and bound in the United Kingdom by the MPG Books Group

A catalogue record for this publication is available from the British Library

Library of Congress Cataloguing in Publication data
Turner, Bryan S.
The religious and the political : a comparative sociology of religion / Bryan S. Turner.
    pages   cm
Includes bibliographical references.
ISBN 978-0-521-85863-2 (hardback) – ISBN 978-0-521-67531-4 (paperback)
1. Religion and politics.   2. Religion and sociology.   I. Title.
BL65.P7T87   2013
322′.1–dc23

                                                                    2012036782

ISBN 978-0-521-85863-2 Hardback
ISBN 978-0-521-67531-4 Paperback

Contents

Acknowledgements

Many chapters in this volume, especially with respect to the notion of 'popular religion', were first presented as working papers to the Religion Committee weekly seminars at the Graduate Center, the City University of New York. My colleagues in the Department of Sociology and the organizing group within the Religion Committee have offered a wonderful platform for testing these ideas. The debates with colleagues were invaluable. I would like to thank John Torpey and John Shean, with whom I read Robert Bellah's *Religion in human evolution* in preparation for the chapters on China and Japan. Berna Zengin Arslan joined with me to write Chapter 11 while she was a post-doctoral fellow at the Graduate Center. I would also like to thank colleagues in the Centre for Religion and Society at the University of Western Sydney, especially Adam Possamai and Julia Howell, for their support. Elena Knox of the University of Western Sydney was an invaluable editor in preparing the references. My wife Nguyen Kim Hoa was my constant companion through these labours.

Introduction

Religion and politics are two fundamental dimensions of human society, and yet they are often at loggerheads. Religion appears to belong to a different realm, signifying matters that are permanent and enduring, residing beyond the everyday. Politics appears to involve the secular struggle for power and influence, being driven by interest. I use this verb (to appear) because in fact religion and politics are almost inevitably entwined and they are both deeply concerned with the control or regulation of everyday affairs. Max Weber at the very beginning of *The sociology of religion* (1966b) said that religion is fundamentally concerned with the things of this world such as health and wealth. He went on to argue that politics inevitably involves power and violence, but that religion (at least organized forms of religion) also involves symbolic violence. Excommunication would be one obvious example of symbolic violence. These claims may not appear to be immediately self-evident, since surely religion also involves the gentle cultivation of the soul, while politics involves the development of the citizen in the public domain. Weber's sociology is ultimately tragic because religion as a universal ethic of brotherly love is inevitably at odds with 'the world', and religion is almost always compromised or defeated by the forces of this world.

In classical thought this relationship between politics and religion was analysed in terms of an important distinction between state-craft and soul-craft. The Good Society required both a successful management of public affairs through the wise leadership of the state and an inner discipline of the citizen to harness passion and to direct interest for the public good. In the modern world we are in danger of losing both. With the growth of the mass media in electoral democracies, politicians are driven by the need for high ratings in opinion polls, and seek celebrity rather than wisdom. We judge them in terms of their performance in economic terms such as the rate of unemployment, and rather less in terms of their religious beliefs and their moral standing. Their policies are typically short term, because in democracies they need to win elections,

1

and hence their political tactics are often based on the findings of the most recent focus groups rather than on the long-term needs of society. The lack of serious attention to the environment as a long-term strategy and willingness to support 'fracking' for oil and gas despite its negative effect on the water supply in the United States is a case in point. The idea of 'politics as a vocation' in Weber's famous lecture of 1919 has been overtaken by 'politics as a game' (Weber, 2009a), and all too often citizens are driven by consumerism rather than by self-discipline. Perhaps only a simultaneous revival of the religious as collective practice and the political as vocation can restore the importance of 'the public' to our otherwise exclusively private lives?

This book addresses the core issues of rulership in classical politics: the One, the Many and the Other. Politics concerns the enduring question: can a unity be forged out of the inevitable diversity of a society that has arisen with the Many, especially when in modern societies with the growth of ethnic diversity and multiculturalism the majority often believes it is confronted by minorities (the Other)? In classical antiquity diversity in the *polis* was thought to emerge from family and gender differences, namely particularistic interests that appeared to confront the unity that underpinned the emergence of the city-state. With conquest there was another diversity arising from the presence of slaves and strangers. In *Fear of diversity* Arlene Saxonhouse (1992) proposed that the very foundation of politics had its origin in these differences which threatened the possibility of the One. Heraclitus spoke of the *nomoi* or the walls of the city as the basis for the rule of the One, but also saw this principle of unity as a metaphor for the order of nature. This idea is the root of the sociological concept of *anomie* or a crisis in the normative ordering of the modern city. In the modern world social diversity has increasingly focused on religious differences emerging from the presence of minorities whose existence in the mega-city is a consequence of a pattern of global labour migration. Jacques Derrida (2000) in a series of seminars and in conversation with Anne Dufourmantelle around the question of hospitality in Greek politics explored the issue of the Foreigner and the City, and the emergence of a pact with such strangers. This democratic debate about the Other and the Many has since 9/11 focused almost exclusively on the growth of Muslim minorities in the West, but in fact the divisions around religious identity are more general than simply a conflict between Christianity and Islam. Indeed, excessive attention to Islam by the media has become part of the problem rather than a contribution to any solution.

Religious conflict may occur when incommensurable claims to a special way of life (the Truth) collide in the same space, and when the secular framework of the state (such as the rule of law and egalitarian citizenship) fails to secure a level playing field between minorities and the majority. These tensions are often magnified when religion becomes deeply embedded in ethnic identity and is further galvanized by the force of nationalism. Many of these conflicts are the legacy of European colonialism, especially in South Asia and Africa, where state borders have little relevance to the complex geography of ethnic communities on the ground. In *The new religious intolerance* Martha Nussbaum (2012) considers many examples of religious intolerance, but the preponderance of cases is concerned with intolerance towards Islam. In fact, her argument about democracies typically comes down to the idea of a 'level playing field', namely that one basic requirement of tolerance is that all religions should be treated equally (by the state) in the public arena, unless there is 'compelling state interest' to do otherwise. She offers many examples where the state in democracies appears to support majorities against minorities, thereby failing to protect the need for tolerance in multicultural and diverse societies. One example concerns permission for religious minorities to construct their own places of worship. In Switzerland a popular referendum voted to ban the building of minarets despite the fact that only 4 out of 150 mosques have minarets. In Chicago the zoning board of DuPage County turned down a plan to build a mosque at Willowbrook despite the fact that the board had already allowed the construction of a Buddhist meditation centre, a Chinmaya mission and an Orthodox church. However, her primary example of discrimination through urban planning is the case of Park51 in New York, in close proximity to Ground Zero (Nussbaum, 2012: 188–239), where the plan by Muslims to build an inter-faith cultural centre in which there would be a facility for Muslim prayer caused a national debate. This issue is complex because even people who supported the site in principle on the basis of tolerance thought that the choice of this specific site was insensitive, and probably unwise. However, Nussbaum points out that the same urban area contained strip clubs, an off-track betting facility, liquor stores, restaurants and so forth. Given that Ground Zero has become a sacred space, why not also object to such facilities rather than concentrating on Park51? Nussbaum proposes that we need to respond to such conflicts not just with laws and public vigilance, but with imagination, insight and sympathy. I propose that we call this imaginative response 'cosmopolitan virtue', which I shall discuss in the final chapter, suggesting that in complex societies we require some degree of personal irony in order to be able to understand our own prejudices in the light of other cultures. Cosmopolitanism in modern societies is one possible response to the eruption of the Many and the challenge of the Other.

With globalization, these historical tensions are further inflamed by conflict over scarce resources, especially the material resources of oil and water. Social conflict is often magnified in circumstances where a majority feels it is threatened by a minority; much of the Islamophobia in Europe has assumed this character. In both Norway and Britain Muslims represent a minority of the population, but in both societies right-wing movements – the Norwegian Defence League and the English Defence League – have drawn enough support, typically from the urban working class, to be able to suggest that there is a cultural threat from the alleged growth of the *shari'a*. Martha Nussbaum also draws attention to differences in response to minorities in the United States and Europe. Societies such as the United States, Canada and Australia are by origin societies of migration and difference, but in European societies membership is defined more in terms of a shared ethno-religious culture than of shared political values. In the United States there has been relatively little public hostility to veiling by Muslim women, whereas in parts of Germany, the Netherlands, Spain and Belgium there are regulations preventing public employees from wearing the headscarf. However, in 2011–12 in the build-up to the selection of Republican presidential candidates there was growing evidence of hostility to the *shari'a* in the United States. These developments raise obvious questions about the future of multi-culturalism and about the role of civil religion in providing a cultural framework within which religious diversity need not be corrosive of the social fabric. Some of these issues relating to the law and religion are discussed in Chapters 11 and 13.

In this volume I argue that in discussion of the political we also have to take into account the core issue of religion, which involves the continuous reproduction of the social through a 'chain of memory' (Hervieu-Léger, 2000). In classical sociology Émile Durkheim saw the role of religion as forging a basis for social solidarity in human societies. Indeed, more fundamentally in his *The elementary forms of religious life*

(2001), the social can be said to have erupted out of the sacred. He took as his basic model for the contrast between the sacred and the profane the symbolic world of the Aborigines of northern central Australia, but modern society no longer enjoys the dense solidarity – or 'mechanical solidarity', in Durkheim's terminology – of such forms of the One. Durkheim never found an entirely satisfactory answer to the question: where are the sources of social solidarity in modern complex societies? He was influenced by Jean-Jacques Rousseau's idea of a 'civil religion', which Rousseau had described in 1762 in the conclusion to his *Social contract* (1973). For Rousseau Christianity could not satisfy the needs of a modern society, and he envisaged a secularized form of religious belief and practice that could provide citizens with a common framework. In contemporary sociology this idea was developed to great effect by Robert Bellah in a variety of articles on the civil religion in America (Bellah and Tipton, 2006). The issue of civil religion is explored in Chapter 7 in the context of a debate about the sources of political legitimacy in democratic societies.

However, in a complex modern society, especially where there has been some fragmentation of the social world, the idea that civil religion could balance the domination of One and the democratic diversity of the Many, while also including the Other, looks unpromising as a solution to the problems of late modernity. In the contemporary world the prospect of a 'clash of civilizations' (Huntington, 1997) is an obvious threat to civil stability, and the rise of religious conflict looks as likely as the flowering of civil religion. There are many sources of diversity in Western societies: the growth of substantial minorities, the political experiment with multiculturalism, the development of legal pluralism, the fragmentation of national educational curricula by the development of separate religious schools, and the privatization of many public utilities. In much of Europe we have also weakened or destroyed public institutions that once contributed to a public world or 'commonwealth' such as universal military conscription, a common and unified system of taxation, the common law, the Christian calendar, the welfare state and public broadcasting. There is a widespread belief among sociologists that the communal roots of society have been undermined by urbanization, secularization and the decline of the family (Nisbet, 1990). The emphasis on the market to increase efficiency, expand consumer choice and control prices (assuming these objectives can be realized by free markets) does nothing to create social solidarity. There are of course many policies to counteract such tendencies towards social fragmentation including support for 'group rights', more flexible forms of citizenship, more generous conditions for the naturalization of migrants, legislation against discrimination on racial grounds and, more broadly, the promotion of normative belief systems that celebrate diversity such as cosmopolitanism (Delanty, 2009). By extension, it is argued that human rights offer certain solutions to communal tensions that are institutionally superior to the social rights of citizenship, which have an inevitably exclusionary character. The 'right to have rights' is seen by many philosophers as the baseline for recognition of membership in a shared community (Benhabib, 2004). In Chapter 3 I look at the history of rights against the background of religious conflict and war. Recent literature on the history of human rights has drawn attention to the importance of Christianity in shaping the contents of human rights values and legislation. In particular, I argue that a sociology of human rights regards these rights as manifestations of what Norbert Elias (2000) called 'the civilizing process'. We can regard the expansion of human rights as an example of 'the civilizing process', offsetting the negative consequences of Huntington's 'clash of civilizations'. There are many examples to suggest that violence (as illustrated by homicide, rape, lynching, domestic violence and so forth) has declined in the late twentieth century as a result of this civilizing process (Pinker, 2011). Nevertheless, the balance between social solidarity, social differentiation and cultural diversity is unstable, if not precarious.

The deeper issue behind both the advocacy and criticisms of human rights, cosmopolitanism and multiculturalism as responses to the Other is the question of secularization. Taking the separation of church and state as a minimal definition of secularization, we can ask whether this constitutional separation, which to some extent had its origins in the Treaty of Westphalia in 1648, is an essential precondition of social harmony. Is liberal secularity capable of securing a peace between contending traditions in the public sphere? There are many who argue that, while liberal secularism achieved a religious peace between Protestants and Catholics, this version of secularization is no longer relevant to a modern society in which there may be an array of religious traditions that cannot be accommodated within these liberal conditions (Spinner-Halevy, 2005). One liberal answer to these dilemmas was developed by John Rawls who, especially in *Political liberalism* (1993), identified a set of conditions that must be met by any community that aspires to be a decent, liberal society with a system of meaningful deliberation and consultation between citizens. This framework has been further elaborated by Jürgen Habermas (2006) in the idea of a post-secular society as a framework for situating religion in the public sphere. In such a society secularists have to take religious beliefs seriously and religious citizens have to give public reasons for their faith. This form of dialogue can contribute to democratic cultures through mutual recognition.

Liberalism can be regarded as an ideal or even utopian characterization of the relationship between religion and politics. In this study we need to keep in mind two significant historical departures from this liberal model, namely Caesarism and theocracy. When the state draws religion into its own sphere we get a form of combined power, or 'Caesarism'. When organized religion draws the state into its orbit we have a theocratic power. Throughout this work, but especially in Part II, I consider a number of different case studies in order to grasp the complexity of the relations between political power and religious institutions, including the Buddhist monarchies of Thailand, Confucianism and Neo-Confucianism in China, Japanese Shinto and emperor worship, and authoritarianism from the Russian state to the soft authoritarianism of Singapore. To take one example, Chinese Communism tried to destroy the religious traditions of ancient China. In particular, Maoism sought to weed out the legacy of Confucianism and feudalism, but paradoxically Mao himself became a god-like figure and the Cultural Revolution had all the hallmarks of religious enthusiasm. In modern-day China I explore in Chapter 9 the revival of religions following the reforms of Deng Xiaoping and also pay attention to the regulation of 'cults' such as Falun Gong. In the West, liberalism attempts to solve these issues by separating religion and politics, but I shall attempt to demonstrate in this volume that the state adopts a 'management of religion' as a strategy to avoid religious conflict in the public sphere. The state management of religious activity, which has been historically described in the Christian tradition as Erastianism, is discussed in the final chapter as a response to problems relating to civil conflict.

In *Religion and modern society* (Turner, 2011c) I explored many contemporary issues surrounding citizenship, secularization and religion. Given the problems raised by religious and cultural identities in societies with sizeable minorities, the state has exercised a management of religion to secure social peace. This strategy involves, as a minimum, various legislative responses such as precluding hate speech in public or censorship of controversial publications; but these interventions can go far deeper into religious life by regulating religious practice – most dramatically by banning the Muslim *burqa* in public spaces. In the final chapter I argue that in the United States and Great Britain the intervention of the state into religious dress, tribunals, and leadership in Muslim communities has the effect of creating an 'Official Islam' (Rascoff, 2012).

In Chapter 1 I take up the issue of the 'fear of diversity' by looking at the Norwegian tragedy of July 2011 when Anders Behring Breivik killed seventy-seven people on the island of Utoya. In his Manifesto he imagined this attack as part of a crusade against Muslims and a warning against the imminent Islamization of European civilization. This tragic event provides me with the pretext for a more general consideration of the political problem in modern Europe, where a majority feels threatened by a minority and where as a result there has been widespread increase in state security and often a departure from previous government policies in support of multicultural diversity. In Chapter 2 I return to the intellectual roots of many of these debates, namely Max Weber's theory of charisma. This sociological framework is developed by looking at aspects of popular religion and the state in the struggle between Fascism and socialism in Italy in the first half of the twentieth century. The chapter looks at two examples – Mussolini and Padre Pio – to develop the theory of charisma via an inquiry into the body and manifestations of the sacred. Both the state and the official religious hierarchy attempt to control the manifestation of charisma, which is inevitably a challenge to established conventions. The body also plays a large part in popular religious movements, where the embodiment of religious charisma is a special source of power. This discussion raises a general problem regarding the burial of charismatic figures.

In Chapter 3 I turn to the history of citizenship by taking three formative moments in the growth of rights: the writing of St Augustine's *The City of God*; the signing of the Treaty of Westphalia; and the proclamation of the Declaration of Human Rights by the United Nations. The background to the emergence of rights has often been violent – the sacking of Rome, the Wars of Religion, and the Second World War – and each of these texts addressed issues about the Other. In the case of Augustine, it was the Jews; in the Westphalian Treaty, the conflict between Catholics and Protestants; and in the twentieth century, the industrialization of warfare.

In Part II I continue with the theme of diversity and unity in the contemporary world by turning attention to a set of comparative case studies which show how and why the state intervenes in religious life in Western societies. These chapters cover the interaction between religion and politics in the creation of kingship, taking as my illustration the rituals that have surrounded investiture. Coronation rituals in the United Kingdom provide a useful example of the role of public liturgies, and raise further questions about the role of religion in public life and in secular society. The persistence of constitutional monarchies presents troublesome questions about the separation of church and state. Some of these issues can be usefully explored by reference to the secular constitution of the United States. Chapter 4 recognizes the fact that liturgical practice has declined in Western democracies and prayer has become increasingly private and personal, playing little role in secular societies as a public activity. Chapter 5 examines the modern paradox of marriage. In the modern world engagement and marriage are typically interpreted as the outcomes of individual romantic choices that are private, but marriage as an institution is also profoundly public. The state has had an interest in marriage for the obvious reason that it is an institution for legitimate reproduction and the stable transition of property. However, many societies have now reached 'sub-optimal fertility'. With low and declining fertility rates, many states are closely and directly involved in monitoring the sex lives of citizens with a view to stimulating higher fertility. With secularization, marriage is both declining and changing profoundly – for example, to include same-sex marriage. In the absence of adoption, same-sex marriage will by definition not contribute to national fertility rate, and we might reasonably ask: why is the state concerned with such arrangements? One trivial answer is that any redefinition of marriage gives rise to considerable conflict in society between evangelical Christians who vigorously oppose these developments and liberal lobby groups who see gay rights as consistent with individual liberties. Same-sex marriage is defended mainly on the grounds that gender should not be a consideration in a marriage contract between two consenting adults. Why not go further in redefining marriage? Recent legislation in the state of New York has recognized gay marriage. Could a liberal society go further to recognize polygamy? In any case American society has a history of polygamy in various stages of the evolution of Mormonism and in contemporary sectarian offshoots such as the Fundamentalist Church of Jesus Christ

of Latter-Day Saints. Feminist critics also argue that polygamy is difficult to regulate, because men will often form secret marriages with other
women or have mistresses, thereby creating a form of de facto or
informal polygamy. These developments raise an issue about the redefinition of marriage by the state. Can the state and the churches work
together, for example in supporting 'covenant marriage', and should the
definition of marriage be handed over to the churches?

Chapter 6 looks at the problem of conversion as a disruptive force
in both traditional and modern societies. Because religious identity is
powerfully interconnected with political identity, religious conversion
has inevitable consequences for secular affairs. For example, the Jews
were a problematic minority in the history of Western Christendom, and
many attempts were made to convert them by the force of law. There
are many other examples of conflicts surrounding conversion, and I take
as a modern example the problem of Christian conversions in Indonesia.
While conversion raises questions about public identities, there is also
a debate about the authenticity of conversions that emerge as a result
of legal constraint or the threat of violence. This chapter also examines
many of the theoretical issues arising in the study of conversion. Through
a discussion of the legacy of the pragmatic psychology of William James,
I consider modern debates about the intentionality and emotionality of
conversion. In the anthropology of religion the notion of conversion has
been repeatedly challenged by anthropologists, who claim that these
features (intentionality, individualism and emotionality) are not general
or universal aspects of religious change. The history of Christian missions
in Asia and Australia raises interesting problems about 'tradition' and
'religion' as general categories. The chapter concludes by looking at the
problem of free will (or intentionality) in Christian doctrine, pointing to
ironic similarities between Augustine's theory of habit and intention and
Pierre Bourdieu's ideas of habitus, embodiment and hexis.

Chapter 7 examines issues about legitimacy in modern societies in
which the authority of natural law and the church has been replaced
by a dependence on more secular sources of authority. Max Weber's
theory of authority or legitimate domination (charisma, tradition and
legal rationality) is developed into a model that argues that modern
legitimate domination can draw on three basic sources: legitimacy,
legality and performance. In modernity these three are typically secular
forms of legitimacy, but they are confronted by serious limitations. In
modern democracies citizens are suspicious of claims to legitimacy and

legality, and instead ask whether their governments can deliver wealth and security, regardless of whether they are legitimate and legal. The capacity of governments to secure performative legitimacy is seriously hampered by a range of conditions (economic, demographic and political) that have in recent years conspired to produce low incomes, poor employment opportunities, inadequate pensions and limited welfare provisions. The chapter concludes by examining whether civil religion in the United States provides a basis for legitimacy.

Part III turns to a comparative study of politics and religion in order to consider the theme of One–Few–Many with examples from outside the West. It could be argued that many of these issues relating to church and state, to conversion and citizenship, and to orthodoxy and sectarian heterodoxy only make sense within the context of the Jewish–Christian–Islamic traditions. These 'Abrahamic religions' have a high God, notions of idolatry, concepts of apostasy and so forth which are absent in most 'Asian religions'. There is one major issue in this discussion of the cultural specificity of Western concepts, which is to ask whether there are any 'religions' in the East. Both Durkheim and Weber were interested in the fact that pristine or original Buddhism rejects the idea that gods can have any ultimate significance or causal agency. These divinities are ultimately merely illusions of the human mind. Is Buddhism originally an atheist philosophy rather than a religion in the Western sense? The relationship between Hinduism and Buddhism was always open and porous. While Buddhism is thought to have radicalized the ethics of the religion of the Brahmins, there was also continuity. 'Hinduism' is largely an invention of Western intervention in South Asia, and hence it makes more sense to talk about the religious traditions of the Brahmins as the foundation of South Asian spirituality. Against this general notion of cultural specificity, I claim that, especially with globalization, one can find parallel issues concerning the political and the religious in Asia. In Chapter 8 I consider Weber's notion of 'acosmitic love' or 'world-denying love' in both Brahminical and Buddhist traditions. In the South Asian story of the dialogue between Krishna and Arjuna we can find one of the persistent themes of civilization more generally, namely how to control and harness violence. Looking at Buddhism in Chapter 8, I consider the history of the monastic tradition (the *sangha*) and the monarchy. There is an established Buddhist tradition that the virtue of the monarch is illustrated by his attempts to purify monastic culture. However, the exercise of kingship requires violent means to defend the society, which makes possible the lives of religious people who embrace an ethic of non-violence. For Weber this is a permanent paradox of social life.

The problem of defining religion and understanding its relationship to politics is even more problematic in the case of Confucianism and Taoism, which I consider in Chapter 9. One can regard Confucianism as a state ideology which proclaimed the importance of the rule of virtue in establishing a social order. The unity of the state against the Many and the Other was to be secured by the coercive role of morality. While Confucianism may be seen in this light as a political ideology rather than a religious doctrine of salvation, the popularity of Taoist belief and practice in China can be recognized as a popular religion of the masses. In Chapter 10 I consider the history of religion in Japan and the relationship between Shinto and a national sense of cultural uniqueness. Japan has been resistant to cultural diversity or to multiplicity (to use the vocabulary of this study). Of all the Asian societies, the Japanese state played a major role in establishing a cultural unity, especially through state Shinto. I conclude by arguing that Japan has been characterized by exceptionalism in the age of globalization, namely that it continues to resist the Other by close regulation of immigration.

In Chapter 11 Dr Berna Zengin Arslan and I consider a critical example of modern secularization, namely the history of Turkey from the decline of the Ottoman Empire to the growing influence of Sunni Islam with the election of the Justice and Development Party. While many observers regard this development as the restoration of religion and the disruption of secularism, we argue that Turkey offers a further example of the management of religion. We question the notion that secularization has been the dominant trend since the time of Mustafa Kemal Atatürk. In contesting this assumption we concentrate on the history and role of the Diyanet (the Directorate of Religious Affairs), which is, we argue, yet another illustration of the management of religion by the state. As a result we develop an argument against the conventional view of republican Turkey as a deeply and uniformly secular society. Critical scholars have remained sceptical about the use of the term *laïcité*, which was favoured by the Kemalist elite to suggest that it was equivalent to French secularism. An examination of Turkish religious groups and institutions in civil society suggests that religion does not function as an autonomous sphere outside the state's control. For example, the state has not been neutral in its relationship with minority religions such as the Alevis.

In the final part I reflect on some of the major lessons of this volume from the perspective of contradictions between the religious and the political. In traditional religious studies and early anthropology it was commonplace to make a distinction between high and low traditions. In Chapter 12 I explore the possibility that in modern societies all religions are popular. In a modern society the state typically manages religion, but it cannot entirely control it. The rise of the Internet and the erosion of established churches have created a religious market in which popular religion can flourish. The result is, by definition, a burgeoning of unorthodox, hybrid and localized forms of religion. These groups are often referred to as post-institutional, post-secular and hyper-religious (Possamai, 2012). The growth of popular religion in the United States is the most significant example, where mega-churches and the prosperity gospel are vehicles of popular involvement, combining religion, corporate capitalist values and popular politics. The argument of the chapter is that there is an elective affinity between popular forms of religiosity and popular democracy, in which religious and secular leaders employ the same technologies and similar values to reach out to a large public. In both cases we might speak of the emergence of religio-political celebrities, who command large salaries in connection with global markets. But isn't popular religion the epitome of religious freedom?

In the final chapter I examine some of the issues around equality and individualism. John Stuart Mill is relevant both to the idea of a dominant popular religion and to the centrality of freedom of religion to a modern democracy. Mill, having absorbed the lessons of Alexis de Tocqueville's *Democracy in America* (2004), believed that a wide and popular political franchise would not be acceptable in Great Britain until the masses had received an education to allow their political preferences to be based on rational knowledge. A democracy based on an uneducated and uncivilized electorate would produce an oppressive conformity, stifling creative beliefs and values. Certainly in the twentieth century the mass media have been responsible for the trivialization of politics and the creation of a cult of celebrities. In Britain and America the major TV channels play a large role in sustaining popularity polls as the basis for the election of prime ministers and presidents. Politicians have to compete in a dynamic market for votes, and hence they have to cultivate the media. These developments are taking place in a context where the educational level of the general public is low, and, in the American case, declining. Can the political liberalism of John Stuart

Mill, to take the most prominent liberal example of the nineteenth century, be refashioned for the needs of the twenty-first century? The debate about religious freedom as a privilege to be enjoyed in private is increasingly problematic in societies with modern information technology. The hacking scandal around the *News of the World* in 2011–12 demonstrated just how far the private domain is now part of the public world.

These chapters when taken as a whole are designed to explore two central issues of politics. The first is the problem of social unity in the classical debate about the One, the Few and the Many. The second is the problem of the Other in the struggle to achieve a social order that is both fair and liberal. How far can politics enforce social unity through the regulation of religion? How far does the unity of civil society rest ultimately on religious foundations? Finally, how can modern societies devise strategies to respond to the Other in a spirit of hospitality without destroying the foundations of an orderly society? My answer is that it requires a return to state-craft and soul-craft, which in turn requires the rebuilding of the foundations of citizenship to cope with a more diverse world and a restoration of public education to develop virtues that can be of service in a post-industrial society where work has been transformed by technology. While recognizing the severe limitations of ideas about secularization, privacy and freedom that had their intellectual origins in the seventeenth century, I nevertheless offer a modest defence of liberalism as a necessary condition of social harmony.

This book is a sociological analysis of the complex relationships between the religious and the political, occurring over time and in different civilizations. I seek to make this long-standing debate relevant to modern societies by considering a variety of difficult issues such as marriage, conversion and legal pluralism. These case studies and the comparative studies of different religious traditions are undertaken from the perspective of Max Weber's sociology of religion with a view to offering a defence of liberalism. In modern political philosophy liberalism is often under attack, and its credentials as a framework for complex societies is often questioned. In this study I argue that without the basic ingredients of liberalism – secularization (in the limited sense of state neutrality), a level playing field and the rule of law – religion cannot flourish, and we need minimal liberal safeguards to avoid religious and secular conflict.

Although this is a sociological study of the religious and the political, there is another underlying dimension here which concerns the relationship between reason and revelation as sources of political authority. Can political legitimacy be grounded solely in secular conditions of validation, and can a political regime be founded on an act of revelation? This is the so-called 'theologico-political problem' that dominated the work of the political philosopher Leo Strauss in his lifelong study of the tensions between reason and revelation, for instance in his research on Spinoza (Strauss, 1965). Are political regimes created by prophets or kings, or both? Much of Strauss's work was directed towards a deep contextual analysis of classical political theory and theology, but his ideas have a profoundly important contemporary relevance (Tanguay, 2007). For example, the foreign policy of George W. Bush appears to have been influenced by religious notions of a war against evil by a country that has become the principal bastion of Protestant Christianity. Among pious Muslim minds the Qur'an, precisely because it is inspired by revelation, has an authority that cannot be questioned, and it too divides the world of men into two separate and opposed houses.

In coming towards the end of writing this book I was fortunate to read Robert Bellah's magisterial *Religion in human evolution* (2011), in which, reflecting on the contradictions in Indian religious culture between the life of renunciation (the monk) and the life of violence (the warrior) that is described in the *Mahabharata*, he observed that the great epic 'opens up for us the abyss between ethical practice and inevitable violence, between religious ideals and political realities, revealing tensions not only in Indian but in human society' (Bellah, 2011: 559). In this comparative sociology my aim is to describe the tragic tension between the religious and the political that constantly emerges in human history, casting a long shadow over attempts to create viable societies that can answer to our vulnerability.

PART I

The religious and the political

1 | *Fear of diversity: the origin of politics*

Introduction: creating diversity

Much of the recent debate about religious conflicts, social diversity and the crisis of multiracial societies, especially in Western liberal states, presupposes a 'fear of diversity'. In the subtitle to her book on religious intolerance Martha Nussbaum (2012) speaks of 'the politics of fear in an anxious age'. Where does this come from? In the West diversity of peoples within the *polis* has been regarded as the cause of political theory, and we can read the classic account of democracy as a response to the perception of difference as the root of the political. Modern social and cultural diversity is bound up with the globalization of the labour market in the nineteenth and twentieth centuries, and the massive migration of Chinese people in and beyond Asia. Consequently, when one talks of migration, diaspora and diversity in Asia, one is mainly talking about the Chinese nineteenth-century migration that created Chinese minorities in the whole of Southeast Asia. These Asian societies were already highly diverse following their exposure to the outside world through trade routes. By contrast, multiculturalism in Europe arose in societies that were by comparison relatively homogeneous. For example, modern ethnic and religious diversity in the United Kingdom was created in the post-war period primarily by Commonwealth – and, more specifically, Caribbean – migration. In more recent times there has been a substantial Muslim migration from Bangladesh, Pakistan and India. In historical terms multiculturalism was probably invented by Prime Minister Trudeau to cope with nationalism in Quebec and the threat to Canadian federalism, but multiculturalism came to be a major plank of liberal Western politics facing diversity as an outcome of both legal and illegal migration. Of course white-settler societies such as Canada, America, Australia and New Zealand have, as it were, a double diversity – from indigenous peoples and from the migrant diaspora. When one speaks of the crisis of liberal multiculturalism, it is important to develop perspectives that take account of these different forms of diversity, and their somewhat separate historical trajectories. The fear of diversity is very different depending on the nature and origins of what we might call 'minorization' – that is, the construction, often by the state, of separate and distinctive minorities.

Ancient Greece and the rise of politics

What is politics? Many definitions are possible, but there has basically been in modern political philosophy a division between those who adopt a liberal view of political behaviour and those who criticize this legacy following the more acerbic arguments of Carl Schmitt and Max Weber. For liberals, politics could be defined as the peaceful management of conflicts of interest emerging from social differences where the management of this diversity requires a state based on a real or implicit social contract and a high level of social consensus. If we follow somebody like Bernard Crick in his *In defence of politics* (1962) the settlement of social and political differences requires not only a shared citizenship but also a set of political virtues – prudence, conciliation, compromise, variety, adaptability and liveliness – to offset the threat of exclusionary ideologies or any 'absolute-sounding ethic'. By contrast Carl Schmitt, following Max Weber's definition of the state as that institution that has a monopoly of violence in a given territory, criticized the liberal view of politics, because it absolves individuals of responsibility for their actions. Schmitt said in *The concept of the political* (1996) that politics is the struggle between friend and foe involving the exercise of sovereignty in a context of emergency. These two traditions are not wholly different, but they do offer very different solutions to the question of difference – the democratic tradition suggests that differences can be settled by consensus, and the Weber–Schmitt tradition by struggle and conflicts. However, what they perhaps have in common is the recognition that politics emerges out of actual diversity in society. With diversity there are different values, and with different values there are different interests. Politics involves the resolution, peaceful or otherwise, of different interests in the public sphere.

Where does this diversity come from? I want to start this discussion of the theme of social diversity and politics to suggest that the very idea of politics grew out of a Greek 'fear of diversity' – the title of a famous study of Greek political thought by Arlene Saxonhouse (1992). The Greek view of the order of things was that there is a unity in nature which we should seek to perfect within society – or, more precisely, in the city. The task of politics was to create or to restore unity out of diversity; but this unity, if it was to persist, had to reconcile the multiplicity of social forms within the city. The science of politics is the study of how to live well in a context where multiplicity may always bring disorder out of diversity. Aristotle in *Politics* believed that hierarchy could always restore harmony out of disorder, but clearly rejected tyranny as such a solution.

What is the source of diversity in the city? There are diverse sources of multiplicity. For the Greeks the first is gender in the natural division between men and women that results in reproduction. The second is closely related, namely generational differences between age groups. These two forms of 'natural diversity' produce a critical social institution that causes disunity within the city, namely the family. Whereas Plato saw the family as a persistent threat to political unity, Aristotle believed that well-ordered households (based on hierarchy) could contribute to the order of the city. The third source of disorder arises from the presence of strangers within the urban world. These strangers, who could arrive in the midst of the city as slaves captured in battle, were the consequence of military victories, and they were now deprived of their freedom and subordinated to the authority of their masters. In addition, because Greek society depended heavily on trade through its maritime economy, there were other strangers who were still free, namely sea-faring traders. Finally, there is the argument pursued primarily by Moses Finley in *Politics in the ancient world* (1983) that the Greek world was also divided by social classes. In short, the argument common to the historical account of states is that 'fear of diversity' is not produced by a deeply rooted xenophobic psychology, but by the state itself.

Urban violence

Modern societies are vulnerable to attack, and becoming more so. Urbanization, population density, social propinquity, standardized mass consumption, mass-transport systems, the global sale of small arms and explosives, the anonymity and alienation of city life, and the presence of large, typically displaced and dislocated, diasporic communities have produced a social environment that is difficult to regulate and control, and hence is exposed to terrorism from small militarized groups operating with devolved authority structures, or from lone individuals equipped with home-made bombs or high-powered weapons. Leaving to one side the instability of war zones in Iraq, Afghanistan, Chechnya, the Democratic Republic of Congo, Somalia, the Sudans and Syria, the list of high-profile attacks in modern times is more or less endless: the Bali bombing, the attack on Mumbai, 7/11 in London, the Madrid bombings, and of course the 9/11 attack on the Twin Towers in New York. An individual with a modern weapon or explosives can cause significant loss of life: Timothy McVeigh ('the Oklahoma Bomber') killed 167 people and injured over 850 in April 1995, Martin Bryant shot 35 people and wounded 21 others in April 1996 at Port Arthur in Tasmania, Australia, and Anders Behring Breivik killed 77 people on the island of Utoya in July 2011.

Although Western cities have experienced civil unrest and terrorist attacks, urban instability in the developing world is obviously far more acute, troublesome and persistent. Karachi is an instructive example. The city has grown from 450,000 in 1947 to an estimated 18 million today; it suffers from a mixture of ethnic conflict between Pushtun and Mohajir communities, organized crime, a weak state and sectarian conflict. Terrorist attacks on key institutions in New Delhi such as the judiciary and on Mumbai in 2011 have become a regular feature of urban life in modern India. The growing instability of Nigeria may be an addition to the general spread of urban violence in Africa. The killing of civilians and violent crime are daily affairs in Pakistan, Iraq and Afghanistan, but in a global world Western cities are not immune from ethnic and religious violence.

One driving force behind these developments is obviously the modern phase of globalization and the consequent emergence of a new type of society based on flows and networks (Urry, 2000). Paradoxically, this intensification of the speed of social flows and the deepening of social connectedness has forced governments to staunch the mobility of populations by creating a system of enclaves in which populations, regions, cities and dwelling places become walled off and developed as safe enclaves as a basic security strategy (Turner, 2007). These enclaves can involve simple devices such as building walls between societies (Mexico and the United States, Saudi Arabia and the Yemen, or Israel and its Palestinian neighbours), or more complex techniques of social segregation through bureaucratic regulation and sequestration. Within the feral city from Cape Town to Los Angeles, the middle classes have to construct their homes as forts, and vulnerable sectors of the population, such as the elderly, move into gated communities. The super-rich seek anonymity for fear of kidnapping and blackmail, hiring private companies to drill them in routines to increase their personal safety. As urban terrorism becomes more complex and more sophisticated, it will be necessary to redesign cities, to transform the character of public buildings, to reduce access to public spaces, to create and store DNA banks, to monitor closely all transport systems, and to upgrade the surveillance of citizens and their dependants. The result, as we have already seen in the United States after 9/11, will be increasing restrictions on and erosions of rights and privileges.

These social conflicts are in turn associated with 'new wars' or irregular, low-intensity conflicts that are 'state-disintegrating wars' (Münkler, 2005: 8). These conflicts are often directed at women and children in order to maximize terror; they also involve an eroticization of violence in which the bodies of women are used to attack the body of the state. Camp rape is a strategy to both humiliate and destroy social groups by destroying their human dignity. The instabilities of feral cities appear therefore to be connected with demography – the growth of large cohorts of unemployed and unemployable young men in the presence of both general consumerism and widespread corruption; the availability of cheap but effective weaponry; and the growth of new opportunity structures such as global shipping lanes that promote modern piracy. This development may explain why with 'some warlord configurations, sunglasses and Kalashnikovs have become iconic signs of a readiness to engage in brutal unpredictable violence' (Münkler, 2005: 16). These 'overpopulation warriors' are the product of unemployment, overpopulation and exclusion from the formal economy (Diessenbacher, 1998).

However, these developments are not simply a matter of demography, new weaponry, urbanization and social inequality. Modern violence is typically fuelled by distinctive ideologies that both explain and counter the instability, degradation and inequalities of global modernity. Of course, many acts of individual terror appear to have little or no ideological motivation. However, when individual alienation and private resentments become attached to a collective movement equipped with a powerful ideology, then isolated acts of violence become coordinated, coherent and cohesive. Within this urban scenario religion appears to be a powerful motivation towards acts of violence, because it (or at least the Judaeo-Christian–Muslim tradition) divides the world clearly into the profane and the sacred, identifies an enemy, offers a justification for resentment and aggression, and promises a future without inequality and suffering. Religion provides an explanation of injustice and the promise of redemption for its warriors by identifying a paradise such as Cockaigne beyond the modern catastrophe. When this religious imaginary is combined with a sense of national degradation, then the motivational force of religion is intensified.

These developments, as we well know, have been described famously as 'the clash of civilizations' (Huntington, 1993). Adopting the phrase from Bernard Lewis, Samuel P. Huntington argued that with globalization identity becomes a political issue as traditional nation-state boundaries become problematic. In a global world it is religion that increasingly defines identity, and that identity no longer sits neatly on political borders and boundaries. The result is that modern political conflicts are almost inevitably conflicts of religions as the primary vehicles of civilizational complexes. These conflicts can be either microfissures within societies or macro-conflicts between religion–civilizational systems.

This political theory lent itself conveniently to understanding the conflict that was emerging between 'political Islam' and the West that has been manifest at the macro level (the Gulf War, the invasion of Iraq, the conflicts in the Sudan and Somalia, the war in Afghanistan, the crisis in Pakistan, the wars in Chechnya) and at the micro level in terms of religious tensions in Europe over the failures of multiculturalism and social integration. Political attempts to regulate the spread of the *shari'a* in Europe and America or the ban on the *burqa* in France or the regulations on minarets in Switzerland can be read as everyday manifestations of these civilizational tensions. The Huntington thesis received dramatic support in the attack on the Twin Towers and the response of President Bush in launching a war on terror that was directed against al-Qaeda. In reaction to 9/11 various blogs such as Jihad Watch, Atlas Shrugs and Gates of Vienna emerged on the Internet to warn against the dangers of the Islamization of Europe. The foreign policy of the Bush administration intensified the idea that the West was pitted against an implacable foe, dividing the world into those who supported America and those that didn't. The idea of 'faith wars' and the growing importance of Karl Rove in the White House confirmed the growing influence of the Christian Right over world politics (Wills, 2007). It appears that a global society has ushered in a new era of religious wars in which the disprivileged of the world are engaged in a global struggle against the West and its promise of secular consumer democracies.

Muslims in Norway

The Huntington thesis – along with the public utterances of Bernard Lewis – has been subject to extensive criticism. The debate about security and the struggle against evil has had the effect of reifying the notion of Islam, thereby neglecting and obscuring its many and varied manifestations. Ethnic identities – Turks, Iraqis, Egyptians and so forth – are often misleadingly replaced by a collective notion of 'Muslim'. Furthermore, Muslims, like Christians, are often individuals who are not observant, but they are given a specific and enduring religious identity. For example, on average only 30 per cent of European Muslims attend a mosque, the headscarf is not ubiquitous, and there are many variations in adherence to and support of the *shari'a*. Other criticisms of Huntington suggest that the tensions between Christians and Muslims need to be set against tensions within religious traditions between Sunni and Shi'ite in the Middle East or between Protestant and Catholic in Northern Ireland, or between Buddhist and Muslim in southern Thailand. The political left, which has made a concerted effort to avoid any victimization of Muslims and intellectuals, in looking for an alternative to the pessimistic implications of Huntington has promoted recognition ethics and cosmopolitanism as alternative possibilities of globalization.

We can take Norway as a case study to illustrate both the weakness and the relevance of the Huntington thesis to modern tensions between Muslims and host societies in Europe. The case against Huntington is that the category 'Muslim' in fact hides a significant amount of internal ethnic and cultural variation. In reality Muslims are a heterogeneous community just like Christians. In Norway Muslims began to arrive as labour migrants in the 1960s, but by the 1970s the governments of all Scandinavian societies began to place restrictions on migration, and hence by the 1980s the principal form of increase in immigrant numbers was through family reunion. Given Norway's military involvement in overseas conflicts there has also been a flow of refugees from Iraq, Afghanistan and Bosnia-Herzegovina. Norway thus has Muslims from a variety of societies, with the largest group, slightly over 30,000, coming from Pakistan and approximately 26,000 from Iraq. Nevertheless, the Muslim population in 2009 of 160,000 represented only 3 per cent of the total population of 4.8 million. Although social research on Muslims in Norway is limited, the data we do have present an unsurprising picture of the difficulties facing Muslim communities. The male employment rate for Muslim men and women is relatively low, especially among the small community from Somalia. There is some evidence of labour discrimination in the sense that immigrants are often overqualified for the employment they actually have. In general, the research on Norway shows that the Muslim population is diverse with variable levels of participation in religious institutions and practices. Looking at Scandinavia as a whole, research on cities such as Copenhagen and Malmo indicates that multiculturalism and social diversity are treated as a resource rather than a problem (Haddad and Smith, 2002; Larsson, 2009; Strabac and Listhaug, 2008).

In the public arena in Norway there have been serious attempts to create a dialogue between the Christian churches and Islamic associations. In 1993 the national Contact Group for the Lutheran Church of Norway and the Islamic Council of Norway (an umbrella organization with a diverse membership) was created by Oddbjorn Leirvik, a theologian from Oslo University. Other initiatives included in 1996 the Council for Religious and Life Stance Communities for different religious traditions, including the secular Humanist Association. Before 1999 government officials had interacted with immigrant associations on the basis of ethnicity rather than religion, but after the Christian Democrat prime minister made an official visit to a mosque the government began to recognize religious institutions. Perhaps the most important change has been the gradual secularization of the state from 2008, when a process of disestablishment was undertaken by allowing the Church the right to select its own bishops.

Despite these efforts at dialogue, there has also been growing right-wing opposition to Muslims from such organizations as the Human Rights Service, which claims that Islam is incompatible with democracy. Various influential journalists have argued that a cohesive Norway is only possible on the basis of a population composed exclusively of ethnic Norwegians and that multiculturalism is therefore a threat to Norwegian identity. These right-wing groups complain that multiculturalism involves cultural relativism in which all religions are treated as equal and having the same validity. While many of these views are extreme (suggesting, for example, that Muslims are incapable of rational thought), these ideas find support in the Progress Party, which has been represented in parliament since 1985 and in the 2009 elections received 22.9 per cent of the vote, making it the second-largest party. Its policies reflect underlying negative views of migration, multiculturalism and Islam. In February 2011 the Norwegian Defence League (a sister organization of the English Defence League) was formed with Lena Andreessen as its leader. These political leaders regard Islam as equivalent to Nazism, comparing the German occupation of Norway in 1940 with a Muslim takeover today. These attitudes are also reflected in studies of the media in which Norwegians treat Muslims as more religious than they actually are and regard Islamic values as incompatible with common Norwegian values.

These developments illustrate two important sociological conclusions. The first is that multiculturalism becomes a problem most significantly when a majority feels that it is threatened by a minority. Second, while the intellectual argument against the Huntington thesis of a clash of civilizations is telling, in the public sphere social groups (Muslims, Christians and Jews for example) are reified by public debate and there is consequently a tendency to 'essentialize' the differences between such groups. In Scandinavia, while both Muslim and Christian associations sought to reach mutual understanding through dialogue, the Danish cartoon crisis of 2005 inevitably polarized opinion. Furthermore, in 2006 Vebjorn Selbekk, the editor of the right-wing Christian journal *Magazinet*, reprinted the Danish cartoons, and received support from the Progress Party and many intellectuals who claimed that it was an issue of the right to freedom of expression. These results show that treating Muslims as a single coherent bloc is misleading, and in fact contributes to the sense of distrust between immigrant and host communities. However, while the Muslim communities in Norway represent only a small percentage of the total population, there has been a negative political response to their presence.

For those committed to multiculturalism and cosmopolitan values there has been an obvious reluctance to accept the idea that Christian and Muslim or Muslim and Jew or Muslim and Hindu are somehow locked into a global civilizational struggle that cannot be successfully resisted or managed or diffused by inter-faith conferences, by improvements in multicultural policies and by intercultural understanding. The defence of multiculturalism and the European welfare state includes the idea that high levels of ethnic diversity arising from migration do not lower trust and social cohesion (Kymlicka, 2009; Letki, 2008). Nevertheless, the Huntington thesis appears to survive these multiple criticisms. The parties to these global conflicts themselves reify 'Christian' and 'Muslim', and 'Hindu' and 'Muslim'. In other words, the actors themselves do not adopt the anthropological notion that social groups (including religious associations) are inevitably heterogeneous, or that they are socially constructed. Breivik believes, however mistakenly, in the existence of a civilizational war, and that an Islamization of Western Europe is taking place. In practice in the European public sphere, ethnicity and religious identities are used interchangeably. In the everyday world people operate with essentialism, not social constructionism. Hence conflicts between Christians and Muslims in the Molukkas in Indonesia, attacks on Catholic churches in Iraq, Muslim and Christian conflicts in northern Nigeria, conflicts between Copts and Muslims in Egypt, violence between Muslims and Christians in Sudan, violence between Buddhists and Muslims in southern Thailand, and the exit of Christians from Israel and Palestine are persistent and fundamental problems of modern politics. The Judaeo-Christian–Muslim traditions provide powerful mythologies and cosmologies that continue to drive these conflicts, and in general terms religion gives the resentment of individuals a collective force and organizational framework. In these examples we might say that the participants lack irony, which is a capacity to recognize the limitations of their own ideas and an ability to use, in Martha Nussbaum's terms, their 'inner eyes'.

There is in the history of twentieth-century Europe ample evidence of a deep-seated conflict between Christianity and other religions, most problematically between Roman Catholicism and Judaism. Hitler's attack on the Jewish communities of Europe was based on his 'redemptive anti-Semitism' which combined his ideas about racial degeneration and religious redemption (Friedlander, 1997). Europe could only be saved through the expulsion or extermination of the Jews. Before the Jews there had been a bloody history of conflict between the Church and heretical groups, and the massacre of 15,000 French Huguenots on St Bartholomew's Day in 1572 remains one of the worst atrocities in European history. The Church's violent opposition to any form of heresy was not finally abandoned until Vatican II. These religious conflicts are significant aspects of the clash of civilizations in modern Europe, where Islam has replaced other religious traditions to become the focal point of alterity.

The Manifesto and European multiculturalism

Anders Breivik's Manifesto *2083: A European declaration of independence* (Berwick, 2011) is a rambling, repetitive and disconnected complaint against political correctness, feminism, cultural Marxism and much more. It claims that a cluster of theories – critical theory, sexual theory, family theory, racial theory and so forth – have gradually chipped away at the social order and have undermined European self-confidence, namely nationalism. These intellectual movements have been especially pernicious in higher education where the classical and Judaeo-Christian traditions have been undermined. The turning point was the 1960s. The 'handmaiden of political correctness' has been the 'multicultural movement' which in the universities has involved 'the systematic restructuring of the curriculum so as to hinder students from learning about the Western tradition'. Through political correctness and 'feminist ideology', the modern student learns about the victims of capitalist society as a result of sexism, racism or homophobia. In summary these ideologies are destroying Western culture through their message which is 'anti-God, anti-Christian, anti-family, anti-nationalist, anti-patriot, anti-conservative, anti-hereditarian, anti-ethnocentric, anti-masculine, anti-tradition, and anti-morality'.

The concrete manifestation of these trends is multiculturalism in Europe, and the principal example is the spread of Islam, the threat of a Muslim hegemony, and the spread of the *shari'a*. Anders Breivik, under the nom de plume Andrew Berwick (Berwick, 2011) and with the self-proclaimed title of Justiciar Knight Commander for Knights Templar of Europe, condemned 'Islamic colonization and Islamization of Western Europe'. He provided a nostalgic picture of Europe in the 1950s:

Our homes were safe, to the point where many people did not bother to lock their doors. Public schools were generally excellent. ... Most men treated women like ladies, and most ladies devoted their time and effort to making good homes, rearing their children well and helping their communities through volunteer work. Children grew up in two-parent households, and the mother was there to meet the child when he came home from school. Entertainment was something the whole family could enjoy.

Although the Manifesto is an exaggerated stereotype of European higher education and multiculturalism, its contents reflect a more general anxiety in Europe about national identity and the growth of multiculturalism, and specifically the growth of Islam. We perhaps forget too easily that multiculturalism was a rather late development in Western Europe. If we take the case of the United Kingdom, by 1959 West Indian migration amounted to some 16,000 per annum, but by 1976 the total number of 'non-white' migrants was only 1.85 million (Judt, 2005). Although British industry was eager to employ migrants at low wages to carry out basic tasks in industrial production, racial conflict in Britain eventually forced the government to pass various immigration acts (in 1968 and 1971) which severely restricted the flow of immigrants to British shores. The point of these observations is to say that multiculturalism was a late development on the basis of societies that were relatively homogeneous, especially when compared to the United States or to Commonwealth societies such as Canada and Australia. European leaders were essentially reluctant cosmopolitans.

Furthermore, contemporary evidence from Western societies is that multiculturalism is in retreat, because there is now growing emphasis on security and careful regulation of migration. More importantly, critics argue that multicultural policies appear often to have divided rather than united societies (Barry, 2001; Joppke, 2004; Levy, 2000). Recent political crises in the liberal democracies – Britain, France, Germany, Italy, the Netherlands and Denmark – have only served to reinforce this critical standpoint. European societies have all faced this post-war cultural and ethnic fragmentation, but in Britain and France, given their colonial history, these social and political changes have been both rapid and profound.

The British problem is not just about multiculturalism and the growth of a Muslim minority, but involves its membership of the European Union combined with the devolution of powers to Scotland, Wales and Northern Ireland. The paradox of these changes has been to create a particular problem of representation for England. One indication of the cultural problems of Englishness is in the emergence of a new right wing outside the consensus of the centre. To take one example, the English Defence League (EDL) was officially formed in June 2009 as an anti-Islamic movement opposed to Islamic fundamentalism and the alleged spread of the *shari'a*. It is closely connected with working-class English football culture, especially in the Midlands and the North. It has staged protests throughout the British Isles. Although its presence has been condemned by the police and senior politicians, it is thought that the views of the EDL in fact reflect an Islamophobia and distrust of multiculturalism that are becoming increasingly acceptable in the political mainstream. EDL politics appear to find a parallel in the 2083 Manifesto. Although the EDL has publicly rejected violence, its protests are typically associated with violence, injuries to the police and minor destruction of property. These developments – extreme political movements, riots in the streets of London, economic decline, the erosion of British military power, the growth of nationalism in Scotland and Wales, the devolution of parliamentary functions, and the decline of the Church of England – are aspects of social change in which Britain in the twenty-first century is a radically different society from the one that emerged in the 1950s.

After the 'shopping riots' of 2011, the prime minister, David Cameron, claimed these urban disturbances were examples of moral failure in Britain, resulting from broken families and inadequate discipline. The riots were thought to be examples of mindless fun, because the rioters were seen to be enjoying themselves. They were also seen as irrational, because in many cases the rioters were middle class and employed. One rioter was convicted of stealing a bottle of water. In summary, the riots were seen to be the result of boredom on the part of young people, the widespread availability of alcohol in British cities, unemployment and low educational achievement, and broken families and lack of discipline. Psychologists argued that bystanders were simply caught up in the exuberance of crowd behaviour. The conservative condemnation of the riots described them as pure criminality – the product of poor schooling, broken families, lack of discipline, and lack of a basic sense of values. The prime minister went on to criticize Britain as a 'broken society'. These views about the absence of discipline, viable families and the absence of national confidence are consistent with much of the outlook and assumptions of the 2083 Manifesto.

With the growing crisis in the European economies it has been argued that the need to restore full employment will replace the debate about immigration and the threat of Islam. It is also suggested that, just as the Oklahoma bombing resulted in a decline of right-wing militia activity, the massacre on the island of Utoya will result in a decline of right-wing political sentiment in Norway and beyond. This more optimistic view of European politics has received some support from the Danish election of 11 September 2011, which brought the Social Democratic Party to power under the leadership of Helle Thorning-Schmidt, who promised a new start in Danish politics. At the same time, the right-wing Danish

People's Party (Danische Volkspartei), which had been the driving force behind the restrictive immigration policies of Denmark, only retained 12.3 per cent of the vote. However, on closer inspection it turns out that the Social Democratic Party received only 24.9 per cent of the vote, and in a multi-party system Thorning-Schmidt's government had no clear majority in parliament. The Social Democrats will in all probability support the economic and social policies of the previous government. It may be premature therefore to think that the rightward swing of Danish, or indeed European, politics has run out of steam.

Conclusion: religion in the public sphere

John Rawls in *Political liberalism* (1993) and *The law of peoples* (1999) sought to describe how public reason would operate in a well-ordered, decent society. In particular, liberal societies have consultative hierarchies in which the people can have a 'meaningful role in making political decisions' (Rawls, 1999: 4). Liberal democracies can therefore function when there is 'an overlapping consensus of comprehensive doctrines' (Rawls, 1999: 16). These ideas have been taken up and elaborated by Jürgen Habermas (2008) in the idea of a 'post-secular society' in which it is incumbent upon both secular and religious citizens to defend their views according to Rawlsian rules of public reason. In thinking about urban conflict and fear of the Other, I have of course drawn upon a wide range of specific cases, and I am reluctant to draw too many generalizations from examples that are very different in terms of scale and motivation. However, there are in the West two important themes in urban conflict: first, the relationship between majorities and minorities; and second, the absence of any public consensus over major issues. What lessons then can we learn from my brief account of the conflicts of modern cities?

The first is that the majority feel that they have not been able to participate meaningfully in political decision making and at the same time they feel threatened by minorities. The economic crisis of the Eurozone has further reinforced many of the underlying problems of declining opportunities, limited incomes, low employment and the marginalization of young men. Growing income inequality and a general absence of social equality have only served to fuel anxiety, resentment and fear. Anders Behring Breivik and political terrorists like him believe that they have been excluded from basic political decisions such as the creation of a multicultural Europe through post-war labour migration in response to labour shortages. Second, there is little evidence in such multicultural societies of an 'overlapping consensus', because there is often little evidence of overlapping social relationships in modern societies (Turner, 2008). In the examples of terrorism committed by Breivik and McVeigh there was low trust in government, and hence a lack of interest in rational communication in the public domain with government agencies and their representatives. These secular terrorists communicated with the government by acts of public destruction rather than public reason.

Contrary to both Rawls and Habermas, religious belief systems do not necessarily lend themselves to public reasoning through engagement and dialogue. If religious orthodoxies are committed to an exclusive notion of Truth, there is little motivation or interest in dialogue. Conversion to religious Truth is not necessarily achieved through exposure to public dialogue, and holding to a religious belief is not like a philosopher holding to a proposition that might turn out to be false or misguided. Religious beliefs in the public sphere can make the achievement of public reason more rather than less difficult to achieve. The fragmentation of society, the drive towards securitization and the erosion of the public domain as a consequence of neo-liberal strategies to deregulate both society and market conspire to make the achievement of any public consensus highly problematic, thereby creating social vacuums within which the motivation towards acts of terrorism can fester. Fear of diversity is both cause and consequence of these political dilemmas.

2 | *Charisma and church–state relations*

Introduction: Max Weber on charisma

Fear of diversity suggests that there is a lack of trust in society, which could hold social groups together. While political leaders often look towards religion as a healing power in society, religions can be highly disruptive, producing difference and division. The paradox of religious charisma is that it is both constructive in forming new social groups and highly destructive of tradition and its conventional certainties. This chapter examines charisma and charismatic authority as a problem at two separate but related levels. First, I consider why charisma is a threat to the stability of existing social arrangements, and why it is in particular seen to be a threat to existing patterns of authority, both secular and religious. Various examples are provided in which we can consider how the state intervenes to regulate charismatic phenomena. Popular charisma in the Roman Catholic Church can be illustrated through the controversial case of Padre Pio of Pietrelcina, whose stigmata appeared in 1918, and whose career caused significant problems for both the state and the Roman Catholic hierarchy. In Chapter 4 I will examine the role of monarchy in democracies as an example of hereditary charisma in societies that are otherwise deeply secular. In Chapter 12 I take a further look at a modern example of a charismatic movement from South India in which the religious leader Sathya Sai Baba created a global movement on the basis of claims to religious authority, often based on his healing powers. Padre Pio and Sai Baba were challenged by external authorities who used scientific investigation to determine whether their claims to extraordinary powers were fraudulent, but these attempts to explain charismatic phenomena by empirical investigation and positivist methodologies failed to contain popular enthusiasm.

Second, I argue that charisma also causes scientific problems for sociology. By demonstrating that charisma is caused by social circumstances, sociology treats it as having natural causes and hence implicitly denies that charismatic phenomena can have any specifically religious causation. Do sociologists, in treating charisma for instance as an outcome of social crisis, thereby imply that charisma is natural rather than supernatural, and if it is natural is it fraudulent? Can secular scientific sociology take the narrative claims of charismatics seriously? In this respect Max Weber's commentary on charisma in *Economy and society* (1978) is deeply confused. On the one hand, he wants to treat charismatic breakthroughs as constituting revolutionary transformations of society. On the other, he argues that charismatic success depends on an ability to produce tangible goods to followers such as health and wealth. However, satisfying the earthly needs of followers does not necessarily engender the radical challenge that is needed to bring about revolutionary moments.

In this respect I analyse the work of Pierre Bourdieu to consider whether his 'reflexive sociology' offers any solution to these long-standing theoretical difficulties. Bourdieu has received an appreciative reception in contemporary sociology of religion (Rey, 2007). However, I am critical of his interpretation of charisma (Turner, 2011b). Does reflexive sociology commit us to paying attention to the beliefs of social actors, and if so can a secular sociology attend comfortably to claims about supernatural inspiration and divine intervention? The core problem in the case of charisma is the question of human intentionality, or in the language of modern sociology the relationship between agency and structure. In addition, most theories of charisma have failed to examine popular religion systematically, and they have ignored the central role of the body in the manifestation and authentication of charisma.

According to Weber's theory of authority, charisma is the most radical challenge to both traditional and rational–legal bases of legitimacy. Weber contrasted the priest and the prophet. While the former operates within an ecclesiastical hierarchy, the prophet stands outside these formal structures and claims a unique authority of conviction rather than convention. In the origin of religions, certain individuals are believed by their followers to have a capacity for ecstatic states that are in turn preconditions for healing, telepathy and divination. It is primarily through 'these extraordinary powers that have been designated by such special terms as "mana," "orenda," and the Iranian "Maga" (the term from which our word "magic" is derived). We shall henceforth employ the term "charisma" for such extraordinary powers' (Weber, 1966b: 2). Charisma (*kharisma*) is derived from the Greek idea of a 'gift of grace', where *kharis* refers to favour or grace. 'Charisma' or 'gift of grace' was originally a theological notion that has been introduced into the social and religious sciences primarily to describe the growth and development of social movements based on religious inspiration. The concept was used to contrast the role of inspiration versus convention. It is also employed to describe a particular type of authority in society generally. In a religious context it means a divinely inspired power, namely the sacred as a force in secular affairs. A charismatic individual is thought to have a special ability or talent or skill, often in terms of therapy or prophecy. In the anthropology of religion it is often discussed under the general category of shamanism. These shamanistic cultures were widespread in the northern hemisphere from Canada to Siberia to China, and involved the use of drums and herbal medicine to achieve healing and ecstatic visions (Eliade, 1964). Shamanism is still prevalent in spirit possession cults in Korea and Vietnam.

Weber's theory of authority remains the basic source of contemporary sociological approaches to the study of charisma. For Weber (1978, I: 216), 'the concept of "charisma" ("gift of grace") is taken from the vocabulary of early Christianity. For the Christian hierocracy Rudolf Sohm, in his *Kirchenrecht*, was the first to clarify the substance of the concept, even though he did not use the same terminology. Others (for instance, Holl in *Enthusiasmus und Bussgewalt*) have clarified certain important consequences of it. It is thus nothing new.' Thus the immediate intellectual influence came from the theological work of Rudolf Sohm and Karl Holl, who had recognized the revolutionary implications of charisma for the development of forms of religious authority and association. Weber's own theory of charisma was an attempt to expand the notion of charismatic change into a wide-ranging theory of authority. From this theological tradition Weber generalized the idea to create a sociological understanding of its radical implications for the study of social and political change. Let us pause to consider the intellectual influences on Weber's development of the sociology of charisma. Frederich H. Tenbruck (1987) has shown how Weber's focus on charisma was a major turning point in the development not just of his sociology of religion, but of his sociology as a whole. The important influences on Weber in this transition in his work were Eduard Meyer and, as we have seen, to a lesser extent in the ecclesiastical research of Sohm and Holl. Meyer published *Geschichte des Altertums* (1884), in which he developed a comparative and universal framework for historical research comparing civilizational clusters – the Orient, Christendom, the Hellenic world – and claimed that it was the universal world religions that had played the decisive part in their evolution. In particular, Meyer had argued that certain personalities, outside the hierarchical order of priests, have been seized by powerful religious ideas, bringing about an internal transformation of civilizational complexes. The parallel between Meyer's universal history and Weber's own comparative sociology of religion is striking. At a later stage he published a history of Mormonism (*Ursprung und Geschichte der Mormonen*, 1912), in which he set out a comparison between Islam and Mormonism. Meyer was interested in the psychological characteristics of two prophets – Muhammad in Islam and Joseph Smith in Mormonism – and developed a critical view of the ecstatic experiences of charismatic leaders as examples of mental illness. This work is of interest to my discussion because Meyer produced a causal account of the origins of prophetic experience in mental illness that paid little attention to the sociological context of charismatic authority. The same tensions between a psychological and a sociological approach are still present in Weber's account, but nevertheless Meyer's influence was decisive. Indeed Tenbruck (1987: 247) observes that it was Meyer's historical work that inspired Weber to engage in 'universal historical [inquiry], empirically anchored in historical research, and operating with a sociology that sought out the comparison of peoples and civilizations according to ideal typical rules of historical events that have a universal significance and validity'.

Turning now to consider in more detail Weber's account in the sociology of religion, charisma is a phenomenon in the emergence of religion in terms of the extraordinary talents of prophetic figures. These religious talents are often understood as an actual substance that may remain dormant in a person until it is aroused by asceticism, visions or trance. Although Weber saw charisma as being important in understanding the origins of religion, he sought to employ the term to develop a general theory of the dynamic of authority and leadership in social institutions. His main intention was famously to compare and contrast three types of authority: traditional, charismatic and legal–rational.

Any theory of authority is also a theory of compliance – why do people obey a leader, or a convention, or a law? Traditional authority involves the routine acceptance of conventions that express existing social arrangements, namely any established pattern of belief or collection of practices. Charismatic authority is by contrast the ability of a leader to inspire disciples to accept the authenticity and validity of a

charismatic vocation that breaks with existing tradition. In more practical terms, an authentic claim to charisma is typically legitimized by
the ability of an inspired person to provide healing or prosperity to a
devoted band of followers, but for Weber these gifts alone cannot be the
ultimate basis of authority. In the case of genuine or authentic charisma,
the disciples obey and support a leader on the basis of a pure commitment to and belief in their leader. In *Economy and society* Weber (1978,
I: 241) argued that pure charisma depends on extraordinary or supernatural powers or qualities. However, pure charisma can all too easily
be shaped and corrupted by the material interests of followers who
may demand that a charismatic figure perform magical activities as a
sign of their power. We can therefore detect a tension in this account
of charisma. On the one hand, the disciples follow an inspired leader
because they have an unshakeable belief in his or her authority. They
follow out of passion or belief. On the other hand, there is the argument
that people follow a charismatic leader because they expect to receive
tangible proof through the performance of magical acts that offer
healing and wealth. The implication of Weber's argument is that pure
charisma can be corrupted by demands for magical practices on the part
of followers, whose compliance now appears to be based on utilitarian
considerations.

The earthly ministry of Jesus was apparently caught in this dilemma.
Stories of magical activities in Jesus' ministry in the New Testament are
absent from the Acts of the Apostles, where Paul concentrates on one
single event: Christ is resurrected (Badiou, 2003). The social pressure
towards magical practices to buttress charismatic authority is intensified
by the competition between charismatic figures for social influence. These
competitive pressures are clearly evident in the New Testament narrative
in which Jesus' pure charisma required his rejection of the Pharisees'
interpretation of the Law. Nevertheless, Jesus' charismatic power also
existed alongside magical activities in critical events in which he is
depicted as walking on water, transforming water into wine or feeding
the five thousand. Furthermore, while the New Testament shows John
the Baptist as preparing the way for Jesus and thus subordinating himself
to Jesus' ministry, we can interpret their relationship as an example of
charismatic competition. Within the competitive field some charismatic
leaders will become sorcerers – that is, religious leaders who through
magical activity such as healing provide services to an audience. Over
time other forms of charismatic activity will be subject to routinization,

being thereby transformed into priestly roles. But some charismatic leaders, although subject to pressure from their followers to deliver substantial goods and services through magical acts, will transcend the conventional world of their followers to issue a message that is both transgressive and innovative. It is only when the message and the audience are not wholly attuned or in line that a charismatic breakthrough can occur at all. If this possibility is not conceded by sociologists, then we should abandon the concept of charisma, since it turns out that charisma is at best a temporary hiatus in the evolution of tradition.

It goes without saying that exegesis of the actions of Jesus in the New Testament is deeply divided, but one common interpretation is that his followers expected him to take on the mantle of David as a messianic king to drive out the occupying Roman forces. Jesus was to bring a sword, not the word of peace, from the Sermon on the Mount. His crucifixion was in this framework the negation of those expectations, and thus it is only when a charismatic leader stands against the mundane expectations of an audience that a radical message can be delivered, and only in such circumstances can one speak about a charismatic breakthrough in history.

Both charismatic and traditional authority are contrasted with modern legal–rational authority, which is typical of bureaucracies. Formal rules of conduct are underpinned by strict procedural guidelines in which commands are handed down from office to office. Legal–rational institutions are defined by officialdom, formal education, transparent methods of promotion, and payment through a structure of salaries. Charismatics are typically supported by voluntary gifts from their followers, and the hierarchical relation between disciples and charismatic leader is not a formal, stable or fixed structure. As we have noted, each form of authority involves a form of compliance. Tradition typically depends on compliance through habituation; legal–rational authority rests on correct procedures and rational argument; and charismatic authority and leadership require unquestioning loyalty. In Weber's methodology these forms of authority are regarded as 'ideal types' in the sense that they do not necessarily appear in pure form in social reality. For example, in some circumstances charisma can be passed from father to son, thus combining tradition and charisma.

Although Weber produced diverse examples of charisma, he argued that charismatic authority is confronted by a common problem of succession with the death of the leader. Both tradition and legal–rational

authority have accepted norms for the transition of authority. In traditional societies patriarchy is a common institution for the regular passage
of authority between generations. Large corporations have systematic
recruitment procedures for selecting new chief executive officers. The
crucial issue is that charismatic authority is unstable. With the death of
a charismatic leader, the movement typically enters into a period of crisis.
If the disciples decide to disband, then the charismatic movement simply
collapses. In the case of the Christian Church, the charismatic authority
of Christ was eventually transferred to the Church itself as the continuing
body of Christ, and the bishops were given authoritative possession of
what is known in ecclesiology as the 'keys of grace' by which they exercise
the authority of the Church through liturgical practices such as baptism
and confession which are the 'means of grace'. This transition of authority was defined by Weber as the 'institutionalization of charisma', in
which charismatic powers are over time transformed into rules and
conventions that are increasingly formal, bureaucratic and impersonal.
As these charismatic powers become conventional, there is a 'routinization of charisma'.

Weber believed that in the pre-modern period human societies were
subject to this endless competition, struggle or oscillation between charisma and tradition, and that by contrast the modern period is dominated
by legal rationality, because the world we live in is fundamentally
secular. This historical struggle between conviction and convention is
somewhat parallel to the conflict between church and sect in the famous
typology of Weber's colleague Ernst Troeltsch. In the church–sect typology Troeltsch (1931) argued that the end of the Universal Church spelt
the end of this creative conflict between form and spirit, and the dominant religion of the modern world would be a form of mysticism as a
vehicle for the growing individualism of the West. Weber had a similar
view, arguing that legal rationality would be the dominant mode of
authority replacing the historical dynamic of charisma and tradition,
leading to a highly routinized world as the outcome of a general process
of rationalization. The increasing application of scientific rationality to
the problems of human society would result in secularization, or what he
called the 'disenchantment of the world'.

Weber was especially sceptical about the rise of a charismatic figure
in the bureaucratic world of Germany, where Prussian militarism and
discipline had become dominant. There was one personality that Weber
took seriously, the German poet and seer Stefan George (1868–1933).

According to Joachim Radkau (2009) Weber became fascinated by George and his followers. Weber respected George, albeit critically, as an important figure with clear capacities as a charismatic leader. Apparently in August 1915 both men were at the Pension Betzner on the Gaisbergstrasse in Heidelberg, and therefore had time to converse directly with each other. George was a famous and influential poet in his own right, and edited the literary magazine *Blatter für die Kunst*. He became the leader of a circle of young men (the George-Kreis), many of whom also became famous intellectual figures. George was profoundly critical of modern society, and sought to create an aristocratic, hierarchical and aesthetic lifestyle to counter the crude vulgarity of the Germany that was expanding as an industrial society. He was critical of the First World War, rejected the jingoism of the time, and predicated the defeat and humiliation of Germany in his poem *Der Krieg* (The war). Given his criticism of Germany and his search for a new social order, his poetry was embraced by National Socialism, but George struggled to distance himself from the Nazi Party. By the 1930s Joseph Goebbels offered him the presidency of an Academy for the Arts, but George rejected the offer and escaped to Switzerland, where he died.

George is important in Weber's theory of charisma since 'the George circle was above all a fascinating experiment in how far, and under what conditions, it was possible to revive old gods in the modern age and to foster a charismatic cult of a prophet and leader' (Radkau, 2009: 296). Although Weber was impressed by George, he concluded that it was a redemptive religious movement but ultimately of little substance or significance. Nevertheless, Weber's ambiguous encounter with the George Circle is important because it illustrates the tension in Weber's work and life between artistic and religious enthusiasm (charisma) and the formal discipline required in any this-worldly calling (for example, politics as a vocation). It presented a struggle between 'acosmic love and charisma, on the one side, and pathos and formed life on the other' (Whimster, 1987: 285). George remains interesting for any theory of charismatic inspiration, since he sought desperately to avoid publicity and his books were privately published, and circulated among his circle. From the perspective of Pierre Bourdieu, George was a charismatic figure in a field of symbolic capital, who went to great lengths to keep outside the competition for immediate influence. This raises an important issue: does genuine charismatic authenticity seek to avoid forms of authentication that are too popular and hence inevitably cheap and superficial?

While most interpretations of Weber's sociology of charisma have accepted the view that charisma disappears when modern societies are subject to a process of rationalization in which science rather than magic promises to deliver tangible goods such as health and wealth, Günther Roth (1975) offered an important alternative interpretation. He took note of the fact that 'Weber moved from the nascent usage of "charisma" in his Sociology of Religion to its systematic usage in the Sociology of Domination: it is less well understood that he also trans-ferred the concept of the congregation or community (*Gemeinde*) from the religious to the political sphere and came to define it as the typical charismatic association' (Roth 1975: 151). Charisma in the modern world is, according to Roth, manifest in people of ideological commit-ment who can be regarded as 'ideological virtuosi'. These figures, which are the secular counterparts to Weber's 'religious virtuosi', cannot be satisfied by the humdrum politics of the party system with its inevi-table politics of compromise. During periods of social disruption these virtuosi can form charismatic groups that enjoy a significant impact on historical developments. These political virtuosi often exist on the mar-gins of the bureaucratic world and outside the business elites that depend on the market, and in a time of crisis their intense commitment to an ethic of ultimate ends is in sharp contrast to the secular pragma-tism of mundane economic and political activity. Interestingly Roth also associated this charisma of reason rather than a charisma of magic with the growth of human rights movements as a modern version of natural law. I shall return to this issue of religion and human rights in Chapters 3 and 7. While I do not reject Roth's interpretation, I am more inclined to believe that political charisma in modern democracies has become merely political celebrity. In addition, we can see in the life of Padre Pio an example of how magical charisma can still flourish in modern societies, and indeed Roth observed that with the growth of the counter-culture the possibility of magical revivals was increased.

The critique of Weber's sociology of charisma

So far I have described charisma as if it emerged free of competition. In reality charismatics typically compete in an oversupplied field of claim-ants struggling to acquire followers. This charismatic struggle can be seen as a phenomenon of social crisis; wars, plagues, famines and civil strife provide the platform on which charismatics claim leadership. In short, charisma is characteristically the outcome of some human catastrophe in which traditional arrangements no longer suffice. We need therefore to understand charisma in the context of social conflict. From the perspective of Bourdieu's theory of symbolic capital, we can think about charisma in the context of a struggle for the monopoly of symbolic power. The general notion of a religious field within which different social groups compete for control and domination is explicitly derived from Weber's general sociology, in which all social relations are relations of power. However, while Bourdieu was deeply influenced by Weber's sociology (Bourdieu, 2000), he was critical of what he believed was Weber's psychological treatment of charisma. Allegedly, Weber interpreted charisma as a property belonging to an individual rather than undertaking an examination of the social relations within which charismatic power resides. Bourdieu (1987: 129) claimed that 'Max Weber never produces anything other than a psycho-sociological theory of charisma, a theory that regards it as the lived relation of a public to the charismatic personality'. Such a model is, for Bourdieu, defective because it ignores the interaction between prophet and laity. Social change can only take place when prophecy 'has its own generative and unifying principle, a habitus objectively attuned to that of its addressees' (Bourdieu, 1987: 131). While Bourdieu accepts the idea that charisma is a lever of social transformation, it can only function as such when the charismatic message is completely attuned to and in line with the dispositions or habitus of disciples and followers.

Bourdieu's interpretation appears in fact to rob charisma of precisely its transformative character by making it look more like traditional authority – that is, a form of authority that is indeed compatible with existing dispositions and disciplines, confirming their existing customs and conventions. By contrast, the New Testament account of Jesus shows how he overthrows traditional authority: 'It is written but I say unto you.' Of course, the New Testament account that was written long after the actual events attempts to show how both Jesus and Paul overturned Jewish institutions ('the Law') in order to create a new dispensation, namely how Jewish conventions were replaced by grace. Nevertheless, Jesus was charismatic despite, as it were, the needs and dispositions of his audience.

Bourdieu's criticism of Weber's alleged psychological treatment of charisma is in fact misleading. To take one crucial feature from the commentary on charisma in *The sociology of religion* (1966b), Weber clearly recognized that disciples or followers of a charismatic figure seek demonstrable and tangible proof of charismatic powers, because they have needs that the charismatic can satisfy. The authority of charisma tends to be confirmed by the capacity of the leader to provide health, wealth or political success for his (and rarely her) followers. Thus Weber (1966b: 47) observed that 'it was only under very unusual circumstances that a prophet succeeded in establishing his authority without charismatic authentication, which in practice meant magic. At least the bearers of a new doctrine practically always needed such validation.' In other words, in the struggle within the religious field charismatic leaders seek social vindication from followers typically through magical means. To understand charisma we need to appreciate its manifestations in social relationships. It is clear that Weber, unlike Bourdieu, was not especially interested in the psychology of charisma, and focused his attention instead on the social exchange between religious leaders (such as prophets) and their potential followers and disciples.

Bourdieu's attempt to 'sociologize' charisma thus distorts Weber's typology of prophet, priest and sorcerer. Of course one can sympathize with Bourdieu's interpretation of Weber, because Weber's account in *Economy and society* contains an ambiguity. A charismatic leader's authority depends on the compliance of his or her followers. Thus the charismatic figure 'gains and retains it solely by proving his powers in practice. He must work miracles, if he wants to be a prophet. He must perform heroic deeds, if he wants to be a warlord. Most of all, his divine mission must prove itself by bringing well-being to his faithful followers' (Weber, 1978, II: 1114). Nevertheless, Weber had to retain some notion of the difference between pure and pragmatic charisma in order to recognize the difference between the radical transformation of secular history by charismatic intervention, on the one hand, and the magical manipulation of charismatic tricks for mundane ends, on the other. For Weber charisma has revolutionary potential. We might therefore reasonably compare Weber's notion of 'charismatic breakthrough' with Alain Badiou's notion of 'the event' as that moment of pure chance dividing history into profane past and sacred future. St Paul recognized that momentous division in the eucatastrophic resurrection of Christ in his proclamation 'Christ is Risen!' (Badiou, 2003). Without some notion of an eventful charismatic breakthrough we are left only with the uninteresting definition of a charismatic as any person who, normally by a few magical tricks, is presumed to have unusual qualities. In brief,

Bourdieu transforms Weber's theory of charisma into a commonsense theory of religious institutions. As a result charisma is hardly distinguished from convention.

The underlying assumption of Weber's theory of secularization was that charisma as a source of inspiration and social change was no longer available to modern societies. Few sociologists, apart from Günther Roth, have since taken up the challenge of rethinking charisma for the present. For another exception I turn briefly to the work of Charles Lindholm, whose main question is why people turn to certain charismatic figures whose message can have devastating negative consequences for their lives. His examples include Charles Manson, who was associated with a number of brutal murders in 1969 in southern California, and the followers of Jim Jones in an alternative community in Guyana, who committed mass suicide by drinking cyanide-laced Kool Aid. He also considers the career of Adolf Hitler, who was unquestionably charismatic, but who was ultimately responsible for the deaths of millions of people and whose misguided military adventures brought about the destruction of the Third Reich. Lindholm's approach is to study, through these troublesome examples, 'charisma as the source of emotionally grounded action' (Lindholm, 1990: 5). Such phenomena are not of course exclusively connected to gruesome acts or to military leaders, but in modern times closely associated with film stars and celebrities of all kinds. He correctly notes that charisma is always about relationships between leaders and followers, and that charisma cannot be learned or acquired through careful training. It is something people have rather than something acquired as a result of coaching. He also notes that in almost all cases of ethnographic research the charismatic figure is male. Whatever happened to female charismatics?

Lindholm makes a number of valuable additions to Weber's original theory, mainly in terms of his attempt to understand charisma within a modern social world that is in Weber's terms disenchanted. He connects modern charisma with narcissism, arguing that the modern world is complex, fluid and fragmented, and the general absence of adequate personal support mechanisms results in anxieties and uncertainties about personal identity. Social groups or movements that are emotionally charged offer an opportunity to fuse an uncertain sense of personal identity with a collectivity that has a clear sense of membership, structure and direction. He quotes David Gutman (1973: 615) as saying that when the internal superego can no longer provide any adequate direction, 'it is reborn externally. . . . It becomes the coercive power of the priest, the prince, the sorcerer – and "the group".' The face-to-face groups of the past have disappeared in modern societies, and when individuals experience a damaging sense of isolation, charismatic leaders and their closely knit social following present an opportunity to be reconnected with the social. Lindholm (1990: 175) concludes by claiming that his examples (Nazi Germany, the Manson family, and the People's Temple) 'are reminders of the intensity of this pressure toward communion and revitalization through charisma'. Given his attention to the role of emotions and action that appears to be driven by intense feelings, it is interesting that Lindholm did not go on to consider the role of the body of the charismatic in these social movements.

Rethinking charisma

In this section I consider three avenues by which a theory of charisma could be revisited and revised. The first is to consider the embodiment of charisma, how charisma as bodily material (blood, sweat and tears) is transferred to disciples, and how the stigmata and embodiment of charismatics are important in their authentication. Charismatic leadership raises one major question: what to do with the body of a dead charismatic? Second, I look at examples of where charisma is hidden from potential followers rather than, as it were, flaunted before an audience. Third, and related to this observation about the secrecy of charisma, I emphasize the fact that often the proof of charisma is that charismatics typically experience the calling as an involuntary event or process occurring against their will. Charisma is given and not chosen. It is for this reason that there is an important difference between what I call celebrity politics and charismatic authority.

Existing theories of charisma have correctly concentrated on how, from a sociological point of view, charismatic authority is authenticated. From a commonsense point of view it would appear to be sensible to start with what people think or believe about a charismatic, that is with beliefs about charisma, but I want to start rather with the body. A charismatic individual often provides gifts or a blessing, and such exchanges typically involve the laying on of hands, or kissing, or touching in some way. Charismatic power is often transferred through the body, and these transfers are often through the human hand. Another conduit of charismatic powers is through the liquids that can come from the body. Christ's blood and Mary's milk in Christianity have been symbolic means of transmitting charismatic healing powers, and medieval paintings of the Virgin Mary show her breast exposed to produce life-giving and life-affirming milk. In much folk religion this transfer of power is actually achieved by material means through bodily contacts. In North Africa Sufi saints among the Hamadsha confer blessings on the crowds that attend their ceremonies by blood that is cut from the head of Sufi charismatics in dance rituals, and women who want to keep the evil eye from their children will capture drops of blood on small pieces of cloth (Crapanzano, 1973). The human hand is also connected with warding off the evil eye, and in both Christian and Muslim folk traditions amulets were important in guarding children from such evils (Hildburgh, 1955). Unsurprisingly, Christ's hand raised in blessing transferred his charismatic healing to the crowds that followed his preaching.

However, a more dramatic and visible confirmation of charismatic (and in this case saintly) authority is associated with the Catholic tradition of stigmata. These physical marks, corresponding to the wounds suffered by Jesus in the crucifixion, especially on the hands and feet, are said to appear on the bodies of saintly people. In a further elaboration of these stigmatic wounds, it was often found that some holy persons gave off a sweet odour that came to be known as the Odour of Sanctity. These stigmatic signs known as the Five Holy Wounds of Christ are associated with the cult of saints. The term is originally taken from a passage in the Letter to the Galatians where St Paul proclaimed: 'I bear on my body the marks of Jesus.' However, the foundational example in the Roman Catholic Church is St Francis of Assisi, who in 1224, while on a journey to Mount La Verna to fast, saw a winged angel. When the angel had departed St Francis was left with stigmatic wounds on his hands, feet and side that often seeped blood. After St Francis had become a dominant saintly figure in Catholicism the Church set up stringent criteria to protect the faithful from false charismatics who might attempt to fake the stigmatic signs by cutting themselves or by using corrosive substances such as carbolic acid. With the growth of scientific medicine and the more recent growth of clinical psychiatry and psychoanalysis these stigmata are often rejected as manifestations of suggestion or hysteria. The Catholic Church has from the twentieth century also employed such scientific methodologies to test whether in its view the explanation of stigmatic phenomena is natural (for example a result of psychological suggestion) or supernatural (the product of divine intervention). From the Church's point of view true stigmatic events (or in sociological terminology pure charisma) are supported by three types of evidence. If doctors cannot stop the bleeding from stigmatic wounds, it is plausible to believe that they are not induced or produced artificially. Where there is no morbid deterioration of the wound, which on the contrary remains free from any infections, there are further grounds to believe that the causality is supernatural. Finally, if the clean and perpetual wounds give off a pleasant odour, it suggests that they are not fraudulently produced.

In raising the issue of stigmata, I am less interested in the explanations offered by the Church authorities, and more concerned to note that bodily marks are often important in proving the presence of charismatic power. These events are also interesting in light of Lindholm's observations about gender in relation to charisma. Michael Carroll in *Catholic cults and devotions* (1989) claims that the overwhelming majority of stigmatics have been female. These include such important saintly examples as Catherine of Siena, Catherine of Ricci, Blessed Anne Catherine Emmerich, Veronica Giuliani, Marie of the Incarnation, Marie Rose Ferron, Therese Neumann, and Rita of Cascia.

One might entertain several objections to these examples. The first might be to argue that they belong to medieval Catholicism and have little relevance to contemporary religion. The changing nature of gender relations in modern societies may also bring about radical changes in female piety. More importantly, one might say that the lives of the saints tell us more about the routinization of charisma, because these charismatic saints through the process of canonization have been subject to what we might call ecclesiastical routinization. In order to begin to address some of these issues, I want to consider how the biographies of Padre Pio and Mussolini offer important insights into charisma in the twentieth century and provide examples by which we can develop the sociology of charisma.

Padre Pio and Mussolini

The experience of stigmata by the Catholic friar Padre Pio appears to be a direct parallel to the experience of St Francis. On the morning of 20 September 1918 Padre Pio was praying in front of the crucifix in the monastery chapel of San Giovanni Rotonda on the Gargano Peninsula in southern Italy when a winged figure appeared. When the strange personage had disappeared Padre Pio was left with stigmata on his hands and feet, which remained with him through the rest of his life, giving off both blood and a pleasant odour. In the coming decades San Giovanni Rotonda became a major site of pilgrimage and the friar, after much early resistance by the Catholic hierarchy, became the most venerated saint in twentieth-century Italy. In order to understand the charismatic movement that his stigmata inspired, we need to consider Padre Pio in the context of war-torn Italy, the rise and fall of Fascism, and the history of Catholic modernism. Put simply, we need to consider this charismatic event in the context of the political and military catastrophe that engulfed modern Italy.

In his brilliant biography of Padre Pio, Sergio Luzzatto (2010) draws our attention to the traumatic character of 1918 in Italian history. The experience of trench warfare had left thousands of families without sons, and the survivors were often deeply traumatized. To the horrors of war was added the 'Spanish flu' in which more Italians died than in the First World War. Paradoxically, while the young men died in the war, the influenza epidemic appeared to kill mainly women and children. In their collective suffering Italians embraced traditional Catholic symbols of grief and mourning such as the *Mater dolorosa*, the Holy Mother with the dead figure of Jesus in her arms. In addition many leading Italian poets and intellectuals came to see the war as a narrative of religious suffering. For the poet Gabriele D'Annunzio, the war was Christ's passion. Luzzatto implies that traumatized Italians needed a saint to make sense of a senseless world. Nevertheless, to accept the wounds of Padre Pio had many controversial and divisive implications: was this a figure to compete with St Francis? Was it possible to embrace the idea that there had come into existence an *alter Christus*, a living Christ in our midst? It is hardly surprising that at first the Holy Office actively resisted the claims of Padre Pio and attempted to isolate him from his followers, because he quickly became the figurehead of a popular religion that was a direct challenge to the authority of the Church – that is, the challenge of charisma against routinized and institutionalized authority. The Church authorities did not believe the miracles that his followers claimed had occurred and feared the groundswell from popular rural religiosity.

In addition to these conflicts between popular and official religion, Italy was also torn apart politically between the left and the right, between secularism and traditional religion, between industrial cities and the impoverished countryside, and between the industrial north and the agrarian south. Padre Pio was, despite his isolated and remote location on the Gargano Peninsula, deeply involved in the political movements that were dividing Italy between the prospect of a Soviet revolution and a Fascist one. It was in the 1920s that 'clerico-fascism' began to emerge in opposition to communism, but more generally in opposition to secular modernism. Clerico-fascism was a response to the social instability produced by war, and the local clergy and Fascists agreed on the need to subdue secular communism, and the importance of family life and high fertility rates for the future of Italy. Padro Pio, at least for local clergy and laity, could become important in reviving the religion of the south through his priestly provision of regular Mass and confession, but more dramatically through the many miracles associated with his bodily presence. The blood that dripped regularly from his body spoke eloquently of his piety.

Despite his obvious humility and piety, Padre Pio offered his symbolic support to clerico-fascism. In August 1920, on the feast of the Assumption of the Virgin, a fleet of cars carrying the war wounded (the *mutilati*) and other veteran groups arrived at San Giovanni Rotonda. They assembled in the town's square, and Padre Pio made the sign of the cross over their banners and pennants, thereby blessing the post-war struggle against the growth of a red Italy. The friar found himself at the centre of a tradition of Christian writing about sacrifice, suffering and pain. It was this linkage between what Luzzatto (2010: 84) calls Christian martyrology and Fascist martyrology that 'lies at the heart of the clerico-fascist alchemy'. These connections demonstrate that, while the friar had a large following of the pious, he also had the support of a political movement.

Despite his local popularity, the Church hierarchy attempted to contain Padre Pio's charismatic activities, and put together numerous scientific investigations of the friar's miracles. Many of the reports and observations of him were sceptical and negative. He was described as a 'psychiatric hospital mystic' with an 'infirm mind' and a limited understanding of the world. His miraculous wounds were in fact simply an example of auto-stigmatization, and hence fraudulent. His intimate relationship with many female followers was regarded with suspicion. The modernists within the Church rejected miracles and stigmata, and Church hierarchy, even when it rejected modernism, nevertheless saw popular religious movements as a direct challenge to ecclesiastical authority. The response was at first to limit his contact with the laity, and later the authorities attempted to remove him from San Giovanni Rotonda. At this stage the local Fascists, who had formed a guard to protect him from the ecclesiastical authorities, threatened to prevent any attempt to remove him.

In the post-war history of Italy these conflicts between communists and Fascists receded as Italy entered into an economic boom, the 'economic miracle'. The term *miracolismo*, first appearing in 1950–1, defined the transition of Italy from an agricultural to an industrial society. In these changing economic and political circumstances, Padre Pio began to gain greater acceptance from the Catholic authorities. The number of pilgrims continued unabated, including a visit from Karol Woytyla (later Pope John Paul II) in April 1948. During this social transition Padre Pio the rustic and simple friar began to symbolize a society that was rapidly disappearing, but at the same time he was also being transformed into a modern Italian celebrity rather than an anachronistic religious figure. Luzzatto (2010: 246) captures this transition as one involving 'a postmodern logic in which the sacred and the spectacular are tightly bound together'. The age of the mass media had an impact on both the Vatican and the friar. Pope John XXIII had sought to remove the media from any involvement in the death and burial of popes, in particular attempting to put in place norms that would prevent his own death becoming a tabloid event. Padre Pio had meanwhile become a favourite object of the worldwide *paparazzi*, who invaded San Giovanni Rotondo to record the friar celebrating the Eucharist with his stigmata highly visible on his bare hands. The front page of the photo magazine *La Settimana Incom Illustrata* in 1959 had an image of the ageing friar alongside a photograph of the beautiful actress Claudia Cardinale. This was also the period in which Federico Fellini was producing his masterpiece of *La Dolce Vita*, depicting the transition of Rome into the new epoch of consumerism and hedonism. Padre Pio survived these social upheavals, dying eventually in September 1968, and his death offered up one more miracle – his wounds had healed and there were no scars left on his body. The struggle between the friar and the hierarchy was concluded when Pope John Paul II celebrated the beatification of the friar, which was followed eventually by his canonization in 2002. The celebrations in St Peter's Square marked the reconciliation between inspiration and convention, between the universal and the local church, and in Weber's terms between the priests and the prophet.

Turning now to another narrative of charisma, Benito Mussolini's life was closely connected to that of the holy friar, and their careers perhaps define the charismatic continuum between religious and secular power.

While Padre Pio's vocation was in one sense involuntary as a consequence of the visit of the winged figure, Mussolini's charisma was essentially voluntary, modern and the product of an emerging system of
mass media. Mussolini's posturing, his jutting chin and his military uni-
forms were designed to impress his followers and to impose his authority.
These bodily gestures of physical power were representative of the
Fascist movement as a political ideology that concentrated on the need
for social order. Mussolini's body was an essential element in his charismatic career. Its solidity and brutality were in many ways the mirror
image of the public architecture that characterized both Italian Fascism
and German National Socialism. For example, Mussolini's head was
the object of much popular attention and the basis of kitsch artworks
that reproduced it for popular consumption. Whereas King Victor
Emmanuel was a slight, mediocre figure, Mussolini, the son of a black-
smith, was imposing and commanding. According to Luzzatto (2005: 16)
in *The body of Il Duce*, in 'Fascist and Nazi ideology, the leader's authority
derived directly from his body'. The main problem with such an ideology –
as Weber's theory of charismatic authority so clearly recognized – is what
happens to political authority on the death of the leader.

For at least two decades after the march on Rome in 1922 the majority
of Italians were emotionally committed to and enthusiastic about the
leadership of Il Duce. However, his authority began to crumble as a
consequence of the social crises that developed during the Second World
War. After Italy's devastating losses on the Soviet front the Church began
to distance itself from Mussolini and his regime. As the fortunes of war
produced shortages and social unrest Mussolini was seen as incompetent,
and he was eventually removed from office on 25 July 1943. In Rome
busts of Il Duce were dragged behind trams. Luzzatto (2005: 39) claims
that his political decline was reflected in his organic decay, and his fall
from authority was associated with his 'bodily decrepitude'.

Mussolini was to have one more experience of limited power. Having
escaped from prison at the Gran Sasso in the autumn of 1943, he was
installed as the head of an Italian Social Republic in northern Italy at
Salo with the backing of the German forces. By this stage Mussolini was
sixty years of age and had lost his impressive commanding presence,
and consequently he appeared infrequently in public. His death was a
pathetic and unheroic ending. Dressed in a German army overcoat and
with a bag stuffed with cash, he attempted to escape to Switzerland
on 27 April 1945, but was arrested by partisans on the shores of Lake

Como at Dongo. Mussolini and his mistress were shot in front of the gates of Villa Belmonte in Giulino on 28 April. From the place of execution, their bodies were then taken to Piazzale Loreto on 29 April and left in a heap, where the crowds showered blows upon them. Mussolini's body was riddled with bullets, and pelted with vegetables. Eventually the corpses were hung by their heels from a crossbar in front of a petrol station. For years afterwards there was a struggle over the remains of Mussolini in which the neo-Fascists and their opponents confronted each other over his corporeal legacy, namely what to do with the body. The death of a charismatic figure always presents problems. The pathetic death of Mussolini raised questions about why Italians had so worshipped and followed him.

Conclusion: charisma in the age of celebrity

What lessons can we learn from Padre Pio and Benito Mussolini? The life of the poor friar suggests that there may be sub-types of charisma that need more attention and careful analysis. The friar was a humble and somewhat secretive figure who appears to have shunned publicity. Mussolini was essentially a theatrical personality whose stage was Italian politics. He flaunted his charisma. Regardless of their intentions, both men were eventually caught up in the world of modern media. They were not only celebrated during their lives, but caught in the moment of death. One can argue that the media in the 1960s celebrated a democratic dream of social mobility and success (Sternheimer, 2011), but this image was hardly compatible with the humble origins of Padre Pio. Nevertheless, the 1960s and 1970s were more compatible with a gospel of prosperity than the traditional gospel of austerity and poverty that had defined the world of the friar's birthplace. This suggests that in the modern world charisma cannot avoid becoming celebrity – a development that Weber could not have anticipated at the beginning of the twentieth century. It is perhaps poetic justice, or at least historical irony, that the best example of contemporary charisma as political celebrity is Silvio Berlusconi.

To conclude, one major argument in the classical sociology of religion was developed by Émile Durkheim, proposing that the roots of the social are ultimately in the sacred. If we accept the direction of Durkheim's sociology of religion, the ultimate roots of community are sacred, and thus that which binds people together into powerful, typically emotional, bonds are religious forces. However, the Durkheimian roots of sacred space are constantly eroded by the impact of Manchester economics, utilitarianism and the individualism of a market-driven society. Weber's sociology of religion is somewhat similar if we take the theory of charisma seriously to suggest that charismatic powers are constantly bursting forward to create new social groups, beliefs and institutions. However, these charismatic powers are transformed by the tragic logic of routinization and rationalization. In our day the sacred roots of collective culture are being eroded by globalization and by the intense commercialization and commodification of social relations. With the growth of global social networks a new form of liquid space emerges that has little stability in community. The 'chain of memory' that is constitutive of community has been broken by a long period of possessive individualism and by a more recent period of neo-liberal economic policies, and hence the roots of solidarity are very weak in modernity (Hervieu-Léger, 2000).

3 | City, nation and globe: the rise of the church and the citizen

Introduction: three events

In order to frame a discussion of space, sovereignty and religion in the construction of modern citizenship, I hang my argument on three events in Western history and three texts. These are the writings of St Augustine, specifically *The City of God* (*c*. 413–26), the Treaty of Westphalia (1648) and the Declaration of Human Rights (1948). All three texts were set against and arose out of a background of violence and destruction. Alaric's sacking of Rome in 410 CE, the legacy of the Wars of Religion, and the civilian casualties of the Second World War and later the emerging recognition of the Holocaust. These violent events were at the time seen to be catastrophic, bringing into question the very bases of civilized life. They exposed the vulnerability of the human body and the precarious character of social institutions. These settlements were woven around problems of difference, violence and exclusion: the Jews in early Christianity; Protestant dissent in relation to the hegemony of the Catholic Church and the authority of the Pope during the Wars of Religion; and genocide, ethnic cleansing and displaced populations as the background to the Declaration. These three texts sought to imagine different social arrangements to control or at least mitigate human violence, and in the process these documents involved a conceptualization of the citizen-subject with respect to the city, the nation and finally the globe. Each stage of the conceptualization and redefinition of rights involved a breakdown of the previous framework such as the imperial city, the ecclesiastical structure of Christendom and the nation-state system.

One could choose other texts – Magna Carta, the Annalects of Confucius, the Federalist papers, or Rousseau's *The social contract*. My choice is necessarily arbitrary and constrained by my own time and place. In this sense each text functions as a pretext for me to consider certain key aspects of the construction of citizenship in relation to religion in the West within three different registers. They are also pretexts for how systems of rights ultimately fail to provide the security we all seek in trying to form social relations and political structures. These documents are consequently conceptual aids to thinking about the idea of social crisis. Consequently I do not treat 'citizenship' as an unchanging bundle of rights, and I am not presupposing any smooth evolutionary growth of such rights. Rather, I treat these texts and events as marking certain ruptures in the organization of European societies in which each text grapples, perhaps unsuccessfully, with the problem of how to package the religious and the political, and to answer the conundrum of the One and the Many.

These historical snapshots mark the growing scale of the discourse of rights from the *polis* of the ancient world to the European city, the rise of the nation-state, and finally to the global framework of politics in the modern world. Once more these are not evolutionary transitions. The imperial Roman city collapsed; the system of nation-states was a prelude to the destructive wars of the twentieth century; and finally many critics argue that the system of human rights can never be adequately institutionalized to overcome regional and national competition. Nevertheless, as a sociological exercise, we need to identify common patterns and to recognize improvements in the legal framework of rights that promise greater social and personal security. For example, this long and uncertain trajectory of citizenship describes an urban phenomenon. The growth of rights presupposed a transition from rural to city life. Obviously we can identify Augustine – a philosopher-saint from the margins of the empire – with the imperial city of Rome. Again the Augustinian city might be a pretext for thinking about the sociology of the city as the nexus within which we eventually encounter civility, civil society and citizenship. It was Max Weber in *The city* (Weber, 1966a) who identified the autonomous medieval city as the cradle of Western rights. He contrasted the military fortifications of eastern empires with the cities of northern Italy. These western cities developed various internal organizations such as the militia, and they often enjoyed a certain autonomy such as an immunity from taxation by the local prince. Within their walls there emerged what Weber called 'the city-commune' involving a network of associations and organizations that began to create a civil society (Weber, 1978, II: 1266). Such a social environment was conducive to the emergence of a merchant class enjoying expanding trading relations with their hinterland and other towns and cities. In the 'patrician city' the burgher assembly, which in Italy was given the title *parlementum*, came to constitute the principal sovereign organ of the commune. We can see from this brief description how Weber laid the claim that out of this burgher culture began to emerge the ethos of modern citizenship with local representation and a culture of public debate. Although this characterization of the occidental city has often been challenged as an example of Orientalism on the grounds that cities in the Islamic world often had urban associations that clustered around the mosque and the public baths, these criticisms often miss an important aspect of Weber's argument. In *The city* he claimed that Christianity had contributed to the breakdown of family and kinship as the principal basis of urban solidarity. Because the early Christian view was that membership of the Church was based on a common faith and not on kinship, Christianity offered a revolutionary picture of social bonds. In the Christian commune there was, at least in principle, neither Christian nor Jew, and neither man nor woman. Membership of the Church required a circumcision of the heart. This observation connects Weber's account with Augustine's view that the Christian community was a spiritual and not an earthly association of kin.

While Augustine's treatise of the secular and the spiritual city said that the human spirit would only find its fulfilment in the heavenly kingdom, Augustine was unintentionally writing the first political theory of citizenship as a type of virtue in the context of a failing empire. His *Confessions* can also be said to have explored in great detail a type of subjectivity that we can recognize as distinctively modern. Augustine worked as a bishop in a large and complex imperial system within which there were many different gods and many centres of imperial power. By contrast, the Westphalian system laid down the juridical foundations of citizenship within the sovereignty of the nation-state, and set the scene for the great land rush of 1600–1900, leaving behind it a legacy of unsolved aboriginal rights. Citizens of the Westphalian Treaty were to be homogeneous (at least in religion) and they were under one prince. In the twentieth century the Declaration of Human Rights recognized that the industrialization of war had exposed civilian populations rather than military personnel to immeasurable harm, requiring a new framework of law and rights beyond the nation-state, and at the same time leaving an unresolved ambiguity between the rights of humans *qua* humans and citizens as members of nation-states.

Modern citizenship as we know it came to be built around nation-states claiming sovereignty over parcels of land in which citizen rights were exclusionary claims over the benefits and privileges of political membership (Turner, 1986). The emergence of the modern nation-state took place alongside three centuries of colonization in which there was a parcellization of land among the sea-going empires – first of Portugal and Spain, and later of Britain, Holland and France. One unintended consequence of the rise of British naval power was that to fund the Royal Navy in the eighteenth century the British monarch created income tax, which was also a necessary stage in the creation of citizenship as a system of contributory rights. Powerful navies made possible a global land grab, and the system of slavery that was associated with this sea-borne imperialism created a subordinated population of slaves and the largely hidden world of the indigenous Other.

In the modern global world many observers believe that these social ties within the nation-state are breaking down. There has been, it is argued, a significant secularization of the West in which the religious foundations of city life are almost non-existent. Furthermore, the growth of mega-cities means that the associational organization of citizens that was envisaged in the work of Rousseau is no longer practical. More importantly, in a global world of mass migration, traditional forms of citizenship are now too restrictive and brittle to contain and express the complexities of modern identities with the growth of diasporas, refugees and stateless people. The idea of citizenship as a national rather than city identity is consequently being transformed with globalization. Many modern theorists such as Seyla Benhabib (2004) argue that citizenship has to be disaggregated, that the *demos* can no longer be understood as an integrated and homogeneous order, and finally that territorial self-sufficiency and sovereignty can no longer operate in a global environment. The real problem here is that the roots of the social itself are changing rapidly and deeply. The social in which citizenship has been embedded is changing with the decline of what I have elsewhere called 'sticky societies' (Elliott and Turner, 2012). In the fluid and fragmented world in which we live, perhaps we are indeed returning to Augustine's idea that in this world we are merely pilgrims on an uncertain journey. The citizen of the second half of the twentieth century is being replaced by the denizen with limited rights and housed in social relations that are thin and mobile. The sticky social forms of the past are being replaced by assemblages that are elastive and ephemeral. The question for which we have no answer as yet is whether the citizens of the Internet (netizens) can form viable 'communities' within which rights can be housed and protected against rapacious corporations and the creative destruction (to use Joseph Schumpeter's terminology) of late capitalism.

St Augustine and the two cities

Two figures – St Paul and St Augustine – can be said to have defined the early Christian community. As we have seen in Chapter 2 on the charismatic authority of the Church, Paul struggled over the relationship between converts from the Jewish community and those from the Gentile world. His solution was to proclaim that the true Christian was spiritually circumcised in the heart. St Paul has been identified recently by Alain Badiou (2003) as the founder of universalism. Unsurprisingly Augustine was deeply influenced by Paul's teaching on original sin, the body and sexual ethics, but of course Augustine was preaching in a very different context. As he struggled with the problems of the Christian Church in relation to the Roman Empire, with internal conflicts over doctrine and with the question of Jews, it has been said that in the process he created many of the concepts and questions that have constituted modern political philosophy. Whereas the classical political thought of Aristotle had argued that the *polis* was necessary for the satisfaction of human needs, Augustine argued that human needs could never be fully satisfied in this world. Men and women are only pilgrims in this world, and their journey leads to a heavenly city that is far more glorious than the earthly city of Rome. It is only in the City of God that human beings can find peace and eternal life. As a result Augustine set up a tension between two cities – between the sacred and the secular – a tension which implied that the loyalty of Christian citizens was never wholly encapsulated within the imperial city. Whereas Plato and Aristotle had recognized that there was a realm of absolute justice, Augustine argued that humans could never find satisfaction in the quest for justice in the earthly city, but only in the commonwealth created by Jesus Christ. In the process of defining the political, he offered a remarkable definition of the social: 'A people is a gathering of a multitude of rational beings united in fellowship by sharing a common love of the same things.' A true community is bound together, not by kinship or familial ties or by material need, but by love. This shared love of the same things refers not to *eros*, which is necessary for the reproduction of humans, but to *agape*, namely a caring and nurturing relationship.

The social nature of the true Church was constructed by the sacraments of baptism and the Eucharist, which created the social around a
mystical feast in which humans were brought into contact with divinity,
and in the process entered into the Church as the body of Christ.
This way of thinking about social relationships represented a real
break with the classical world. Sheldon Wolin in *Politics and vision*
(1961: 130) expresses this transformation by noting that 'the crux of
these contrasts lay in the inference that *civitas dei* was more perfectly
"political" because it was more perfectly "social". The superiority of
the "social" category over the "political" was a fundamental proposition in Augustine's thought.' The social came to be seen as a natural
and spontaneous gathering together of people to satisfy the deep needs
of sociality (or love, in Augustinian terminology), whereas the political,
which is represented above all by the state, is an artificial and involuntary world of secondary relationships. Human beings are therefore
created and nurtured within this social world, but they are regulated
and controlled by the state. This relationship between the political and
the social was given a spatial definition in the sense that the state was
'above' society, and this imagery entered modern thought via the work
of authors such as Antonio Gramsci, for whom the civil sphere of moral
conduct was a site existing between the coercive power of the state and
the dull compulsion of the economy.

The underlying purpose of Wolin's *Politics and vision* was to lament
the triumph of the social over the political in modern thought. From
Saint-Simon and Auguste Comte to the theories of the organization of
man and industrial society sociologists had subordinated the political to
the social, and in the work of Émile Durkheim the problem of modern
society was identified as the weakness of social solidarity, the pillar on
which everything else comes to depend. In this struggle between two
contrasted visions of the relationship between the social and the political
we might also understand the rise of 'citizenship studies', because the
modern theory of citizenship has involved a social rather than a political
theory. Political science has understood citizenship to reside in voting
behaviour, military service and taxation – that is, in a set of institutions
that connect individuals to the state and thereby to a national identity.
Sociology, by contrast, has seen citizenship as an assembly of social
relationships within civil society that binds individuals together into a
viable community before they can enter into relationships with the state.
For sociology, the community of citizens exists before they enter into

contractual relationships with the state, and without those primary connections the social contract cannot have any force. Citizenship gets its political significance from the assembly of social relations that provides the supportive framework for acts of citizenship. This view of the social and the political was of course the famous argument of Durkheim that the validity of the social contract presupposed a prior set of social norms and values. In modern times this vision of the relationship between the social and the political was famously challenged not by a major political thinker but by the conservative agenda of Margaret Thatcher when she claimed that society does not exist, only individuals and their families. We can argue therefore that the neo-conservative agenda is profoundly anti-Augustinian in claiming that familial ties are primary, and hence the market is now the public sphere and the family is the private arena of the individual. In Augustinian political theology the true community is neither the family nor the state, but the Church as a gathering of rational creatures bound together by the love of common things. In the neo-conservative view society disappears, leaving only the particularity of familial relations and the impersonal exchange of goods and services on the market, and the only site for the agency of the citizen is the market, in which the citizen is redefined as the consumer.

The legacy of Augustinian theology is the idea of the community as a gathering of individuals who, while loving each other, are also connected together by rituals, namely by liturgies and sacraments of the Church. They are assumed to share a common life that transcends other attachments to both the family and the imperial city. The Church-community of believers is a *corpus mysticum* into which individuals enter by baptism, and membership is then reinforced by the Eucharist and a calendar of liturgical activity. This corporate community is assumed to be unified and coherent. The growth of any divisions within this body would require the imposition of order, and so Augustine was forced to recognize that political issues would inevitably arise within the Church. He had therefore to develop some ideas about authority and control within the visible Church even if its members were destined for the invisible Church at the end of their earthly journey. He was forced therefore to produce rules about order, discipline and authority within the Church while maintaining the idea that the secular city was a polity based on coercion and the holy city was a society of love. The City of God is not a visible city; rather, it is a standard against which all human cities must ultimately fail (Weithman, 2011: 248).

To understand Augustine we need to consider in more detail his idea of love which he employs to describe what moves people to want or not to want things. There are two types of love: to love things in themselves and for their own sake; and to love things for their use. Only the first – to love for its own sake – can give humans true happiness, because to love in such a way is to secure justice in human affairs. Sin by contrast arises from our pride when we love things for their usefulness to us. In the City of God, where humans love for the right reasons, a true harmony arises out of diversity, but in the secular city men love out of a sense of pride and there is disharmony. What characterized the earthly city was the quest for domination or power. We need to understand this contrast between two cities as not referring to visible cities, because in the visible Church Augustine recognized that the pious and the unholy exist side by side; indeed, all human beings are divided by these two forms of love. After the event of original sin, the exercise of power is inevitable and necessary. The authority of political power comes ultimately from God, and it is necessary to subdue the pride in humans that leads to conflict.

In one important respect the Roman world, in which Christians were merely sojourners, was highly diverse and divided. There were inevitable conflicts between pagan and Christian, but there were also deep divisions within the Christian community. The conflict with the teachings of the Donatists was especially divisive. The Donatists condemned those whom they accused of being traitors in subjecting themselves to the secular authority of Rome during the persecution of Christians. Donatists were strict with respect to their sense of orthodoxy, arguing that only through re-baptism could these traitors, who had sold out to the Roman authorities to save their skin, re-enter the Church. Augustine rejected their narrow and exclusive doctrines, claiming that his Church was 'catholic' – that is, universal – and rejected the idea of a second baptism. Confronted by this diversity and the ever-present threat of schism, Augustine came to accept the necessity of coercion within the visible Church (Brown, 1964). One division in Roman society that has special importance for an understanding of citizenship was between Jew and Christian. In order to understand this categorization we need to digress briefly to clarify the understanding of membership in fourth-century Rome.

In the ancient world 'religion' typically referred to the cult surrounding practices directed towards a local god who protected the household. More narrowly it referred to scruples required by the cult, or more broadly it defined an ethnic group. In this sense the cult 'functioned as a type of ethnic designation, binding a group together across time as well as space, defining one's kinship group, the *genos* (Greek) or *natio* (Latin)' (Fredriksen, 2008: 7). Kinship was defined by blood, but in turn blood was characterized by sharing the customs that defined kin. In ancient Rome religious differences were a fact of everyday life, because different social groups were defined by their scrupulous adherence to the customs that pertained to different gods. Baptism defined a new type of kinship between individuals within the Church, and indeed we might say that baptism transcended family and kinship by creating a spiritual family that was extended into the coming Church.

In this world of cults, where piety or scrupulousness was embedded in ethnicity, there was no such thing as conversion in the modern meaning of the word. When an individual crossed these ethnic–religious lines the transition took the form of a fictive adoption in which the incoming person adopted the customs of the host community. Jews had from the dawn of the Christian community lived as a diaspora throughout the Hellenistic world, and they had become a target of Christian hostility, because the New Testament, and John's Gospel in particular, had defined them as a community responsible for the betrayal of Christ. Jews were not only to blame for Jesus' betrayal and crucifixion, but they were in the eyes of ascetic Christians also associated with the flesh, whereas Christians were associated with the spirit. Augustine accepted and embellished this legacy to claim that the Jews were locked within the Law and had neglected its spirit. They had received the message of salvation, but rejected it, and as a result they had embraced the world of the flesh, turning their backs on the spirit. However, as Paula Fredriksen (2008) demonstrates in *Augustine and the Jews*, Augustine came eventually to ground his understanding of the Jews in Psalm 59.11–12: 'Do not slay them, lest at some time they forget your Law; scatter them by your might.' This scattering of Jews was to act as living proof of the message of Jesus. For Augustine the Jews were not to be slain, because they shared the same scriptural origins that had shaped the early Church, and they had received the same message of salvation. The Jews and the Christians were not defined by their allegiance to their ethnic or hearth gods, but to the one supreme God. However, while the Jews were scattered, in theological terms they remained committed to their own land, whereas the universal Church of the Christians was everywhere.

To conclude this discussion, Augustine can be said to have forged a new notion of citizenship as an aspiration for membership of a city held together by love rather than by coercion, and by spiritual ties rather than by blood. The Christian Church was bound by the body and blood of Christ given to them in a common festival. In this sense the Church was a new type of 'family' that was unlike the secular family. Whereas the human family was the product of human lust, the Christian family was the product of a spiritual love. The human preference for kin was for Augustine equivalent to the same mindless character as the behaviour of animals towards their offspring, and he called this preference a 'carnal custom' because it comes from habituation rather than from rational behaviour. The love for one's neighbour is superior to the merely habitual regard for kin. The Church held celibacy in high regard precisely because it offered a life without sexual distractions and familial involvements. In this Augustinian contribution to political theory, citizenship is above all a public identity founded on the social relations of civil society, and kinship and family stand in the way of the growth of social citizenship.

Augustine's *The City of God* has to be seen against the background of the entry of the Visigoths under Alaric into Rome on 24 August 410. The Visigoths remained for only a few days, and hence the attack was only of modest importance in comparison to the military disasters of the late empire. The initial impetus for the *City of God* was to defend Christians from the accusation that their neglect of the ancient gods of Rome had caused the military weakness that had guaranteed the success of Alaric's invasion of the imperial city. Edward Gibbon's *The decline and fall of the Roman Empire* (Gibbon, 2005) has nevertheless provided the classic account for subsequent historians of the conditions that contribute to the end of empire. The fall of the Holy Roman Empire and the final break-up of the system created by Constantine ultimately paved the way for another development in the idea of citizenship as a post-imperial form of membership.

The Treaty of Westphalia: religion and modern sovereignty

The Treaty of Westphalia was equally framed by a century of religious violence and persecution involving significant loss of life, population decline and widespread devastation. The Peace of Westphalia was in fact brought about by two separate treaties, the Treaties of Osnabrück and Münster. These treaty arrangements brought to an end the Thirty Years War (1618–48) and the Eighty Years War (1568–1648). The treaties were the outcome of the first modern diplomatic congress involving over one hundred separate delegations which met on an irregular basis between 1643 and 1646. The two treaties produced the Westphalian system of sovereign states, which was based on the idea of a state ruled over by a sovereign person. The sovereign rulers of the Imperial States were to determine the religious worship of their subjects in a new system where Roman Catholics and Protestants (or at least Lutherans and Calvinists) were to be regarded as equal before the law. While the Treaty of Westphalia is typically regarded as the diplomatic and legal framework of European constitutional secularism, it was in fact based on an earlier legal recognition of territorial sovereignty and the right of the ruler to determine the religion of the inhabitants of his sovereign terrain by the Treaty of Augsburg in 1555. This was the famous principle of *cuius regio, eius religio*. However, the only options in this official recognition of de facto religious pluralism were Catholicism, Lutheranism and Calvinism. Of course these arrangements did not automatically solve the problem of majority–minority relations, and hence protection was to be offered to those Christians living in states where they were a minority. These minorities were given the right to practise their faith in public during specified times, and thus these provisions recognized the right of individuals to practise their faith in private. The treaty did not give a clear foundation for religious tolerance. Rather, it allowed for the establishment of Protestantism within the realms of various German princes without opposition from the imperial central government.

Augsburg had implicitly recognized the weakness of the Catholic Church. The Council of Trent of 1563, after many adjournments, gave the Church a stronger sense of purpose and discipline, but it also gave clear recognition of the division between Catholicism and Lutheranism, and as a result it prepared the way for conflict between Protestants and Catholics. It was the attempt to suppress the Protestant sects in Bohemia that brought about rebellion by the Protestants and the Defenestration of Prague (when two ministers were thrown out of the fortress of Hradshin into the surrounding moat) that brought about open warfare. The conflict involved the invasion of a Swedish army into northern Germany, Dutch resistance with English support to Spain, the involvement of Denmark, the clever interventions of Cardinal Richelieu, and the exhaustion of the various parties that brought them eventually to the Westphalian settlement. The Westphalian settlement involved significant territorial adjustments. Both the Netherlands and Switzerland were formally recognized as independent from the Empire. The treaty offered the French control over various parcels of European land, but its arrangements were unable to resolve many land disputes such as those between Sweden and Brandenburg. The treaties were, however, successful in removing barriers to trade, and open navigation was restored to the Rhine.

From the perspective of the principal theme of this book, Westphalia was important because, in attempting to remove some of the causes of religious wars, it involved a step (however small and hesitant) towards eventual acceptance of religious tolerance. The Treaty of Osnabrück recognized three types of worship: public religious services, private worship and the worship of minority faiths. It also recognized that northern Europe was to remain Protestant and was the constitutional foundation of religious tolerance. Westphalian tolerance is often described as the separation of church and state, but it would be more accurate to say that it involved the political control of the sovereign over religion in the interests of social peace. As such it looks more like Caesarism than modern tolerance, involving pragmatism on the part of the princes whose principalities were exhausted by war and whose populations had been decimated by unceasing conflict.

Hobbes's Westphalian theory of the state

Thomas Hobbes can be regarded as the theorist of the Westphalian system, because he viewed any division in the unity and sovereignty of the state as a recipe for civil war, and he famously declared that a house divided against itself cannot stand. He grew up in one of the most turbulent periods of English history, and his theories clearly reflect the political crises of his time, culminating in the English Civil War and the execution of Charles I. The English Civil War broke out in 1642, and Hobbes was closely involved with some its leading figures, becoming eventually a mathematical instructor to Charles, Prince of Wales. Born prematurely at Malmesbury in April 1588 when his mother heard the approach of the Spanish Armada, Hobbes declared that she gave birth to twins: 'myself and fear'. This observation in many respects is a useful summary of Hobbes's political theory, which offers a rational argument in favour of absolutism.

Leviathan, which was completed in 1650, contains his political theory of the state of nature, social contract and state sovereignty, famously claiming in chapter 13, 'Of the natural condition of mankind', that without a sovereign power and in a state of nature, humans live in 'continual fear, and danger of violent death; and the life of man, solitary, poor, nasty, brutish and short' (Woodbridge, 1930: 253). Hobbes's solution was that, given their capacity for rationality, human beings would surrender a significant amount of freedom in order to commit themselves to a social contract that would bring about peace in civil society. He rejected any division of powers, arguing that the sovereign should have control over military, judicial, civil and ecclesiastical powers.

Clearly the experience of bloody strife in England during the Civil War had provided Hobbes with ample empirical material to come to such a conclusion. One cannot be certain, but it would be a reasonable supposition that Hobbes had seen or knew about William Shakespeare's play *King Lear*, which was written between 1603 and 1606. If Hobbes is the theorist of Westphalia, perhaps Shakespeare is its dramatist. The play opens with King Lear attempting to divide his kingdom equally between his three daughters, assuming that, no longer burdened by office, he could lead a life devoted to hunting and entertainment in the company of a small band of knights. Two daughters – Goneril and Regan – have other views on how much power he should retain. The division of Lear's kingdom results in civil war, the eventual destruction of the leading characters and Lear's madness, culminating in the storm scene when Lear is locked out of society. His exclusion casts him into a state of nature which is symbolic of the decay of the regime. It is Hobbes who provides us with a blunt summary of the play: 'a commonwealth, without sovereign power, is but a word without substance, and cannot stand' (Woodbridge, 1930: 382).

Hobbes's political theory is well known and hardly needs comment. It is, however, his views on church and state that are most relevant to this study, since in his rejection of any autonomy for ecclesiastical institutions he most clearly articulates the implications of Westphalia. Hobbes is adamant that any attempt to protect the autonomy and authority of the church outside the unified sovereignty of the state is the greatest political mischief. Consequently Hobbes's *Leviathan* could be said to definitively suppress the legacy of St Augustine's *City of God*, in which the great theologian spelt out the division between the Roman imperial city and the divine City of God as the ultimate goal of Christian life. For

Hobbes the Christian is first and foremost a loyal subject to the king, who in turn is the head of church and state. Only by this inclusion of the church into the body politic can the peace and security of the commonwealth be secured. We do not need to enter here into the debate about whether Hobbes was an atheist who disguised his true beliefs in order to save his life. It is enough here simply to sketch his views of church and state as the intellectual counterpart of the Treaty of Westphalia.

Hobbes's definition of the church is in striking contrast to the legacy of Augustine. For Hobbes a church is 'a company of men professing Christian religion, united in the person of one sovereign, at whose command they ought to assemble, and without whose authority they ought not to assemble' (Molesworth, 1839: 459). In this passage Hobbes ruled out the possibility of a universal church by defining it as a national church under the authority of a single sovereign. He justified this subordination of ecclesiastical authority to the sovereign by reference to the Old Testament, claiming that the idea of a covenant had always been associated with figures such as Abraham and Moses, who combined ecclesiastical and civil power. In the New Testament Christ the King is both the divine and secular ruler. In these references to biblical authority, and in terms of his interpretation of natural law, Hobbes provided a clear defence of the Westphalian principle of *cuius regio, eius religio* – whoever rules, also rules religion. This argument was clearly a defence of the English Reformation, because he recognized that it was the Pope who challenged the idea that the monarch shall also be the head of the Church of England. In an ironic question, he asked 'For who is there that does not see, to whose benefit it conduceth, to have it believed that a king hath not his authority from Christ, unless a bishop crown him?' (Woodbridge, 1930: 248–9). Leo Strauss (1952: 74) gives us this simple but definitive summary of Hobbes's position: 'religion must serve the State and is to be esteemed or despised according to the services or disservices rendered to the State'. We can see the Treaty of Westphalia and Hobbes's defence of it as the definitive rejection of the Augustinian legacy in which human beings inhabited two worlds, in which the secular city was only a temporary and inferior resting place on the spiritual journey.

The origins of British citizenship

The assumptions about religious homogeneity, the sovereign power of the monarchy and the institutional dominance of the Church of England were not particularly problematic in what we might call the 'national consensus' of the British Isles from the union of crowns to the First World War. The twentieth century saw Britain become increasingly multicultural and multifaith, and the religious hegemony of Anglicanism slowly perished in face of growing social diversity. The late tranquillity of the Victorian era was shattered by the Boer War and the First World War, and hence it was war rather than religious diversity that promoted both the idea of and the need for social reform. The improvement of social provision for the working class goes back to the parliamentary leadership of Herbert Asquith and David Lloyd George. Social legislation had been patchy but cumulative from the Workmen's Compensation Act of 1897, the beginning of compulsory health insurance in 1912, the Pensions Act of 1908, and the Unemployment Act of 1934, but the most significant development of a national welfare state was the result of the Report on Social Insurance and Allied Services which was subsequently known simply as the Beveridge Report of 1942.

The committee that produced the report was ironically seen by Ernest Bevin as a way of getting Beveridge out of the way by occupying him with a somewhat minor inquiry, but the Beveridge Report turned out to be a revolutionary document aimed at removing the five 'Giant Evils' of an industrial civilization: Squalor, Ignorance, Want, Idleness and Disease. The report contained among other things recommendations for changes to pensions, unemployment benefit and health care. It enunciated what from the perspective of the twenty-first century is a revolutionary proposal: 'Medical treatment covering all requirements will be provided for all citizens by a national health service organised under the health departments and post-medical rehabilitation treatment will be provided for all persons capable of profiting by it' (Beveridge, 1942: 11). The report recognized that one challenge for Britain in the future would be a low fertility rate and an ageing population, and the solution was to introduce for all citizens 'adequate pensions without means test by stages over a transition period of twenty years while providing immediate assistance pensions for persons requiring them' (Beveridge, 1942: 8). The underlying assumption of the report was that poverty was caused by unemployment, whether resulting from lack of economic demand, sickness or old age. One can see immediately the connection with J. Maynard Keynes's concentration on the causes of 'sticky money' (low investment and weak labour demand on the down side of the business cycle) and with T. H. Marshall's foundational work on citizenship in *Citizenship and social class and other essays* (1950). The Beveridge Report basically describes Marshall's notion of the growth of social rights as a third stage in the history of citizenship which was intended to give citizens a modicum of civilized life.

The Beveridge Report was rejected by Bevin, who argued that higher wages and not social security was the answer to working-class poverty, and by the Treasury on the grounds that a universal scheme was too expensive; Winston Churchill warned the country that such a scheme could not be considered until the war had come to an end. However, the report was immensely popular with the general public and its recommendations were eventually adopted by the Labour Party after their electoral victory in 1945 in a series of acts relating to family allowances, national health, national insurance and industrial injuries stretching from 1945 to 1949. The resulting welfare state was based on contributory rights in which everybody paid into a national insurance scheme supported by the state, the employers and the workers. These contributory rights were the foundations of Marshall's social rights of citizenship, combining duties and entitlements. The welfare state was thus national, secular and compulsory. It is perhaps ironic that Beveridge (later Lord Beveridge), who was the son of an Indian civil servant, should be the chairman of what amounted to a socialist revolution. While the resulting social security scheme was the product of a secular economic interpretation of the social requirements of post-war Britain, the report was welcomed by William Temple as 'the first time anyone had set out to embody the whole spirit of the Christian ethic in an Act of Parliament' (Barnett, 2001: 29). Temple, who was Archbishop of Canterbury from 1940 to 1944, supported the working-class movement and social reform, defending his combination of socialism and Christian faith in *Christianity and the social order* (Temple, 1942).

Citizenship rights versus human rights

I have dwelt on the Beveridge Report as the foundation of the Marshallian view of national citizenship, because by the middle of the twentieth century there were two competing visions of social rights as a foundation for human security, namely a contrast between the contributory rights of citizens within a sovereign nation-state and universal human rights regardless of national identity or political membership. The implication of contributory rights, however, is that they are exclusionary; Marshallian citizenship says nothing about the rights of migrants and minorities, and it presupposed a rigid division between the public and private worlds, whereby women were implicitly relegated to the domestic sphere. The Declaration of Human Rights of 1948 was a utopian (indeed, religious) document with universal ambitions, while the Beveridge Report developed a national platform for social reform, which was nevertheless seen by the Cabinet as a utopian document beyond the economic means of the country. It is important to keep in mind the fact that the rights of human beings and the rights of citizens typically stand in a contradictory relationship.

One issue that runs throughout this study of religion and politics is the conflict between sovereign states, on the one hand, and human rights and the individual, on the other. One feature of rights utopianism is that politics can be replaced by morality and that totalitarian states and their leaders can be brought to justice. However, enforcement remains a persistent problem of human rights. The other aspect of this long-standing problem, as I have already indicated, is the tension between the rights of citizens and the rights of humans. The French Declaration of 1789, which is seen as the foundational document of secular rights, was a proclamation regarding the Rights of Man and Citizen. This issue is perfectly illustrated in a recent study by Samuel Moyn (2010) in *The last utopia*, in which he argues that human rights have been stymied by the claims of national self-determination to promote national goals.

The idea in the late 1940s that the actions of states could be constrained or checked by human rights was never taken seriously. In a nutshell, the uncompromising emphasis on the Westernization of rights discourse guaranteed their irrelevance and, 'postponed in the focus on declaring rights, the prospect of moving to legally enforce human rights across borders that a few observers still considered a live possibility as late as 1949 was dead by 1950' (Moyn, 2010: 69). Within the cultural framework of Christian conservatism and Western property rights there was no socialist renaissance to offer an alternative vision of rights instruments, and human rights remained incompatible with the national requirements of the modern state.

The anti-colonial movements from the Bandung Conference of 1955 onwards were grounded in the idea of *national* independence and self-determination, and hence these movements were not in any meaningful sense movements for or of human rights. There was an intersection of the claims of the 'new states' and human rights within the UN, but these UN resolutions against colonialism only reaffirmed the priority of nation-states, their borders and their legal sovereignty. The doctrine of self-determination did nothing to institutionalize human rights. The tragedy of the anti-colonial era was that, while self-determination was achieved through political struggles for independence, it was too often the case that post-colonial autocracy crushed the seeds of individual liberty and freedom. In September 1975 Daniel Moynihan, writing to Henry Kissinger, advised him that, if there was to be a new world order free from poverty and hunger, the United States should insist that a minimum standard of political and civil liberty was as fundamental as a right to basic welfare. However, by 1975 America's authority as the champion of liberty for Third World societies was already deeply compromised by the war in Vietnam.

The peculiar upshot of these contradictions between national self-determination and human rights, between individual and social rights, and between liberty and economic development was not, according to Moyn, the rise of human rights but their failure as a system of binding international law. This political failure was by the end of the Cold War replaced by the comforting myth that human rights had in fact flourished in the aftermath of the Second World War in response to the Holocaust and in recognition of the human misery caused by the displacement of millions of people. This reinvention of legal history laid the foundations for the 'contemporary utopian imagination' (Moyn 2010: 82).

Although human rights had as a result struggled to gain recognition and influence, several developments in the 1970s eventually brought them into prominence. Growing dissatisfaction with conventional politics, especially with state politics, and widespread recognition of the failures of communism produced what the Polish dissident Bronislaw Baczko described as the distrust of utopia combined with the desire to have one anyway. Human rights emerged as the most serviceable utopia for a variety of social movements such as women's internationalism and the worldwide explosion of NGO activity. The presence of human rights was further orchestrated by the creation of Amnesty International. In addition, Jewish activists and intellectuals such as Moses Moskowitz formed agencies and councils to promote the cause of Jewry under the banner of human rights. These developments gained further support from President Jimmy Carter who at his inauguration in 1977 declared an absolute commitment to human rights as the foundation of American foreign policy. With the establishment of university courses in human rights, the creation of various institutes for human rights and the support of the Roman Catholic Church for rights based on personalism, human rights became the language of dissent in Eastern Europe and of protest and opposition in Latin America.

Although the Declaration of Human Rights is an overtly secular document, its formulation was nevertheless heavily influenced by Christian ideas. One figure who was central to the growth of human rights and the reassessment of natural law was Jacques Maritain (1882–1973), who played a major role in the drafting of the Declaration. He was critical of the underlying positivist empiricism of science and, influenced by Henri Bergson, he developed a critique of these dominant assumptions, converting eventually to Roman Catholicism in 1906 and becoming a philosopher in the Thomist tradition. In particular, Maritain was deeply influenced by Aristotle and St Thomas Aquinas. The key issue in Thomism, as opposed to Augustinian Christianity, is that Aquinas did not see human nature as essentially evil, and believed in the capacity of human reason to direct action. On these somewhat eclectic foundations (Bergsonian vitalism, Aristotle's virtue ethics and Thomist rationalism) Maritain (1968) came to develop 'integral human-ism' which, while rejecting Western secularism as barren, sought to build a bridge between Christianity and politics. The result was two works of political philosophy – *Christianity and democracy* (1986a) and *The rights of man and natural law* (1986b) – in the 1940s, in which he insisted that without a strong moral foundation democracy and freedom could never flourish. The West required a vital Christianity grounded in a proper appreciation of natural law and expressed in human rights as the modern vehicle of natural rights.

Maritain stood out from most critical social theorists in taking a largely positive view of the United States (Howard, 2011). While both the French left and European conservatives often dismissed America as a mass society and the conduit of crass consumerism, he thought that individual freedom and the separation of church and state in America had produced a pluralistic and dynamic society that came close to realizing his goal of integral humanism. His *Reflections on America* (1958) warned against the dangers of a democracy based merely on the will and opinions of the majority and argued the case for an organic democracy based ultimately on natural law. He was also enthusiastic about Franklin D. Roosevelt's ambition that freedom of religion – so central to the American spirit – should be a basic right of all nations, but for Maritain such freedom was very different from the notion that every religious opinion was valid. Rather, freedom of religion meant freedom for rational debate and dialogue, and hence it meant that the state should never coerce belief.

In any discussion of this contrast between the national rights of citizens and the global rights of humans, the jurisprudential debate typically refers to a position taken up by Hannah Arendt in her analysis of totalitarianism in which she argued that, without the power to enforce rights claims, these universal Rights of Man are empty words. In turn she referred to Edmund Burke, who had famously complained that the rights of an Englishman under common law were a more efficacious protection against tyranny than any number of abstract rights. For Arendt the German Jews were a tragic example of a people who, once deprived of citizenship, could not be easily accepted by any other country, and the absence of any documentation of their social membership effectively expunged their right to rights. This formulation of the problem is well known. John Rawls, for example, treats human rights as rights of last resort, namely as a special class of urgent rights, because they come into play when everything else has failed. In the absence of effective global governance human rights are typically enforced by nation-states, and yet it is nation-states, especially failed states, that are the main perpetrators of human rights abuses. Consequently criticisms of human rights argue that such rights are not in fact 'justiciable', because they cannot be effectively enforced without the cooperation and involvement of states.

Violence and the civilizing process

Many observers believe this situation is changing. In his recent work *The better angels of our nature* Stephen Pinker (2011) questions our taken-for-granted assumptions that modern times are violent, certainly more violent than the past. He presents a wide range of statistics to show that rates of homicide, lynching, rape, domestic violence and so forth declined steeply in the twentieth century. For example, in the United States lynching of African Americans decreased sharply between 1890 and 1940, and hate-crime murders also declined in a similar fashion. Turning to homicide rates, the United States has a history of violence that has no parallel in the developed world. Frontier violence explains part of the American history of killing. There was a homicide rate in the eastern colonies of 100 per 100,000 adults, which ended in 1637 when state control was consolidated. Those regions that remained backwaters beyond the reach of state consolidation continued to have high homicide rates, and the Californian Gold Rush of 1849 also witnessed a significant increase in lawlessness. The South, where self-help justice prevailed alongside the culture of honour, was far more violent than the North. The annual rate of rape has also fallen from 250 per 100,000 women over the age of twelve in 1973 to 50 per 100,000 in 2008. The Violence against Women Act of 1994 is further evidence that sexual violence against women was being taken seriously by the law. There has been a similar decline in reported cases of domestic violence, and the recognition of rape in marriage signals that women are no longer regarded as merely the property of husbands.

How does Pinker explain the decline of homicide rates in the United States? First, most of the violent crime in society is committed by young men between fifteen and thirty years of age. History shows that frontier violence began to lessen as women arrived in greater numbers and violent men settled down to become husbands and fathers. Second, violence declined as state power became more systematically established. The civilizing process required the state and marriage to bring violent men into peaceful domesticity. Similarly, lynching declined as a result of state action, law reform and changes in values about slavery. Pinker recognizes that this explanation involves a Hobbesian solution. Violent young men form a social contract with society through the mechanism of marriage and family life, but religion has played a part in creating a more peaceful society: 'As with the pacifying of the American West a century before, much of the moral energy came from women and the church' (Pinker, 2011: 125).

The United States and Europe are different in terms of state building. In Europe the state disarmed the people, created a monopoly of violence, and became a sovereign power. In America the people took over the state and, as the Second Amendment affirms, they retained a right to bear arms. In presenting this historical material Pinker draws heavily on the work of Norbert Elias. In *The civilizing process* (2000) Elias developed a theory of self-control against the background of the rise of the modern state in Europe. Describing the transition of the man-on-horseback in warrior societies through feudalism to the rise of court society to the bourgeoisie household, Elias argued that norms of self-restraint and control meant that society depended less on external violence and more on self-control to achieve social order. He examined etiquette books, manuals describing correct knightly behaviour and guides to courtesy and refined manners at table to demonstrate the decline of interpersonal violence. However, interpretations of Elias often neglect his state theory. Personal forms of violence – such as the duel – declined because the state, to use Max Weber's terminology, acquired a monopoly of violence. English aristocrats abandoned swords in public spaces, and carried walking sticks, umbrellas and handkerchiefs; they left the battle-field for the City to become gentlemen capitalists, and acquired norms of good conduct on the cricket field. Elias's work is widely respected, but it has also been widely criticized. Elias's parents died in the German concentration camps and, against the background of the destruction of the Jews of Europe, his critics have asked how he could ever believe that Europeans had become more civilized. One possible answer is that, if you read the Norse epics in the Prose Edda, you encounter warriors who killed with enthusiastic gusto. This type of killing contrasts with modern wars of the twentieth century, in which men kill at a distance and when destruction by drones occurs through computers. In modern professional armies rampage is the exception, not the rule.

Pinker explains these developments by reference to changing culture (a greater respect for human autonomy and dignity) and social structure (more effective means of social control). However, the principal cause of the reduction in violence appears to be the Matthew Effect. For example, the decline in violence against women is connected with a set of 'wholesome factors' – 'democracy, prosperity, economic freedom, education, technology, decent government' (Pinker, 2011: 413). These factors cannot be the whole story, because developed societies such as South Korea and Japan have relatively high rates of domestic violence. The difference may be explained by societies in which women have greater representation in government and the professions, and by indi-vidualistic cultures that promote women's rights to empower women to function equally alongside men in the public domain. In short, the Matthew Effect is not so much causation as correlation. The decline of violence against women in the West is 'pushed along by a humanist mindset that elevates the rights of individual people over the traditions of the community' (Pinker, 2011: 414). The language here is rather loose. Perhaps this passage suggests that the legacy of filial piety in Asia treats women as inferior to men, daughters as inferior to sons, and the ruled as inferior to the ruler. It is often said that Confucianism elevated rule of virtue over rule of law.

Pinker treats the rise of human rights, including animal rights, as an outcome of a general civilizing process in Europe and North America – a civilizing process that has global significance. These developments imply the end of the Westphalian system of nation-states, given the emphasis on autonomy and individual dignity that are inscribed in the Declaration. There are many international institutions that defend human rights, bring war criminals to trial and enforce social rights – for example, through the International Labour Organization. With globalization there has been some erosion of state sovereignty and a corresponding growth of legal pluralism. Dual citizenship, international marriages, international tribunals and multiculturalism are seen as evidence of these social changes. Contrary to Pinker's conclusions, I am less sanguine about the peacefulness of the modern world, because his arguments tend to neglect the growing emphasis on state security, the rise of nationalism and increasing xenophobia, the criticism of multiculturalism by European politicians, the enforcement of borders to prevent illegal migration and the development of surveillance technologies to monitor the movement of people. I have elsewhere referred to these negative developments in terms of the rise of an 'enclave society' (Turner, 2007).

What we might call 'the crisis of the Westphalian system' under the impact of globalization is in some respects anticipated by the Declaration of Human Rights, which assumes that human beings now live in a post-national political environment. These human rights stand in some tension therefore with the institutions of national citizenship, and human rights can be regarded as utopian in the sense that their defence rarely takes into account the resources that would be required for their implementation. The economic foundations of national citizenship are by contrast rather obvious – they derive from taxation and from other services performed by citizens in the support of the national community. In modern societies, therefore, there are often two inconsistent vocabularies of rights for humans and for citizens. Nowhere is this confusion more evident than in the case of the United States, where the social rights of citizens in relation to the state are characteristically formulated in a language of individual rights. This problem of the relationship between the state and the individual has become fundamental to modern American politics, where the agenda of the Tea Party is to dismantle state provision of welfare in the name of liberty. The confusion that surrounds the ideas of citizenship rights, civil liberties, individual rights and human rights is perhaps indicative of the breakdown of the tripartite organization of Western history into city, nation and globe.

Conclusion: from citizen to denizen

Denizen: *n.* 1. an inhabitant; occupant; resident. 2. *Brit.* an individual *permanently* resident in a foreign country where [they] enjoy [only] certain rights of citizenship. 3. a plant or animal *established* in a place to which it is not native. 4. a naturalised foreign word [or thing]. *vb* 5. (*tr.*) to make a denizen [C15: from Anglo-French *denisein*, from Old French *denzein*, from *denz*, within, from Latin *deintus*, from within] (Hanks, ed., 1979, *Collins Dictionary of the English Language*, London).

I conclude by arguing that with globalization and the growing geographical mobility of labour, there is for many people a sense of the loss of home. In Augustine's theological vocabulary we are pilgrims once more, sojourning in political spaces. We live in a time of collective nostalgia for the certainties of the past, and people are now denizens rather than citizens. While the concept of citizenship originated with residence in a city-state – the citizen was originally a denizen of a city – and was later developed in the context of the nation-state, the need for a concept of denizenship has developed in the context of international relations during the twentieth century and relies on the idea of the geographical mobility of people from one country in which they usually have citizenship rights (however limited these might be in any particular country) to another country where they live and work – perhaps even permanently – but are not entitled to anything more than limited rights. As more people live and work in countries in which they were not born – and according to the UN Department of Economic and Social Affairs, 191 million persons, representing 3 per cent of the world population, lived outside their country of birth in 2005 (Turner and Khondker, 2010: 105) – and as nation-states increasingly struggle to raise enough taxes to provide comprehensive political, social and cultural rights to all citizens who are entitled to these, then these nation-states will increasingly attempt to deny or to limit full citizenship rights (naturalization) to economic migrants however long they might live and work in that country, where the costs of social and cultural citizenship outweigh the benefits to the state in the form of direct taxation. In short, since the concept of citizenship and the rights that go with this are unavoidably linked with the development of the nation-state (no nation-state, no citizenship), and given the continued predominance, despite all the current talk of globalization, of the nation-state in world affairs in the twenty-first century, there is a growing theoretical need for a concept of 'denizenship' with the increased settlement of people throughout the world in countries in which they are denied full citizenship rights. Various attempts have been made to refine the idea of citizenship for a global world, such as semi-citizenship, flexible citizenship and post-national citizenship, but I am not sure this conceptual transition can be easily achieved (Ong, 1999, 2008). In Asia and elsewhere the great movement of peasants from the countryside into global mega-cities means that modern societies are increasingly societies of strangers.

It is because of the dominance of the market over civil society in the neo-liberal phase of modern capitalism that people are either increasingly able or, according to their means, are increasingly *forced* to buy citizenship rights on the open market in the societies in which they live and work. The new global elites can purchase rights of residence fairly easily, whereas the majority of impoverished migrants have little security and limited access to citizenship rights. Throughout Africa the majority of children have no official birth certificates and hence are excluded subsequently from effective citizenship rights (Manby, 2009). Whereas citizenship rights depend on the state, and ultimately on taxation, denizenship rights increasingly depend on what individuals can buy in the marketplace. Being a citizen with comprehensive entitlements is therefore increasingly a *privileged* position not enjoyed by large sections of the labour force, who are simply mobile guests. The result is a widespread sense of rootlessness and a lack of attachment to place.

The crisis of citizenship is that the Marshallian model of entitlement is breaking down in a global neo-liberal market environment. The problem with contributory rights is that in the new global economy there is a scarcity of meaningful employment at adequate levels of remuneration for young workers to form households in which they can enjoy some level of security, or the levels of pay in the modern economy are too low for workers to enjoy the modicum of a civilized life envisaged by Marshall. At the same time, the decline in personal taxation means that the state cannot provide the benefits required for adequate health care, and the resulting problem with pensions means that, for many, retirement is an entry into poverty. Human rights cannot fill the void created by the decline of the social rights of citizens. Whereas citizens have a capacity for political activity, on the one hand, and duties to perform collective services, on the other, there is little notion of duty in claims to human rights. Basically human rights are the rights of victims rather than of active agents. This erosion of citizenship (Turner, 2001) is one cause of the emerging waves of protest against social inequality, injustice and exploitation that we have seen in the Occupy Wall Street movements, but it is also at the root of modern populism in the Tea Party. Whether these forms of resentment can congeal into organized movements of social change remains to be seen. It is unclear whether this collective resentment will produce effective social change through political action or simply create destructive outbursts against the social order that have no lasting consequences (Lammy, 2012). The world is crumbling apart but as yet we have not found the text – the equivalent of St Augustine's *City of God* – that can make sense of our predicament, or a modern version of the Beveridge Report that could offer a model of global citizenship.

PART II

State management of religion

4 | *Religion and kingship: liturgies and royal rituals*

Introduction: liturgies

Coronations, and related rituals of monarchy, are public liturgies combining religious and secular elements. *Liturgy* is from the Greek *leos* ('people'), and hence *leitourgia* is a secular notion referring to the public duties of the citizen. In the public culture of Athens wealthy citizens performed duties at their own expense, such as the *choragus* who paid for the singers of a chorus at the theatre. It refers therefore to any work of the people directed towards some public duty, and in a religious context it refers to ritual services in a temple. Over time liturgy began to acquire a more precise meaning, for example in the New Testament where it refers to the official services of the Church, corresponding to the public performances in the Temple in the Old Testament.

In the early Church the performance of public rituals such as the Eucharist was not fixed by any exact calendar. In addition, the performance of these rites was not determined by a set of written instructions, but was rather simply delivered by a bishop. While there was no uniformity of practice, thereby allowing local churches to develop their own customs, the basic elements of a liturgy emerged from the performance of the Eucharist in which the bread and the wine were served and the words of the Last Supper were uttered. To some degree these early liturgies simply followed the pattern of worship in the Jewish synagogue, in which passages from the holy books were read, psalms were sung and homilies were read. Over the first two centuries of Christianity these improvisations were standardized as a formal list of basic activities, and the liturgies of West and East also evolved into two distinctive and alternative services. In the West, although there was a uniform liturgy for the whole Church, there remained local variations of the rite corresponding to the patriarchal cities of Antioch, Alexandria, Rome and Gaul. As the liturgical traditions of the West further evolved the Roman rite became dominant, and by 1570 Pius V published his revised Roman Missal that established the official pattern for the whole Church.

Liturgy thus contrasts with any private act of devotion such as the private prayer of an individual. In Roman Catholicism it took on the meaning of the assemblage of services, ceremonies, rituals and sacraments that are delivered in a regular pattern of activities according to a religious calendar. It is an official guide to public practices. The effect of the Protestant Reformation was to limit the role of liturgy in public worship by giving greater emphasis to personal devotion such as Bible study, private prayer and inward self-inspection. After the Reformation pilgrimage and saints' days gradually disappeared from the calendar of Protestant churches in northern European societies, and the sermon now stood at the centre of Protestant worship.

Among other things, the idea of a liturgy serves to remind us that language is not just about informal communication in a social context; it can also involve a performance in which a collection of actors have to bring about a public event through a sequence of acts that require some degree of discipline, skill and competence. These performances – marriage ceremonies, court sentences, funerals and the like – are typically conducted in accordance with some set text. Such performances can be usefully described within the framework of Pierre Bourdieu's notion of the 'logic of practice' (1990). In a modern society that has been deeply influenced since the end of the Second World War by a democratic commercial culture, there is little sense of the liturgical role of language in public spaces. This absence may be connected with the fact that in modern society we no longer easily recognize the role of liturgies in public life. The explanation for these developments is, in my view, related to the weakness of public life itself, and in turn this absence can also be taken as further evidence of secularization.

However, what is lacking in Bourdieu's sociology of practice as illustrated by language is any understanding of the history and politics of liturgy within the public sphere. My argument in this chapter is that the public sphere in late capitalism has been eroded by the emphasis on individualism, the privatization of public utilities, the private consumption of media in the home, and by our obsession with celebrities. The growth of an Internet society has privatized much of our social engagement, further undermining the social role of collective practices. In short, the decline of liturgical practice, at least from the perspective of Émile Durkheim's sociology of religion, is not only an indicator of the secularization of society, but also of a transformation of the very nature of the social. It is an example of what can be called 'an elastic society' in which social relations are typically temporary and transitional (Elliott and Turner, 2012). In short, the decline of liturgies signifies an important transition in the contrast between the sacred and the profane.

The sociology of monarchy

Of course, liturgies have not entirely disappeared in modern societies, and those that remain are typically connected with the power of the secular state. The swearing in of presidents to public office is clearly liturgical, but if we want to grasp the remnants of liturgical ceremony we have to look towards sovereignty and constitutional monarchies. Here again the body is prominent in liturgical recognition of power, often in ceremonies in which the body of the monarch is anointed. The bodies of kings and the problem of sovereignty were the topics of a famous study by Ernst Kantorowitz (1957), who argued that in medieval monarchies the king was thought to have two bodies, one sacred and the other profane. Whereas in ancient times the power of the king resided in his physical body, with the development of political theory and the evolution of the state the king acquired a more profound and enduring sacred body. The king's body became abstract and free from decay, and thus when the king died his attendants shouted out 'The king is dead, long live the king!' Defending the king's physical body was an important defence of sovereign power itself, because any threat to the monarch was an attack upon the state and hence regicide was a most serious crime. Michel Foucault (1977) famously described the brutal destruction of the bodies of regicides in the opening passage of *Discipline and punish*. Eventually revolutionary movements in France and America shook the very foundations of the *ancien régime* and opened up the age of secular government with limited powers. Nevertheless, monarchies have survived in many European societies that have secular constitutions. The British monarchy is perhaps the most significant example. What might the Crown tell us about liturgies in a secular society?

To understand the constitutional nature of British monarchy we need to turn to the most important statement of its functions from the nineteenth century. Walter Bagehot's *The English constitution* of 1867 clearly defined the symbolic and religious significance of the Crown as well as its political and constitutional functions. First, he argued that, while the majority of the British people could not understand the meaning and importance of the constitutional implications of mon-archy as a legal framework in abstract terms, they could readily grasp the symbolic significance of the monarch. In this respect, the people were inevitably connected to the monarchy more by emotion than by reason. For example, while the emotional appeal of the marriage of the Prince of Wales might appear 'childish', women 'care fifty times more for a marriage than a ministry' (Bagehot, 2009: 37). Furthermore, he noted that 'the Americans were more pleased at the Queen's letter to Mrs Lincoln than at any act of the English Government' (Bagehot, 2009: 37). Second, the British monarch is the head of the Church of England, and therefore it is through the monarchy that religion effec-tively contributes to the enhancement of government. While Bagehot was critical of the actual person of George III, he believed that the oath of allegiance was enormously important in securing the loyalty of the people to the underlying principles of the constitution. The monarch was seen to be above politics. While the country was divided into com-peting political parties, 'the crown is of no party' (Bagehot, 2009: 40), and hence it can function to stabilize the society as a whole. Third, the monarch was the symbolic head of society. While he readily admitted that the prime minister could quite easily be the head of society, the authority of prime ministers is inevitably limited by elections, forcing them to leave office on a regular basis. The monarchy could where necessary function to disguise the actual underlying changes taking place in society and government, and thus the monarch expresses the symbolic continuity and coherence of a nation, otherwise divided by class, ethnicity and religion. The monarchy could obscure some of the underlying tensions in Victorian society around religious minorities such as Jews and Catholics, and disguise the obviously profound divisions in terms of wealth. Finally, monarchy is the vehicle of public morality, because the virtues of Queen Victoria and George III, he suggested, had had a significant impact on general values and behaviour.

Despite the prominence of the British monarchy in the institutions of government and church in the United Kingdom, monarchy has not been a topic of serious research among sociologists of religion, and even less so among sociologists in general. Understanding the public func-tions of monarchy has mainly been left to historians. One important exception was an article by Edward Shils and Michael Young, 'The meaning of the Coronation', in 1953 in *The Sociological Review*. The article opens with a critique of 'political science and philosophy' for their neglect of the important role of monarchy in British society, arguing that the reason for this neglect lies in the 'intellectualist' and secular bias of the social sciences in assuming that religion no longer plays any significant role in modern society and more specifically that the political role of the monarch in a democracy is negligible. The palpable enthusiasm of the crowds in celebrating the Coronation is therefore an anomaly from the perspective of a secular sociology. According to Shils and Young, popular support for the Queen during the Coronation celebrations was explained by some critics as 'the product of commercially interested publicity, others that it is the child of the popular press, others simply dismiss it as hysteria or "irrationality"' (Shils and Young, 1953: 71). More plausible explanations suggested that the collective enthusiasm of the nation was caused by British love of pomp and ceremony, or simply by the attractiveness of a young woman and her husband.

Much later Shils reflected on the context and reception of the article in his *A fragment of a sociological autobiography* (2006). In his autobiography, which was edited by Steven Grosby from Shils's notes from 1991 to 1992, he had been reading William Robertson Smith's Aberdeen lectures from 1889, published as *Lectures on the religion of the Semites* (1997), and made the obvious connection between the Coronation as a public ceremony and the notion that 'societies intermittently seek contact with and infusion with the sacred' (Shils, 2006: 87). Shils described his co-author Michael Young as 'a friend and former pupil' whom he had supported in the development of the Institute of Community Studies in Bethnal Green in London. Apparently it was Young who had conducted interviews in east London about working-class attitudes towards the Coronation, and it was left to Shils to provide the theoretical framework in which the Coronation appeared as a moment of 'intense charismatic experience' (Shils, 2006: 87).

Shils and Young approached the Coronation of Queen Elizabeth II from the perspective of Émile Durkheim's notion of public rituals and the celebration of the sacred through collective representations. Following Durkheim closely, they claimed that all societies are based on a set of moral rules, and this collection of values, rituals and disciplines restrains egoism and reins in egoistic individualism. Furthermore, the 'sacredness of society is at bottom the sacredness of its moral rules' (Shils and Young, 1953: 66). Given this understanding of the nature of moral values, 'it is barely necessary to state the interpretation of the Coronation which follows from it: that the Coronation was the ceremonial occasion for the affirmation of the moral values by which society lives' (Shils and Young, 1953: 67). Their article concluded with an even more assertive affirmation of the Durkheimian perspective, namely that the Coronation was 'a great act of national communion' (Shils and Young, 1953: 80).

These observations about British life were admittedly based on scanty evidence. Apparently Shils and Young had toured the East End of London to observe the many street parties that were taking place to celebrate the event. They also noted the public hostility to a cartoon by David Low in the *Manchester Guardian* on 3 June which had been critical of the public expense required for its celebration. They took note of public observations that saw the Coronation in the same light as other major national events such as Armistice Day in 1918 or VE Day in 1945. In their view the Coronation ranked in importance alongside the Blitz, the Fuel Crisis of 1947 or the London smog of 1952, during which there had also been a sense of collective involvement in response to a national crisis. They also commented on a police report that had noted a decline in minor criminal activity around the time of the Coronation. In addition, the Coronation service itself required the Queen to affirm her commitment to the defence of moral standards, and to govern in accordance with the laws and customs of the land. Perhaps a more interesting sociological argument was that Britain in the post-war period was a relatively harmonious and cohesive society, and that it enjoyed a 'degree of moral consensus' that was absent in similar industrial societies.

The Shils and Young argument received a very critical reception, at least in British sociology, partly because Shils's theoretical orientation was closely associated with the sociology of Talcott Parsons. Much of the early version of Parsons' theory of values had appeared in *Toward a general theory of action* (Parsons and Shils, 1951). The Shils and Young article was consequently taken to be representative of the tradition of American sociology in which sociologists such as Parsons allegedly exaggerated the coherence of modern societies resulting from a central value system. In British sociology in the 1960s there was an overall criticism of the assumptions of functionalism which were associated with Parsons' *The social system* (Parsons, 1951), and by contrast there was an emerging interest in 'conflict sociology' associated with the work of John Rex, whose *Key problems of sociological theory* (Rex, 1961) had become a textbook in many sociology departments. Much of the opposition to Parsons in American society was also driven by a sympathetic reception of C. Wright Mills's criticisms of functionalism and 'Grand Theory' in *The sociological imagination* (1959).

For British sociologists in the 1960s, British society was seen to be deeply divided by social class rather than held together by common values, and the Queen was at the apex of the Establishment rather than a symbol of national unity. Sociologists were thus inclined to argue that, while the media often create the impression of a society with unified and coherent attitudes, media studies and specifically audience research showed that audiences are diverse and differentiated, if not fragmented. Consequently events such as the Coronation have different meanings for different social groups, and many attitudes will consequently be discordant with the official view. The Coronation was designed to reaffirm the bonds of family, community and nation within a religious rite, but there was only partial and limited evidence that these harmonious attitudes were shared in the wider community. In her anthropological study *Symbol and privilege*, Ilse Hayden (1987: 157–8) argued that, while the Coronation affirmed the moral values of British society, 'those values were the solidarity of the upper class, the exclusion of the lower ones, the importance of social distance, the unequal distribution of social honor, and the domination of society by an hereditary elite'.

Shils on centre and periphery

In retrospect the Shils–Young argument does appear to be wildly optimistic in claiming that in 1953 the Coronation was a celebration of core moral values and a national communion. What is undoubtedly true is that, in a period of economic scarcity, the Coronation was an opportunity to display national pride and to enjoy street parties in a context of peace. Basic food rationing in Britain did not end until 1954, and consequently British society was, in a period of post-war austerity, notoriously drab, grey and pinched. Contrary to the assumptions of conflict sociology, Shils and Young were correct in detecting a national consensus in the 1950s, and these consensual attitudes were perhaps nowhere better expressed than in taciturn acceptance of endless queues for rationed goods.

The Coronation came at a turning point in post-war Britain where national achievements were being celebrated such as the conquest of Everest in 1953 and the four-minute mile in 1954. A Conservative government had come to power in 1951, and Britain entered a 'new Elizabethan age' in which the popular films of the time (such as *Genevieve* in 1953 and *Doctor in the House* in 1954) portrayed southern England as 'rather perky, youthful, affluent and self-confident' (Judt, 2005: 300). The mood in Britain had changed by the early 1960s to give greater recognition of social class and regional divisions, as illustrated by a series of plays and films exploring social inequality: *Room at the Top* (1959), *Saturday Night and Sunday Morning* (1960), *The Loneliness of the Long-Distance Runner* (1962) and *This Sporting Life* (1963). These 'kitchen-sink' dramas exposed class inequalities, but they also played on the regional accents and attitudes that divided north and south in British life. The 'Queen's English' was the regimented language of the BBC, but not of Birmingham, Preston and Newcastle. In 1936 Victor Gollancz had commissioned George Orwell to visit areas of high unemployment in Lancashire and Yorkshire, and *The road to Wigan Pier* (1937; Orwell, 1989) was a searing indictment of the poverty and despair of the north. While those regional and class differences were still part of the British landscape in the 1960s, they were slowly overlaid and masked by the emerging consumerism of the 1970s.

The celebrations at the time of the Coronation have to be understood therefore in the context of economic scarcity in the immediate aftermath of the war and modest signs of economic improvement by the middle of the 1950s. This period was also followed by the abandonment of what was left of the British Empire, and the Suez Crisis of 1956 had demonstrated that Britain no longer had the resources to sustain its global colonial presence. Under the Conservative government of Harold Macmillan Britain gave up overseas interests in favour of increased domestic consumption. It was Macmillan in 1957 who famously said 'most of our people have never had it so good' and in 1963 he accepted the inevitability of African independence, recognizing the process of decolonization in his 'wind of change speech' to the South African parliament. The rise of a consumer society in Britain and the end of empire produced a national nostalgia, creating a demand for history and giving rise eventually to the heritage industries. In the Macmillan years Britain embraced his political and social strategy, which was based on 'selling colonial retreat abroad and prosperous tranquility at home' (Judt, 2005: 301). By the 1980s Britain was becoming a post-industrial society which was economically dominated by the financial interests of the City and which in cultural terms was increasingly apathetic and nostalgic. The growth of the heritage industries is one important measure of the social transformation of imperial power.

The English problem

Perhaps the most sustained attack on Shils and Young appeared in Tom Nairn's *The enchanted glass* in 1994 in which Nairn described their article as the 'Sociology of Grovelling'. Recognizing the fact that the article was not commissioned by the Buckingham Palace press office, Shils and Young had nevertheless with 'Durkheim's help' given 'a little theoretical gloss to the Old Regime' (Nairn, 1994: 120). He went on to review Birnbaum's critique of Shils and Young, arguing that, while Shils and Young represented a right-wing mythology of Britain as a consensual society, Birnbaum represented a left-wing mythology that the real moral values of Britain were lodged in the working class, who would eventually overthrow the system. Both positions contrasted the 'show' of the monarch and the reality of 'society'. His own position, following Ernest Gellner's interpretation of nationalism as a modern phenomenon, was to argue that the British monarchy with its mythical claims about history and continuity was an essential component of the peculiarities of British society in which modernity is shrouded in and postponed by the archaic rituals of the House of Windsor. The persistence of the British Crown is part of an institutional apparatus that prevents Britain from becoming a modern democracy; its presence has allowed British society to resist and to some extent reverse the modernization of its core institutions and culture.

This thesis was part of the general orientation of the *New Left Review*, where it was argued, most famously by Perry Anderson, that Britain lacked both a valid sociology and a genuine socialist tradition, because it was based on liberalism, political gradualism and class compromise. Nairn refers correctly to the seminal article by Anderson (1964), 'Origins of the present crisis', as the key statement of the *New Left Review* position on British backwardness. In this respect, the Crown itself was seen not only as the foundation of this historical compromise, but as the principal ingredient of Britain's failure to modernize. Nairn's views on British backwardness, the need for Scottish independence, the merits of federalism, and the importance of electoral reform have remained constant across a range of publications from *The break-up of Britain* (1977), *After Britain: New Labour and the return of Scotland* (2000a) and *Pariah* (2002). He has been successful in promoting the humorous idea of 'Ukania' as a fictitious country resembling the Austro-Hungarian Empire in a state of deep decline. In 'Ukania under Blair' (Nairn, 2000b) he argued that under Blair's New Labour government there had been a missed opportunity at genuine constitutional reform of both the House of Lords and the Crown. As a result Britain had lapsed into 'corporate populism' in which citizens are now customers, and New Labour had substituted 'brand loyalty and ordinariness for hope and glory' (Nairn, 2000b: 95).

The real problem in modern Britain is that, while there has been some devolution of power to Scotland, Wales and Northern Ireland through the creation of democratic assemblies, this development leaves England and the English in an anomalous position with respect to parliamentary representation, creating a problematic position in the constitution of the United Kingdom. The Union of Scotland and England came into force in 1707, but it was not uniformly welcomed in Scotland, and many Presbyterian parishes held a day of fasting. It was believed that independence had been sold too cheaply. Despite this early lack of enthusiasm, the Scots did well out of the British Empire, finding employment as administrators, engineers and soldiers in Britain's expanding imperial markets. However, these economic and political advantages have been eroded with the loss of empire, and by the general decline of the United Kingdom as a significant economic and military force. The Scottish National Party came to prominence after the 1974 election, and the discovery of oil and gas in the North Sea gave material substance to the separate cultural identity of the Scots. In addition, the European Union has fostered the autonomy and viability of smaller nations, and therefore an independent Scotland would no longer be regarded as an anomaly. A referendum is to be conducted in 2014 on the specific issue of independence, and there is some degree of agreement among political commentators that Scotland, having achieved greater independence in the short term, will claim full independence by 2020. At present only 30 per cent of the Scottish electorate has expressed any commitment to full separation from the Union, and independence may not extend to real secession. The main problem for Scottish independence would be economic, namely whether declining oil revenues would be enough to avoid increasing taxation and reduced spending on social services. The result is more likely to be creeping autonomy rather than a bold move towards maximum independence.

In Wales the nationalist party Plaid Cymru also sought independence, but eventual devolution was driven by the administrative changes brought about by the New Labour government of Tony Blair. Differences in religion, language and culture have not found expression in a radical demand for independence in Wales, where there has been increasing provision for the use of the Welsh language in public and greater recognition of its regional needs. Conflicts between Catholic nationalists and Protestant Unionists in Northern Ireland have been far more problematic and violent, and remain troublesome despite the Good Friday Agreement that brought peace to the province in April 1998. These political developments pinpoint the fact that the Crown is one of the few remaining institutions that binds the United Kingdom of Great Britain and Northern Ireland into a single political system. If the British monarchy does eventually fail, there will be little social glue – or tradition as Shils would have it – to hold 'Ukania' together. With the disappearance of the House of Lords and the monarchy, Britain would indeed be constitutionally modernized, but the social price might be rather high.

Monarchy and celebrity

Despite these major transformations of British society in the half-century following the Coronation the monarchy has survived, albeit with significant changes in the image it presents to the public. Although the criticisms of the Shils–Young article are well taken, there remains an interesting sociological problem: how to explain the continuing popularity of monarchy in Britain. One might argue that the death of Princess Diana posed an acute crisis for the House of Windsor, and nobody could have predicted the outburst of public grief surrounding her death. Sociologists of the media have argued that responses to Princess Diana's death have to be read carefully, because the public response represented a range of meanings and attitudes (Thomas, 2002). Perhaps the interpretation and meaning of her death were diverse, but the volume of national grief still defied satisfactory explanation. If the death of Diana represented a deep crisis for the monarchy, then the wedding of Prince William and Kate Middleton might be taken as a restoration of public confidence in and commitment to the Windsor monarchy. The royal wedding of William and Kate, as so many noticed, was also an attempt to heal the legacy of the divorce between Charles and Diana, and her subsequent tragic and very public death. In a society where the majority of marriages end in divorce within the first seven years, the 'fairy-tale' royal wedding was a public celebration of the imaginary weddings and happiness that the majority of the population never experience. The marriage promise of loyalty and commitment fulfils this *illusio* of stability and contentment. Such an interpretation, however, misses the fact that coronations, royal weddings, the Queen's Christmas message, the changing of the guard and other military ceremonials are liturgies in a society that otherwise has few collective rituals to mark transitions in the history of the nation. This decline in a shared public space and collective experiences is compounded by the decline of the Church of England. Other institutions, such as the British Broadcasting Corporation and the House of Commons, might compete to provide the public with moral guidance, but generally speaking they do not have liturgical functions.

In the absence of a liturgical calendar, the global response to the royal wedding was overwhelmingly positive, with over three million people on the streets of central London and with an estimated worldwide audience of some three billion. By contrast, the response of intellectuals was uniformly critical and cynical, namely a repeat of the negative response of the left in the 1950s to the Coronation. In the *Financial Times* Philip Stephens (2011: 9) referred to the 'fuss and flummery surrounding the royal couple' and predicted that 'the institution's long-term survival will depend on whether it manages to adapt to straitened circumstances'. The headline of the *FT Weekend* (24 April 2011, p. 1) warned that the royal family is 'a changed, chastened institution, and no one is banking on its future' (Engel, 2011: 1). In its 'Week in Review' *The New York Times* (24 April 2011, p. 7) under the banner 'This tarnished crown' asserted that for many British people the royal marriage is 'a step toward saving a sullied monarchy – an uncertain step, at that' (Burns, 2011: 1). The distinguished historian Simon Schama (2011), writing about the wedding and royalty in *The Financial Times* (30 April, p. 7), observed that the royal couple were 'two good-looking kids at the altar, doing their I-dos for the nation and for each other, at worst a harmless distraction; even perhaps worth a bit of a national knees-up'. How then to explain the spectacle of three million people on the London streets and the billions around the globe watching this 'harmless distraction'?

The enthusiasm for the royal wedding was subsequently matched in June 2012 with the celebration of the Queen's Golden Jubilee, marking sixty years of her reign. After the crises confronting the royal family in the 1990s, there is general agreement that the monarchy has not only survived, but enjoys widespread social support. The two princes have been successful in presenting an image of youthfulness and public service, and enjoy considerable public support and sympathy not only in the United Kingdom but in the Commonwealth and especially in Jamaica and Africa. There is little sign of any enthusiasm for republicanism, and media praise for Queen Elizabeth has been generous with Max Hastings (2012: 9) in *The Financial Times* describing her reign as 'an unflagging display of discipline, discretion and dutifulness'. While the succession remains problematic, given the lack of public support for Prince Charles, there is no sense in which the monarchy is in question.

Centre and periphery

Shils clearly believed that charisma and charismatic experiences were essential in keeping alive the tradition that he believed was fundamental to the continuity of society. The Shils–Young article was thus an early statement of his lifelong interests in charisma, tradition and the role of intellectuals. However, he recognized that, when for example Rousseau or Durkheim wrote about civil religion, or a general will, or social solidarity, these notions have very different significance depending on whether one is talking about small or large societies. The obvious fact about modern societies is that people can know or interact with only a small section of the total society. He argued that the 'collective self-consciousness is a pattern constituted by a plurality of minds oriented towards an image – of an objective symbolic configuration – of their own society and towards the individuals who participate in that objectivated symbolic configuration' (Shils, 2006: 165–6). The dominant image of a society is concentrated at its centre, but no 'center ever fully pervades and dominates its peripheries' (Shils, 2006: 166). In 'Society, collective self-consciousness and collective self-consciousnesses' he stressed repeatedly that a large and complex society could never have anything approaching a dominant and coherent moral system. His early work in military sociology on the integration and coherence of fighting groups in the army had taught him that there is a significant difference between 'the primary group' and the larger society. Thus in the modern era 'large societies have a tendency towards internal differentiations' (Shils, 2006: 186).

Given Shils's long-term interest in tradition, centre and periphery, and consensus, we might conclude that in 1953 the monarchy was indeed an important component of the British tradition. It was situated in a cluster of institutions – the Crown, Parliament, the Church of England, and the law courts – that were fundamental to the system of power, and the cultural framework of Britishness. The Coronation could be seen as a symbolic celebration of that system of privilege that recognized and endorsed the Establishment. Despite the obvious presence of class differences in Britain – marked by income, education, speech, religion and disposition – he correctly saw that Britain was nevertheless a relatively coherent society. We might recall that when Marshall published his famous account of citizenship in 1950 in *Citizenship and social class and other essays* he felt no need to include any reference to ethnicity, migration, gender or nationalism as issues in the sociology of citizenship. These all lay in the future.

Shils published an interesting reflection on social change in his article 'Max Weber and the world since 1920' (Shils, 1987). In a similar reflection, we might ask how the monarchy and British tradition have changed since 1953. The short answer is that, particularly after the death of Diana, who was cleverly described by Tony Blair as 'the People's Princess', the monarchy has survived as the result of a process of modernization. Here again Nairn is useful in providing a picture of Britain as a 'populist corporation'. The Royals have now become an important part of the British celebrity system, in which Kate Middleton may well replace Princess Diana as an influential figure in the fashion world. Whereas the Royal Family was secretive and exclusive in the past, their lives have been increasingly open to public view. Another change has been that the financing of the monarchy has been more openly discussed and debated. In short, monarchy has been radically changed since the Shils–Young article.

We might summarize the social change in Britain within the framework in terms of Shils's idea of centre and periphery. The Establishment now represents a far weaker cultural centre, because the Church of England has experienced a major decline and the changing nature of the Established Church was perhaps indicated by the publication of the Bishop of Woolwich's *Honest to God* in 1963. Britain is increasingly a multifaith society. The landed aristocracy has been marginalized in

British politics as a consequence of the transformation of cabinet government by Margaret Thatcher. The monarchy is no longer the centre of 'Society'. In Victorian Britain 'State Balls at Buckingham Palace, Royal entertainments and Royal attendance at certain functions gave a stamp of authority to the whole fabric of Society' (Davidoff, 1973: 25). The role of the court has changed dramatically, especially in relation to the function of marriage among the social elite. Young women no longer 'come out', and are no longer under the watchful eye of a chaperone. One can perhaps measure public opposition to aristocrats in politics by public criticism of the appointment of Sir Alec Douglas-Home (fourteenth Earl of Home) as prime minister (1963–4). A product of Eton and Christ Church, he was seen to be more at home on his estate shooting grouse than conducting the business of Parliament. His stuffy and elitist demeanour confirmed the general view that he was out of touch with domestic politics. The influence of Parliament has been significantly reduced, while the power of the prime minister has been much increased, assuming in modern elections a presidential aura. The popular press has found ample opportunity to criticize the monarchy, and events in the life of Prince Charles have raised difficult issues about succession. In December 2010 Prince Charles and Camilla Parker Bowles were on their way in a black limousine to the Royal Variety Performance at the London Palladium. They were suddenly attacked by rioting students, who shouted 'Tory scum' and 'Off with their heads'. Charles unwisely waved to the rioters, and the damaged vehicle eventually carried the occupants to safety. These developments, at the very least, suggest that the harmonious and consensual society that Shils and Young described in the early 1950s has been replaced by a society that is uncertain, divided and fractious. We now have a weak centre and a long and differentiated periphery.

Following Bagehot's argument about national coherence, Queen Elizabeth II in the twentieth century (like Victoria in the nineteenth) remains a symbol of national continuity, given the length of her reign and her capacity to survive domestic and national crises. She survived the many domestic crises of the Royal Family in what became known as the *annus horribilus* of 1992. The monarchy during the reign of Elizabeth II has been a benign force in providing some stability to British public life (Pimlott, 2001). We might therefore recast the Shils–Young argument to suggest that these public events are secular rituals or liturgies that reaffirm what Danièle Hervieu-Léger (2000) has called the 'chain of memory'. They revivify our own memories of marriage, of our connection to our parents and grandparents, and our hope of continuity within our own families, and they form a connection, however fragile and uncertain, between family and nation.

Conclusion: religion, royalty and politics

It is important to understand the British monarchy within a longer historical trajectory, as shaped for example by the American Declaration of Independence of 1776 and the French Revolution of 1789. Conservative reactions in Britain to the French Revolution were memorably stated by Edmund Burke (1955: 98) in his defence of tradition against the radical rupture of the past in France: 'In England we have not yet been completely embowelled of our natural entrails; we still feel within us, and we cherish and cultivate, those inbred sentiments which are the faithful guardians, the active monitors of our duty, the true supporters of all liberal and manly morals.' While British conservatives turned against the creation of radical republicanism in France, Burke supported the demands of the American colonists. Through much of the twentieth century, political and cultural relations with the United States have been close, if complicated.

In terms of political systems, the two societies – American republicanism and British constitutional monarchy – are allegedly separate and different. America is formally a secular democracy with an elected president, while the United Kingdom is a constitutional monarchy with an established church. While the powers of monarchy are thought to be arbitrary and expansive, the powers of an American president were in principle limited by the separation of powers and the absence of an established church. The founding fathers sought to avoid the perils of European absolutism by limiting presidential power. However, the actual practice of religion and politics has been very different.

It is widely believed by political observers that presidential power in the United States had grown considerably by the end of the nineteenth century and continued to expand throughout the twentieth in response to the need to conduct total war and, more recently, in response to global terrorism, real or otherwise. Writing in the late 1890s, Henry Ford Jones (1898) in *The rise and growth of American politics* observed that the increase in presidential authority could not be explained by the personal ambitions and intentions of presidents. It was the outcome of changing political conditions in which Congress itself appeared to aggrandize the presidency. In the second half of the twentieth century international crises enlarged the powers of presidents. From President Kennedy's confrontation with Khrushchev in the Cuban missile crisis in 1962, Lyndon Johnson during the Vietnam War, Ronald Reagan in response to the Iran crisis, George W. Bush in response to 9/11, or Barack Obama's management of the Iraq and Afghan wars, there has been a notable increase in 'executive power'. Writing of these developments in his *Presidential power and the modern presidents*, Richard E. Neustadt (1990) noted the growth of a new dimension in American political life, namely the capacity to launch nuclear war that could not only devastate an enemy but also destroy America itself – socially, politically and morally. This development has not only consolidated executive power but also isolated the president, who must take these decisions in a social vacuum. The combination of isolation and power may partly explain the sense of paranoia in the case of Richard Nixon that was the background to the Watergate debacle in 1972 (Fulsom, 2012: 187). In the presidency of George W. Bush partisan loyalty and total commitment to the war on terror were defined in terms of unswerving patriotism. The result was that 'under the cover of war, executive power was asserted and concentrated, and secrecy was justified' (Wilentz, 2008: 441). While the British monarchy has been shorn of power through the twentieth century, the power of American presidents and their isolation in power has grown immeasurably. How is religion bound up with these developments?

In a critical discussion of God and king in modern America, Robert Bellah (2006: 370) observed that the church and world in America are now deeply entangled, and 'the entanglement goes much deeper than liberal Protestant theology, and that it is even difficult to see where the church leaves off and the world begins in our country'. The connections or 'entanglement' between church, state and patriotism were intensified during the presidency of George W. Bush who, in projecting American power over the world as a struggle against evil, was able to conduct the war by means that often conflicted with or defied international legal agreements including rendition and the construction of detention facilities at Guantanamo Bay in which detainees had little recourse to legal aid. Bush, who saw himself as called to the presidency by God in the period leading up to the 2000 election, also interpreted the global mission of the United States in biblical terms. While Americans wholeheartedly reject the notion that America is an imperial democracy, they believe in American eminence and its special role in making the world a better place. Bellah concluded by proposing that America might have developed a new Constantinianism, namely 'a society that recapitulates the archaic fusion of religion and state in a way unique among modern nations (Japan excepted)'. The few liturgies that are available to American society celebrate this entanglement in which the inauguration of the president carries the same aura as the coronation of monarchs.

5 | Religion and reproduction: marriage and family

Introduction: sex and death

Individual decisions to marry and to create a family are, from a liberal point of view, supremely private matters, and in modern societies where such decisions are clothed in a romantic language of love and fidelity they appear to belong exclusively to the private sphere. In reality, social conventions have largely determined whom we marry and under what circumstances. Because marriage has important consequences for the economics of households, in traditional societies these decisions were often determined by the kinship group. Marriages represented important alliances between families, and hence in many societies cross-cousin marriages were preferred. Before the rise of modern individualism and the related notion that marriage involves a romantic attachment, marriage was typically regarded as a secular contract in which there were mutual obligations and entitlements. These contracts were not simply between individuals but between families. The logic of dowry is to reinforce the presence of these contractual obligations. In these contractual negotiations, the social status of the woman meant that rights and obligations were characteristically uneven. Given the unequal relationship between men and women within the wider society, women have typically found it difficult to enforce their claims on divorce. To guard against such eventualities, many marriage systems allow for pre-nuptial agreements that anticipate the complexities of divorce. In short, the idea that choosing a spouse is simply a matter of individual choice is sociologically unrealistic. In many societies the state can also intervene to determine who is an eligible or lawful partner by for example creating laws that prohibit or regulate inter-faith marriages. Indonesia is a good example. Despite these objective constraints on marriage as an institution, it is overlaid with romantic conventions in which the marital union is grounded, not in contract or an exchange of economic resources, but in a personal and emotional decision.

Unsurprisingly, religion is deeply embedded in the conventions of marriage and family formation. The case of Christianity is somewhat unique, because, while all religions encourage human beings to reproduce, early Christianity was deeply ambiguous about marriage as an institution that allows for the free exercise of desire. In *The body and society* Peter Brown (1989) gives a brilliant account of the issues surrounding sexual renunciation in early Roman Christianity. For Christian believers, while death was the inescapable fate of all human beings, only certain categories of persons were exposed to the dangers and perturbations of unbridled lust. It was a problem for the young, but women in general were regarded as dangerous and as the cause of the disturbances of desire. Early Christians nevertheless recognized the need for sexual intercourse simply as the only way to produce offspring who would become their heirs. In the second century, however, sex and death became ever more conjoined as expressions of human vulnerability, and as a result renunciation of sex came to be seen as an act of redemption that restored human freedom. The Gospel of Luke, composed around the year 80 CE, gave an uncompromising view of the dangers and disadvantages of marriage, and saw sexual asceticism as a necessary step on the path to paradise.

From the second century onwards Christians more persistently proclaimed their wish to avoid sexual relationships and to engage in a life of ascetic discipline. The message of ascetic Christianity was profoundly anti-marriage and anti-family, calling men and women to renounce sexuality and the kinship ties that bound parents and children. In the theology of Marcion, a Christian theologian from Asia Minor who settled in Rome around 144 CE, Christianity was seen to be a completely new revelation that had overcome and transcended the teaching of the Old Testament, and Marcionism 'was to draw the ascetic individual out of the narrow embrace of family and to launch them into the unexpected openness of a missionary, celibate church' (Brown, 1989: 90). The story of Adam and Eve was now interpreted as demonstrating that the union of our first ancestors had created a false society, and that redemption required a new basis for human freedom outside the chains of sexual union. It was through the pathway of ascetic denial that humans could ultimately escape their animal origins. The body in this theological worldview was 'deeply alien to the true self' (Brown, 1989: 209).

There are obviously many different versions of the Christian tradition, but nevertheless the Christian churches inherited a deeply ambiguous vision of women, marriage and fertility. Sexual desire was something to be closely regulated and controlled by personal discipline and ecclesiastical institutions, and where necessary by the intervention of the state. This legacy marks Christianity off from other world religions, and clearly distinguishes it from both Judaism and Islam. One obvious social characteristic of Jesus of Nazareth was that he never married, and since he had no offspring there was never any sibling rivalry over succession. The life of Jesus as described in the New Testament gives ample warrant for the view that celibacy is a spiritual status. In this regard, Christianity inherited the ascetic doctrine and practices of the Essene sect, including celibacy. Consequently the Gospels indicate that Jesus gave scant attention to marriage and family life, and it is only in Paul's first letter to the Corinthians that we find anything definitive. Paul argued that, unlike pagans and Jews, Christians do not divorce; in marriages with non-Christians, the non-Christian spouse should be encouraged to convert, and celibacy is promoted as superior to the married life. This letter was an ad hoc response to a growing movement of ascetic Christians at Corinth who were rejecting all sexual relationships as a barrier to piety and ultimate salvation (Grubb, 1995: 66). In later centuries the absence of a family life for Jesus in the biblical narrative created a theological space within which Mary and the Holy Family could be presented as a model of the perfect familial union.

Islam provides an instructive contrast to this Christian legacy. Muhammad the Prophet of Islam was a merchant who was married and who had children. He also took additional wives, polygamy has a sanction in the Qur'an, and unilateral divorce by a husband remains valid within the *shari'a*. In Islamic countries marriage is essentially a civil contract, but generalizations are difficult because there are different forms of marriage. Because widows and single women are regarded as a problem in Muslim societies, temporary marriages often function as an institutional solution. In Egypt so-called *urfi* or customary marriages are unregistered and often novel arrangements. For example, in a *misyar* marriage husband and wife agree to live apart, and the husband has no financial liability for the agreement. Critics of these often secret arrangements claim that, especially in Saudi Arabia, they allow for a de facto polygamy in which men can easily avoid responsibility for wives and their children. In Iran many women's movements have opposed attempts to change the laws relating to marriage and family life that would have changed the status of women, giving them less legal security

(Voorhoeve, 2012). In many Muslim societies *mahr* is a contractual agreement that aims to protect a woman against a husband who wants a divorce. While *mahr* is gender specific in protecting the wife, secular pre-nuptial agreements can be used to protect the property of either spouse, and indeed *mahr* has often been treated in secular courts in the West as equivalent to a pre-nuptial agreement.

In all of these circumstances there have been many social movements such as 'Islamic Modernism' to change the status of women. However, it is generally the case that 'a woman' (*nisa*) in Arabic societies has less public standing and fewer legally guaranteed rights than men, and women have exercised power primarily within the domestic environment. Arranged marriages between cousins are common in many Muslim societies, but they are often resisted by young women (Dahlgren, 2012: 26). Orthodox Muslim views about women have been grounded in two notions: *qiwama* (protection or maintenance) and *wilaya* (friendship and mutual support) from the Qur'anic verse 4:34. In this Qur'anic passage men are defined as the protectors of women, and righteous women are obedient. The juristic ideas arising from this passage give men the right of sexual access to their wives, and a duty to support them. A disobedient wife loses the right to protection and maintenance, and the man can terminate the contract by repudiation (*talaq*); in the majority of Muslim societies a woman cannot obtain a divorce without her husband's consent. While these traditional views are strongly supported by conservative clerics, they are equally contested by Muslim feminists from the Sisters in Islam in Kuala Lumpur in Malaysia to Muslim women in Australia (Akbarzadeh, 2010).

While generalization about marriage in Islam is problematic, the fact that the Prophet was a married man has had major significance for the character of Islam as a religion. Because the Prophet had descendants there was far more scope for conflict over political authority, such as the conflict between Sunni and Shi'ite Islam. Unlike Jesus, the Prophet had descendants who to this day claim a genetic and spiritual legacy, and Islam has retained a more consistent and positive religious and ethical attitude towards sexuality and reproduction. Over time these aspects of the life of the Prophet have through the evolution of traditions (*hadith*) created a set of norms about sexual relations and married life that has established important differences between Christianity and Islam. Whereas Islam had nothing approaching a Gnostic tradition celebrating an ascetic life free from sexual entanglements, the Christian churches have had to invent traditions in which married life is seen to be the normal state of a sanctified Christian believer rather than a haven from irrational desire. Modern critics of the Vatican's attitudes towards women and marriage argue that the Church is out of touch with the life and needs of the laity, and that recent scandals around payments to sexually abusive priests in Milwaukee to leave the priesthood in 2003 were indicative of problematic attitudes towards sexuality.

Sexual citizenship, the state and the status of women

As I have argued throughout this study, religious individuals are also citizens, or at least they have identities within social and political spaces that are controlled by states. Marriage is not simply an agreement between two individuals who may or may not have religious convictions. Marriage, especially in Islam, is a civil contract that is ultimately enforceable by civil law. Perhaps more importantly, the state has an interest in reproduction, because the offspring of legal unions constitute the next generation of citizens. The state inevitably becomes involved in enforcing marriage agreements and in determining the identity and legal status of children. With the evolution of citizenship rights in modern states there has been an important growth of legislation to guarantee women equality of condition – that is, women have equal rights with men as citizens of the state.

One aspect of the principle of equality in a liberal society is the notion of 'the level playing field' – that is, the state and the law must treat individuals and social groups on the same basis. The state must not be seen to treat certain groups with special and unique favours; for example, white males should not be given special privileges over the rest of the population. This principle is very important when it comes to the recognition of religious practices and the status of women in society. Generally speaking, in the twentieth century the status of women within religious traditions collided with the growth of citizenship rights and gender equality.

Citizenship is composed of a bundle of rights and duties that define an individual's identity and status within a political community, typically a nation state. T. H. Marshall (1950) identified three types of citizenship rights, namely the juridical (such as *habeas corpus*), the political (the right to vote and form political parties), and the social rights associated with the welfare state. Social rights are said to mitigate the negative effects of market forces by providing some minimal protection from accidents, unemployment, poor health and old age through collectivized social security. The emergence of citizenship has presupposed the creation of a modern taxation system that makes possible the maintenance of a collective system of security against risk. In a capitalist society citizenship is often contrasted with social class, because the entitlements associated with citizenship limit the full impact of class inequality. While critical sociologists have been sceptical of the claim that citizenship can significantly change the logic of economic exploitation, citizenship is seen to be a fundamental basis of modern democracies. It has, especially in northern Europe, through the twentieth century institutionalized some degree of equality between social classes, ethnic groups and between men and women. As a generalization we may propose that at least historically in the Abrahamic religions there is an enduring assumption that men should exercise authority in the home and that women have special domestic obligations to do with caring and nurturing. There is in many instances the additional assumption that there should be respect for if not submission to male authority (Browning and Clairmont, 2006). The conclusion must be that at least historically there has been a tension between the view of gender relations embedded in secular citizenship and the understanding of those relationships in organized religion.

The original notion of citizenship has nevertheless been subject to constant revision, mainly to accommodate changes brought about by growing cultural diversity associated with multiculturalism, labour migration (both legal and illegal), the pressure of refugees and asylum seekers associated with globalization, the employment of women in the formal labour market and demands for equal treatment of women in terms of incomes and pensions. Despite these social developments, feminist critics of the legacy of Marshall's theory argued that the persistence of gender inequality in industrial societies (with respect to employment, wages, child support and social mobility) indicates the limitations of the liberal model of citizenship. The effects of 'the glass ceiling' on the social and economic advancement of women have demonstrated the limitations of liberal contract theory and the Marshallian theory of citizenship, wherein the consequences of the public–private divide have been systematically ignored (Pateman, 1988). While demanding the full range of rights of secular citizenship (including the right to vote and to participate fully in the public domain), the rights of women have focused on issues relating to sexuality, reproduction, marriage and divorce.

The notion of 'sexual citizenship' raises interesting criticisms of the traditional divisions between the public and private. Feminists argue that heterosexuality and domesticity have been constructed, more or less implicitly, as necessary conditions of citizenship. For example, the model of citizenship and the welfare state in Marshall's sociology presupposed the presence of a stable nuclear family, a working husband in the labour market and a reproductive wife in the home. In this combination of a Fordist economy, liberal citizenship and the nuclear family, women, it is claimed, are exposed to exploitation at work, where their wages are lower than their male colleagues, and in the home, where their role is to provide unpaid services to their husbands. According to these criticisms citizenship has been closely connected with hegemonic forms of heterosexuality, especially in the institutions of inheritance, marriage, divorce and adoption.

Early feminist criticisms of traditional notions of citizenship have now been extended to consider the rights of gay and lesbian individuals. The relationship between entitlement and gender can be viewed as an important aspect of the emergence of sexual citizenship. Modern theories of citizenship regard identity, subjectivity and gender position as in many respects more politically and culturally salient in modern societies than traditional issues about social class, income equality and employment opportunities. Gay and lesbian movements have claimed that sexual liberation, especially the right of individuals to decide on their own sexual orientation, is a necessary entitlement of autonomous individuals in a democratic society. These arguments have promoted claims for enhanced sexual rights under the umbrella of 'intimate citizenship' or the right to sexual pleasure without state interference.

We may divide these rights relating to sexuality into two categories. First, there are rights to reproduction: with whom may one reproduce, and under what social and legal conditions? These rights serve, among other things, to protect under-age children from sexual exploitation by adults, and they may also be construed as giving every woman in principle a right to reproduce whether or not she is married. The second perspective concerns the rights of sexual consumption: with whom may one enjoy sexual intimacy, and under what conditions? These claims to rights are more ambiguous: is there a *right* to intimacy and sexual pleasure? Reproductive rights are closely connected with the so-called capabilities approach to human development of the American philosopher Martha Nussbaum, in which the education of women and the achievement of literacy are necessary stages towards achieving personal health, including reproductive health. Expanding the capabilities of women is important in giving them control over their own fertility. The second form of sexual citizenship, promoting the idea of sexual intimacy as a right, makes no assumptions about reproduction and is more concerned about promoting the idea of freedom of sexual expression, experience and association.

These notions of gender equality are not confined to the West, and there have been significant developments in women's rights in Muslim societies. In the early twentieth century there were important developments in Egypt, starting in 1922, when Britain granted Egypt partial independence. However, the constitutional arrangements made no provision for women's political equality, and women, who had been politically active in social movements, were expected to return to their domestic duties. Nevertheless, women came to play a significant part in the subsequent evolution of Egyptian nationalism. The Second World War radicalized political consciousness in Egyptian society, and in 1944 the Egyptian Feminist Party was formed on a political platform for social reform, birth control and the right to abortion. Active in the rise of Egyptian nationalism through the Women's Committee for Popular Resistance in 1951, women supported the struggle against British imperialism during the Suez Crisis. They enjoyed support from the Islamic modernists who argued that the Qur'an gave women equal social and political rights, and eventually the nationalist government of Gamal Abdel Nasser introduced social reforms that enhanced women's status in post-colonial Egyptian society. However, Nasser's 'state feminism' undermined the power of husbands and fathers, and ironically made women dependent on the state, giving rise to a form of state patriarchy. In more recent times both Anwar Sadat and Hosni Mubarak shored up their political authority by forging alliances between fundamentalists, state officials and the middle class. However, in the 1980s many of the social advances of women were challenged by the politics of 'Islamism', which attempted to re-establish traditional values. Among conservative clerics the 'politics of reversal' sought to enforce the *hijab* (headscarf) as a potent symbol of the (re)domestication of women.

Western critics have often regarded Islamic tradition as a major hurdle to the growth of citizenship for women outside the liberal democratic societies of the West. Veiling, female genital mutilation and polygamy are often cited as key disadvantages confronting the enjoyment of equal rights of citizenship for women in Muslim communities. These traditional patriarchal structures severely limit Muslim women's chances of adequate education, social mobility and control over their own sexuality. Although there have been many oppositional voices against the West demanding change within the Islamic world and calling for a spiritual renewal, their pleas for Islamic modernization did not always include the modernization of the family, or improving the status of women, or recognizing gay and lesbian rights. Women have been politically active especially through local engagement in non-government organizations in defence of sexual citizenship (Hafez, 2011), but recognizing sexual rights remains one of the most contentious and unresolved issues in contemporary Islam. The same arguments would apply equally to ultra-orthodox Jews and fundamentalist Christians, who are also confronted by legal recognition of same-sex marriages.

The French philosopher Mohammad Arkoun has been a lone although powerful voice among contemporary Muslim intellectuals. With a doctorate from the Sorbonne and as an influential commentator on the need for a critical reading and demystification of the Qur'an and *hadith*, he argued in *The unthought in contemporary Islamic thought* (2002) that Islamic thought had to break out of its 'dogmatic enclosure' and that Muslims needed to rethink gender relations, because in Islam only men have full legal status as persons and citizens. While early Islam had broken the tribal structures of traditional societies, creating a community based on faith, socially conservative practices around women, marriage, inheritance and the family had acquired sacred status. While the revealed Word of God had opened up the thinkable, socially conservative values had produced the unthinkable.

Religion has played a major role in defining citizenship in the Arab world, especially its gendered nature. Religion is a necessary component of the patriarchical structures that underpin the power of men within the family, tribe and state. More importantly, citizenship as a legal entity has in the Middle East often been constituted through membership of a religious community, and hence the distribution of rights and resources is organized on the basis of membership of religious sects (Joseph, 2000). Consequently the nation is imagined as an assembly of sub-communities that are in turn defined by religion. Political conflicts between and within the nation-state often assume the form of religious conflicts, and establishing peaceful relations between different religious communities is a complicated and protracted process. In recent years a flourishing opposition to patriarchy by Muslim women through the agency of voluntary associations and the Arab Spring of 2011 have created opportunities for Islamic organizations such as the Muslim Brotherhood in Egypt to enter legally into democratic politics.

In Indonesia, during the presidencies of both Sukarno and Suharto, human rights were often treated as the unwanted interventions of Western liberalism. The international emergence of rights discourse appeared to clash with the more pressing claims of national self-determination and economic growth. Women's organizations played a major role in the downfall of the authoritarian New Order regime of Suharto, who ruled over Indonesia from 1967 to 1998. Women's associations also emerged as important social and political forces in the Reform period after 1998 (Blackburn, 2000; Robinson, 2009). In their confrontation with the government, women activists led public campaigns condemning the systematic rape of women in Aceh and East Timor as state-sponsored attacks on women, and in the process of criticism they sought to establish rights associated with sexual citizenship. The prominence of women in the development of democracy is important, since Indonesia is the largest Muslim society with a population of 217 million, of whom 80 per cent are Muslim. Criticism of polygamy and female genital mutilation became widespread through the activities of Nahdlatul Ulama, the largest Islamic organization, under the leadership of Abdurrachman Wahid (1940–2009). The election of women to high office in predominantly Muslim societies, such as President Megawati (2001–4) in Indonesia and Prime Minister Benazir Bhutto (1988–90; 1993–6) in Pakistan, gives some confirmation of the growth of the political rights of citizenship for women.

Across the Islamic world, as women acquire entry to secondary and higher education, and control over their own fertility through access to contraception, their voices are no longer easily silenced by traditional values and patriarchal institutions. The global growth of women's organizations is indicative of an emerging civil society and patterns of active citizenship that are the foundation of popular demands for rights. One paradox in the conflicts between the West and Islam has been that many movements for social change within Islam have had their origins in Muslim communities in the West. To understand modern Muslim attitudes towards women and marital rights, we often have to pay special attention to Muslim communities within the United States and Europe.

While sociological studies of 'Islam and the West' often fail to distinguish between conditions in Europe and America, it is important to note that Muslim communities in America have characteristics that distinguish them sharply from Muslims in Europe. American Muslims trace their ancestry back to the arrival of African slaves in the seventeenth century. Approximately 15 per cent of African slaves came from Muslim communities, and today African Americans represent around 30 per cent of the Muslim population in the United States. With the rise of the Nation of Islam movement around such charismatic figures as Elijah Muhammad and Malcolm X in the 1960s, Islam has often had a turbulent history in the United States. Nevertheless, prior to 9/11 Muslims were relatively successful in integrating into American society, especially in northern cities such as Detroit, Chicago and New York, and they remain more highly educated and socially mobile than South Asian Muslims in the United Kingdom or African Muslims of France. Adopting the headscarf in the United States is a relatively recent practice, and this adoption can have multiple meanings: identification with Islam, an expression of piety, a desire for security in public spaces, or a wish to appear 'cool'. While there is widespread suspicion of Muslims and prejudice against veiling, in political terms there has not been a headscarf debate as such in the United States to match attempts to ban veiling in various European societies, especially France.

Perhaps more serious and problematic have been the attempts to control the spread of the *shari'a* (Islamic law) in both the United States and Canada. In 2011 senior figures in the Republican Party, most notably Newt Gingrich, called for a ban on the *shari'a* to prevent judges making reference to Islamic legal norms in decisions relating to marriage, divorce and child custody. A variety of court cases in the United States have exposed the fact that there are legal inconsistencies between American and Islamic law, regarding marriages contracted outside the United States that are dissolved in secular courts. As a result, secular courts are making decisions about religious traditions, and these interventions begin to trespass onto constitutional ground concerning the separation of church and state in the First Amendment, or the so-called Establishment Clause, by in fact requiring government to decide on the theological content of religion. However, in order to understand these legal issues we need to look more closely at the tensions between the authority of the Supreme

Court, the growth of legal pluralism and the possible development of the *shari'a* as an informal method of regulating family life.

Marriage and legal pluralism: legal debates in the United States

In the discussion so far there has been an implicit assumption that when we consider the relations between church, state and marriage we are dealing with societies that are primarily homogeneous and, more importantly, have one legal tradition. The problem with religion and marriage in modern societies is that we are now forced to consider different religious traditions in multifaith societies, where there are a growing number of inter-faith marriages and where as a result there may be competing legal traditions with respect to the nature of marriage and divorce (McLain, 2010). These circumstances are perhaps exceptionally complicated in the case of the United States, which has inherited a Christian interpretation of marriage that is now challenged by international and inter-faith marriages, and by the growth of legal pluralism that rubs up against the legal supremacy of the Supreme Court. Furthermore, the definition of marriage itself has become increasingly controversial, with the political role of the Moral Majority and its defence of heterosexual marriage, on the one hand, and the growth of the gay and lesbian movement, which demands the right to single-sex marriage, on the other. Recently several states such as the state of New York have legalized gay marriage. The legal argument is essentially that a marriage contract between two adults should not be prejudiced on arbitrary grounds of gender. The legal debate is still unresolved in the United States. For example, a federal appeals court in Boston in 2012 made a ruling asserting that a federal law declaring marriage to be explicitly and solely between a man and a woman discriminated against married same-sex couples by denying them the legal and social entitlements of a heterosexual marriage. The Supreme Court may nevertheless take legal decisions in favour of preserving the traditional Christian notion of marriage as necessarily heterosexual.

There is a long tradition of legal battles with polygamy (both formal and informal) in the United States, especially with respect to the Mormon Church. There have been controversial attempts to control the polygamous traditions of the Fundamentalist Church of Jesus Christ of Latter Day Saints, for example in 2008 when federal agents in Texas attempted to take custody of over four hundred children (Jacobson and Burton, 2011). Polygamous marriage is not legal in the British and American legal traditions, and hence in both jurisdictions there are tensions with religious traditions, primarily with Mormonism and Islam, over polygamy. Evidence of polygamy in Britain is often exposed when a Muslim woman presses for divorce where she suspects that her husband has contracted a marriage with another woman, who may be living abroad. If gay men can contract legal marriages, thereby redefining the conventional notion of marriage as a more or less permanent and exclusive relationship between a man and woman for the purpose of legitimate reproduction, why not allow polygamy for Mormons and Muslims, or indeed other forms of marriage such as polyandry? The problem we have to examine here is attempts by the law to balance freedom of religion in the First Amendment and the rights of children. I suggest in the ensuing discussion that the state rather than the churches comes to define 'marriage', and conclude that there are good reasons for predicting the erosion of conventional marriage in the West, thereby raising acute questions about the status of religion, especially the Christian tradition in the West.

Let us begin this discussion with a brief reference to the idea of legal pluralism (Turner, 2011a). Leaving to one side the issue of the legal consequences of post-colonialism, the principal cause of modern legal pluralism is said to be globalization (Teubner, 1997). With economic and financial globalization there has been an inevitable growth of commercial law, which is not specific to state boundaries (Twining, 2000). The growth of human rights legislation has also constrained states to behave according to legal norms, thereby further contributing to legal pluralism (Moyn, 2010). Furthermore, with mass migration and open labour markets, the flow of migrants across borders has intensified cultural diversity, necessitating the partial recognition of legal differences within states. Questions about legal pluralism tend to emerge around international marriages when divorce brings different legal traditions into conflict, forcing secular judges in courts in the West to refer to or consult norms influenced by the *shari'a*.

Academic debates about legal pluralism became important in the 1970s in response to the research of legal anthropologists working on the study of law in post-colonial societies. In anthropological studies legal pluralism was understood to refer simply to the incorporation of customary law into state law or its maintenance alongside the state system. The concept has subsequently been embraced by legal theorists, often influenced by postmodernism and pragmatism, to describe the differentiation of law emerging from multiple legal systems in modern societies (Tamanaha, 1997). For many contemporary legal scholars the problem in defining legal pluralism is simply a consequence of the broader issue of defining law itself (Tamanaha, 2008). There is a conventional distinction between law as consisting of rules that apply to conduct, and secondary rules, or the rules that determine which primary rules are valid, how they are found, and how they should be applied (Hart, 1961). However, every institution by definition applies rules, and there is therefore no obvious way to determine which are public and which are not. These jurisprudential issues are important for any discussion of *shari'a*, since crucially there is no clear view about whether the enforcement of norms by religious arbitration tribunals is in fact equivalent to law. For some legal theorists law can only exist where there are judges sitting in courts with the ultimate backing and authority of the state, and in this sense tribunals are not courts (Pound, 1966). There is much conceptual confusion as a result, and some writers who welcome postmodern interpretations of this situation accept the view that 'legal pluralism' simply defines any form of normative or regulatory pluralism (de Sousa Santos, 1995). Whenever 'legal pluralism' is invoked 'it is almost invariably the case that the social arena at issue has multiple active sources of normative ordering' such as official legal systems, folkways, religious traditions, economic or commercial regulations, 'functional normative systems' and community or culturally normative systems (Tamanaha, 2008: 397). As a consequence, the notion that a single, coherent and integrated legal system is constitutive of a modern society has been widely challenged. The problems associated with legal pluralism often arise from the pressure from conservative Muslim scholars to have the *shari'a* recognized in the West (An-Na'im, 2008).

In any discussion of legal pluralism it is important to recognize that ultimately the state intervenes to exercise authority, and where necessary compels individuals and groups who are engaged in disputes to accept the state's legal judgments. More precisely, we have to recognize the difference between state law and non-state law, especially with the growth of tribunals, religious courts and customary 'normative ordering' (Turner and Zengin, 2011). Given the growth of alternative forms of arbitration, it may be more appropriate to define 'legal pluralism' as in fact 'jurisdictional pluralism'. If the United States and other Western societies evolve towards such a form of jurisdictional pluralism, then in effect the state is ceding aspects of its authority, for example over marriage and divorce law, to religious groups. The differentiation of jurisdictions can be seen to parallel the growth of different forms of marriage or 'multi-tiered marriage' in America, such as the emphasis on 'covenant marriage' among fundamentalist Christians in Louisiana, or *get* statutes among Jewish groups in New York (Nichols, 2007). When anti-feminist fundamentalist movements defend conventional marriage in which the husband has ultimate authority, women are encouraged to multiply and contraception and abortion are condemned, such as the Quiverfull Movement, then we have a normative ordering that some would regard as law. These changes in jurisdiction have been compared to the *millet* system that operated in Ottoman times, in which different communities enjoyed a certain degree of autonomy, and limited freedom to follow their own customs. The Ottoman *millet* system has been seen as a model for the development of group rights in multicultural societies (Kymlicka, 1995). It is not self evident, however, that a *millet* system can guarantee gender equality through the mechanism of secular citizenship.

In the United States a *millet* system already exists to some degree in that Judaism, Catholicism and Islam have their own system of tribunals to oversee family issues (Estin, 2004). These arbitration systems do of course require the civil law and civil courts to enforce their judgments in domestic matters. In a number of well-publicized cases religious arbitration has come under considerable public criticism, either because it fails to protect women's rights or because it departs too easily from religious orthodoxy. The crisis in Canada over attempts to recognize Muslim arbitration tribunals in Ontario, where these provisions were eventually discarded, is the most noteworthy example of these disputes.

Legal pluralism has been severely tested by the movement to legalize same-sex marriage, which is seen by many as in fact redefining the very nature of marriage, and one response to these debates has been the proposal that marriage should not be a matter for the state, thereby leaving the 'marriage business' to religious groups. The implication of this position is to create a marriage market in which for example couples might opt for a civil contract that would assign jurisdiction of the marriage to religious institutions. These debates inevitably point to a radical redefinition of marriage, and hence some critics have suggested that the word 'marriage' should retain its traditional meaning and that a new terminology should be created to deal with these new forms, such as 'coupledom'.

The paradox of these solutions is that they may enhance the influence of the state over religious marriages. The idea of a covenant marriage is a good example. In religious circles this form of marriage offers Christian couples an opportunity to abide by stricter religious norms than can be enforced by the law. It is argued that under this arrangement the church and the state work in harness to enforce a Christian view of marriage as an enduring and exclusive relationship between a man and a woman. By contrast, a marriage market might take marriage out of the control of the state (Spaht, 1998). However, marriage and family life are too important to leave to free-market solutions which provide too little protection to those who are particularly vulnerable. State oversight of marriage has become especially important in the case of international marriages where legal systems that are incommensurate come into collision, especially over understanding dowry arrangements (*mahr*) in marriages from Muslim societies. These disputes, where one of the parties to the dispute cannot achieve a satisfactory resolution, often encourage 'forum shopping' between different jurisdictions. In these examples the principal problem is the opportunity created for the development of informal systems of 'normative ordering' which do not protect women's rights in terms of equal citizenship.

Conclusion: the end of marriage?

To some extent this discussion of law, religion and marriage has so far been conducted on the assumption that conventional marriages are viable in modern society and that some form of marriage will continue well into the future. To make these assumptions is to ignore the profound changes taking place in marriage, family and divorce in the West. We can briefly provide a list of these changes and then consider their implications for religion. First, with the extension of life expectation in developed societies marriages can in principle last over a much longer part of the life cycle, because in Britain and America the middle classes are surviving into their mid-seventies and in Japan into their late seventies. Along with 'no-fault divorce', longevity contributed to steeply rising divorce rates in the second half of the twentieth century, simply because the chance of marital breakdown and ultimate divorce are more likely over a long period of the life cycle. Second, there has been a worldwide decline in total fertility rates (the number of live births in a woman's reproductive life cycle). In Europe this rate has declined to 2.0, and in America, with its high migration intake, it is 2.4. In many Asian societies the fertility rate is hovering around 1. For example, in Singapore in 2012 it had fallen to 1.15. In the whole world only four countries have a fertility rate over 5. There is a convincing argument that the decline in fertility is a major foundation of gender equality for women (MacInnes and Perez, 2009). With serial monogamy, high divorce rates, low fertility and long life, the implication of these changes is that, especially for men who are divorced and separated from their children, old age will be a lonely and socially isolated experience. Third, it is predicted that American children born in 2012 will live to 100 years, but many future-oriented bio-gerontologists are anticipating the widespread possibility of a life-extension project, driving life expectancy well beyond 120 years. Medical technologies – nanotechnology, cryonics, stem-cell research, organ production and anti-ageing cosmetics such as 'mesotherapy' – will convert ageing into a bio-engineering problem for which there are practical solutions. The result is the idea that we are gradually moving into a post-human or trans-human society (Bostrom, 2005; de Grey, 2008; Drexler, 1986; Juvin, 2010). We might say that the post-human society has arrived only in so far as we are evolving towards the post-body. If we assume that religion has been historically bound up with the problems of suffering and death, what are the implications of these techno-medical changes for religion, and for the relationships between religion, marriage and family?

Demographers have argued that there have been historically only two family strategies (Caldwell and Caldwell, 1986). In the first strategy the economic and social effort of humans is to sustain a large number of children and an extended family. We might add that in this system religion is often concerned with placating ancestors and sustaining gift relations with relatives. In such a system it is rational for individuals to have a large number of children to sustain them in old age. In the second system parents invest all their efforts into a limited number of children and pay little attention to either ancestors or surviving relatives. When wealth passes from children to parents it makes sense to have a large number of children. When wealth passes from parents to children it makes little sense to have many children. To understand these changes we might appeal to the metaphors of sticky and elastic societies (Elliott and Turner, 2012). In the past the family represented a 'sticky society' in which it was hard to join and costly to leave. Family members, often brought together initially by expensive arranged marriages, could only exit through a costly and emotionally challenging divorce, and as we have seen women could not as a general principle leave the family without the husband's consent. A modern family is characterized by its social elasticity, because the family is easy to join and easy to leave. Marriages rarely depend on the consent of an extended family of relatives, because romance rather than economics is thought to determine engagement and marriage choices. Infidelity and high divorce rates demonstrate the relatively low costs of entering and leaving married life. In societies with low fertility, people move in and out of marriage without the encumbrance of numerous children. Couples that remain childless maximize the elasticity of social relationships.

However, we may be passing into a third type of family system where many children are conceived with the aid of medical technologies, while other couples practise voluntary childlessness. Today sexual desire has been separated from reproduction, which can now be achieved without sexual intercourse, and in the process parenting is being transformed. Children become items of consumption, but with increasing life extension we may begin to move into a largely childless environment. It is difficult to know how religion would fit into this new environment of the post-family. Elsewhere I have argued that we have shifted from a theology of unhappiness, in which life was nasty, brutish and short, to a theology of happiness, in which life is long, tedious and meaningless (Turner, 2009). The task is to imagine what religion will become in a future world of the post-body without families and children, and without personal pain and mortality. For the rich global elites living a life in principle without either suffering or meaning, it is difficult to know how the Cross – the quintessential symbol of Christian ethics and religion – could have any existential significance.

6 | Conversion and the state

Introduction: collective identities

From a common-sense perspective it may sound paradoxical that, while conversion, at least in the Protestant tradition, involves a profoundly private turning to a personal God, it comes under regular public scrutiny, especially where conversion movements threaten to disrupt the social balance between majorities and minorities. Conversion concerns the transformation of individuals and their identities, but it also typically involves an important change in membership of a community. Because religion is often constitutive of national identity, a change of religious identity can have important implications for national character. In this sense, conversions may be disruptive, especially when they occur systematically to social groups rather than apparently at random to individuals. Conversion is not just the experience of an isolated individual; it can also involve the transformation of the status and identity of whole communities. For these reasons the state may often intervene to quash evangelical movements that seek to convert citizens to a new religion, or to some reformed version of an existing religious tradition. Such conversion movements may threaten to disturb the balance of populations in societies that are diverse rather than homogeneous. Furthermore, when evangelism is perceived to be associated with colonial powers, conversion can also be interpreted as a cultural threat to an indigenous community from a colonial power. The religious response from a local community to such invasions can be violent, setting off an aggressive religious competition resulting in a civil conflict.

We can consequently see why conversion is important socially and politically. First, in changing individual subjectivity conversion almost inevitably changes social and political identities, and therefore conversion movements can often represent a challenge to the cultural definition of membership and to the criteria of inclusion in society and the state. In many societies, such as the Philippines, Poland, Malaysia and perhaps increasingly Russia, religious membership is more or less equivalent to citizenship, especially where state institutions are weak or corrupt. Many states in Asia and Africa cannot provide adequate and reliable documentation of their own citizens, and hence identities as national citizens are typically unstable and uncertain. In *Paper citizens* Kamal Sadiq (2009) offers a criticism of the 'distinguishability assumption' in conventional studies of citizenship, namely the assumptions that receiving societies have carefully documented populations, and that host populations can be definitively distinguished from migrants, both legal and illegal. Standard theories of citizenship often fail to grasp the crucial role of documents in the informal pathway to rights. Citizenship emerged with the rise of the modern nation-state, in which documentation was necessary to define individuals who could legitimately claim entitlements. This process of bureaucratic consolidation, involving taxation and conscription, produced top-down citizenship. By contrast, the contemporary growth of 'paper citizenship' with economic globalization is a bottom-up process. Modern states often fail to provide adequate registration of their citizens, such as birth certificates. In Indonesia only four out of ten children receive such a certificate, and in Bangladesh birth registration rates are as low as 7 per cent. Naming practices can also create uncertainty. For example, in Pakistan and Malaysia 'Mohammad' may be sufficient to name a boy, and marriage registration is not common in many traditional Muslim communities in South and Southeast Asia. This registration vacuum is then filled by paper citizenship, in which migrants acquire a documented, if falsified, identity. Illegal citizenship is a function of immigrant networks which subvert the formal gate-keeping activities of the state, creating blurred membership, and the complicity of state functionaries (border guards, registration officers, local police and others) who are willing to ignore or conspire with the illegal acquisition of documents. The spread of fake documentation has caused considerable conflict in Asia with the flow of illegal migration into Assam in India and Karachi in Pakistan. In Malaysia thousands of illegal migrants, such as Filipino Muslims, have acquired identity cards illegally, often with the connivance of political parties. Uncertain registration of citizens and migrants creates political conflicts that add further fuel to political strife around conversion.

As a result the state may seek to control or to exclude evangelical religions if they begin to change the existing composition of ethnic identities in a society, or if they are in general seen to be a disruptive force that may alter the ideological composition of civil society. This fact explains the nervous response of states to the growth of Pentecostalism in Vietnam, Singapore, the Philippines and Malaysia. Evangelical religions must in all probability confront the authority of the state. If the state demands loyalty from its citizens and if it has a monopoly over force within a given territory, can it tolerate any religious challenge to its authority?

The tensions between Islam and Christianity have often involved issues about state control, national identity and the balance between majorities and minorities. In this respect Algeria is an interesting case. Protestant missionaries have been active in Algeria since the end of the nineteenth century, when for example the British 'Mission to the Kabyles' was established in 1881 in the small village of Djemaa Sahridj. The Algerian state defines Islam as the state religion, but also recognizes freedom of conscience and the right of Algerians to create associations, including religious associations. However, in 2006 the government passed an Ordinance that specified the conditions in which other religions can be legally practised. It specifically criticized evangelical movements that might disturb or unsettle the faith of Muslims, and it also stressed the need for religious practice to take place in buildings that have been officially registered. In her study of Christian conversions in Algeria, Nadia Marzouki (2012: 76) argues that this 'one-sided policy' is not based on some assumption about the superiority of Islam but arises rather 'from a broader effort by the Algerian state to monitor and monopolize religious practice'. The state resists conversion movements in its effort to safeguard social stability and to contain pressures towards cultural and religious pluralism. In turn, conversions to Christianity involve a critique of existing relations between state and religion in which Islam is transformed into state law, and in converting new adherents insist that they are embracing a unique relationship to Jesus rather than joining a 'religion'. At the same time, converts construct a new identity for Algeria that connects the nation with the Maghreb or with Africa rather than with the Middle East. Converts interpret their conversion as the adoption of a new lifestyle that dramatically rejects their previous identities, but this narrative transformation also involves a redefinition of their relationship to the state. In my terminology, conversion in Algeria and elsewhere has to be understood in the context of the state's attempt at the 'management of religion'.

Subjectivity, intentionality and conversion

It is difficult to write about conversion in the modern period without quickly realizing that sociologists are often operating with notions of conversion that have been implicitly influenced by Protestantism, and especially by Protestant subjectivity, which had its origins in the pietist movements of the seventeenth century. In evangelical Protestantism conversion is characteristically defined as a sudden, sincere and voluntary turning towards God, typically in the person of Jesus Christ. It cannot be coerced or interested, and it is often accompanied by deep emotional experiences. As a consequence, the individual changes his or her lifestyle to lead a more disciplined and ethical existence. This personal event is an aspect of the general notion in evangelical Christianity of being 'born again'. This conversion model in Protestantism is represented by religious movements such as Methodism. In his conversion narrative John Wesley recalled how his heart was 'strangely warmed' by the message of the New Testament. Wesley preached sobriety and perfectionism, but his followers often experienced violent emotional reactions during Methodist preaching, and the ecstatic response of some Methodist converts produced a sect known as the Jumping Methodists.

This Protestant approach to the conversion experience also influenced psychological theories, for example in the work of William James in his famous *The varieties of religious experience* of 1902. Approaching the question of conversion from the perspective of pragmatism, James sought a rational interpretation of the phenomenon without denying its positive social and moral benefits. If conversion produced more reliable, happy and adjusted individuals, it was pragmatically beneficial. If 'the fruits for life' of conversion were positive, then we should welcome conversion 'even though it be a piece of natural psychology' (James, 1929: 237). His approach therefore emphasized the moral consequences of conversion, but as a psychologist he was particularly interested in those conversion experiences that appeared to be sudden, dramatic and unexpected. The majority of his examples involved strong emotional experiences, such as the case of Mr Stephen H. Bradley who in November 1829 at a Methodist meeting 'began to feel my heart beat very quick all of a sudden ... it was the Holy Spirit from the effect it had on me' (James, 1929: 191). James went on to regard conversion as 'in its essence a normal adolescent phenomenon, incidental to the passage from the child's small universe to the wider intellectual and spiritual life of maturity' (James, 1929: 199).

In reflecting on these sudden transformations on the journey to adulthood he distinguished between voluntary and conscious, and involuntary and unconscious, conversions, which he defined as the 'volitional type' and the 'type by self-surrender'. However, in actual cases there was always a mixture of 'explicitly conscious processes of thought and will' and 'the subconscious incubation and maturing of motives deposited by the experiences of life' (James, 1929: 230). Conversions arose from intentionality and 'the subliminal regions of the mind' (James, 1929: 235). In summary, conversions in Jamesian pragmatism are short and sudden emotional events that bring about a happy state of mind, and in many cases provide a resolution to what he called the 'divided self'. One classical example was the experience of St Augustine who after conversion 'emerged into the smooth waters of inner unity and peace' (James, 1929: 175).

St Augustine and St Paul: the problem of intentionality

Let us then turn to the famous account of the conversion of St Augustine. We can start by noticing one major difference between conversion in the ancient world and in the great age of Protestant evangelism. Augustine in the famous account in *Confessions* throws himself down under a fig tree and weeps bitter tears, because he feels captive to his own sins. With 'bitter sorrow in my heart' he by chance heard the voice of a young boy or girl singing 'Take it and read, take it and read'. He rushed home to open the Bible at the place where he had been reading St Paul's Epistles, and there found the passage commanding him to 'spend no more thought on nature and nature's appetites'. He then recalled in *Confessions* VII xi: 27 that 'it was as though the light of confidence flooded into my heart'. This conversion took place in 386 when Augustine was thirty-two years of age, and it has all the characteristics described by James: emotions, a sudden turning associated with a specific event, and a conclusion involving a resolution of uncertainty. This event in Augustine's life is however much contested, because the conversion was retrospectively described – and, more importantly, it was preceded by a long history of engagement with Platonism. The conversion was a turning to Christianity, but it was also a resolution of an intellectual argument between Greek philosophy and Christian theology. James's account neglected the social context of Augustine's conversion, because it overlooked the fact that Augustine's entry into the Catholic Church occurred with his baptism. We know only from his own account that in 387 he was baptized by Ambrose in Milan and abandoned his life of the flesh to become an ascetic.

In the Roman world of the fourth century, membership of the Church was achieved not so much through conversion, but through the sacrament of baptism. Furthermore, the secular and powerful individuals of imperial Rome would often delay baptism until old age in order to continue to enjoy the pleasures of a secular lifestyle. Augustine's mother Monica, who was herself a devout Christian, delayed the baptism of her son to ensure that his final entry into the Church would be sincere and genuine. Was baptism a once-and-for-all entry into the Christian Church? During persecution by the Roman authorities many Christian clergy had forsaken their Christian convictions and handed over the scriptures to the secular powers to be burnt. These were the *Traditores* (traitors), and the question was: could they be rebaptized in order to re-enter the Church? This issue perfectly illustrates the importance of the sacrament of baptism as the 'gate' to membership of the Church as a community of those sharing a common liturgy. Augustine was closely involved in a conflict against Donatism, the doctrinal position that argued against rebaptism and rejected the re-entry of the *Traditores*. Augustine argued in favour of a universal – that is, catholic – Church that had wide arms of acceptance, and by 411 had persuaded the Roman commissioner Marcellinus to deny any legal status to the Donatists. As bishop of Hippo Augustine would administer baptism at Easter to congregations entering the Church as the grace of salvation passed through his hands.

Interpreting Augustine's conversion to Christianity presents some important problems, because his major publications, for example the *Confessions*, are typically retrospective conversion narratives that were designed to present his life as a defence against his critics. *Confessions* was written late in his life in a manner that reconstructed the conversion experience of his youth. Augustine's famous conversion was at first a conversion to Philosophy, since Augustine and his circle of educated Romans saw the contemplative life of the philosopher as the model for the Christian soul (Brown, 2000). Augustine's Christianity was a mixture of 'Plotinian intellectualism and ritual purification' (O'Donnell, 2001: 18). Augustine was steeped in the philosophical and literary works of Plotinus, Cicero and Virgil, and for some (O'Connell, 1969) his Christianity was Neoplatonism, in which human souls had entered the material world by a fall from the purity of a spiritual world. The Christian vocation was to shed this corporeal shell through baptism and discipline. This view of the meaning of conversion is strikingly different from the emotional conversions of working-class Methodists in the early nineteenth century, with their implicit endorsement of Protestant individualism.

Despite these differences between the Catholic and Protestant traditions, there would be general agreement that the classic figure of conversion from the early Church is presented in the New Testament account of the story of St Paul's transformation on the road to Damascus. Turning once more to the figure of St Paul, his initial hostility to the Christians was transformed into a passionate devotion to the cause of the primitive Church and a desire to demarcate clearly the differences between the old beliefs of Judaism and the new reality of a life committed to Christ as Lord. Paul's conversion had three characteristics: it was involuntary; dramatic rather than incremental; and it created an entirely new subjectivity. In symbolic terms Paul's conversion took place on a road or journey, in which he discovered subjectivity in a new place. Paul received a 'gift of grace' or charisma that gave him an authority over the Christian community (Gager, 2000) – albeit a disputed authority, as we can gather from his letters.

I have chosen to consider St Paul not only because his conversion has become paradigmatic in Christian theology, but also because he is the topic of two major studies in contemporary philosophy, by Jacob Taubes and Alain Badiou. I am especially interested in Badiou's approach precisely because it gives such prominence to the idea of an 'Event'. In *Theorie du sujet* (Badiou, 1982) he argues that Christ's crucifixion and resurrection were conceived as a subjective intervention, proclaiming the Event as the dividing point between the old Adam and the New Creation. As a result the primitive Church was the first institution in human history to claim universal significance. The argument here is that any evangelical religion with a universalistic set of assumptions must confront the problem of the Other, and out of that dialogue with otherness an early or 'primitive' form of universalism and cosmopolitan consciousness can emerge. My first example would be the problem that confronted the apostle Paul when faced by the conflicts between Jewish and Gentile Christians over the relevance of Judaic legalism to the early Church. In Galatians 5:6 Paul rejects the idea that salvation can come from the old Law, claiming: 'For in Jesus Christ neither circumcision nor uncircumcision availeth any thing; but faith which worketh by love.' To achieve salvation one must be transformed into 'a new creature'.

In claiming that there was neither Gentile nor Jew, slave nor free person, man nor woman, Paul laid down a universalistic doctrine that challenged any allegiance based on blood and kinship (Badiou, 2003). The early Christians had to be spiritually circumcised, in their hearts rather than in their bodies. On these grounds, Jacob Taubes (2004) claims that Paul is our contemporary, because he engaged with the problem of conflicting visions of religious truth. In short, Pauline 'political theology' contains a reflexive understanding of Otherness and offers an incipient cosmopolitan vision of the problem of 'the world'.

The conversions of Paul and Augustine can be regarded as paradigmatic from a Christian perspective; they are markers of authenticity. Their conversions did not result from any overtly materialistic interest in secular advancement or promotion. Their validity is confirmed by the fact that their conversion experience was, according to the narrative, involuntary. While the focus of these accounts was on the transformation of their identity, we might also note that both stories involve the Roman state. Paul represents the imperial power of Rome, but his conversion starts the process of the gradual acceptance of the Christian sect as a legitimate religion within the empire. Augustine's endless literary struggles with paganism, neo-paganism, Donatism and Manichaeism were not just theological struggles; they were also political struggles to establish a particular version of the 'catholic' Church. The status of these Christian sects – as we saw with Donatism – was important to the Roman authorities because religious identity had juridical and political significance. The point of Augustine's *The City of God* was to advise Christians about how they should live in this world as a preparation for the next – that is, how to be good Roman citizens before they became citizens of an eternal city. Conversion (or baptism) was not just a personal statement of commitment.

So far I have been addressing the issue of conversion as if it was an individual act with implications for the secular world. We need also to consider situations in which conversion is enforced either by religious authorities or by religious authorities working in tandem with the state. The problematic status of the Jews in the history of Christianity was often solved either by banishing them or by employing the law to compel them to convert. The persistence of Judaism was a theological as much as a political problem for Christendom. If Christianity was the true message of a personal God, and if God had sacrificed His own Son to bring about the salvation of humanity after the Fall from a state of grace in the Garden of Eden, why did the Jews stubbornly and wilfully retain the 'old faith'? Why not embrace the new dispensation offered in the sacrificial blood of Jesus? As we have seen, Paul appealed to the Jews to embrace the new law and struggled to reconcile the differences between Gentile and Jewish Christians by a message of universalism. The continued existence of Judaism in the Mediterranean world, however, remained an enduring problem. We can see this difficulty come to a crisis in Spain, which was subject to various conflicts between Jews and Christians. After anti-Jewish riots across Iberia in 1391, pressure for the Jews to convert increased significantly. Some Jewish converts rose to influential positions in the royal court, for example Paul of Burgos, who became the tutor of King Juan II of Castile and bishop of Burgos. On other occasions, such as the famous Disputation of Tortosa in 1413–14, rabbis were forced to debate their faith with Geronimo of Santa Fe, a convert to Christianity who had been born Joshua Halorki (Kruger, 2006).

Conversions and colonialism

The intervention, often brutal, of the state in the affairs of religion is not of course confined to the Middle Ages. Many important explorations of conversion have been presented by anthropologists looking at conversion and Protestant missions in the contexts of colonialism and post-colonialism. These studies typically bring into focus the clash that took place between the missionary view of conversion involving emotions, intentions and sudden changes in values and identity, and the ways in which the theology of the missionaries was adopted and adapted to indigenous cultures. Anthropologists argue that Protestantism embraced a notion of religion, as distinct from culture, that emphasized the idea of religion as belief with universal implications (Asad, 1996). The effect was simultaneously to 'dematerialize' religion (making it into a collection of beliefs and values) and to disconnect religion and culture in the societies to which they brought their missions. In so far as missions were successful and local churches evolved, it raised a problem about the status of, for example, 'Indonesian Christianity': could the universal message of Pauline Christianity be transformed into a specific cultural location? Webb Keane also makes the important observation about the local character of conversion in Sumba, an island in eastern Indonesia which has been exposed to missionary activity by the neo-orthodox Reformed

Churches of the Netherlands from the early years of the twentieth century. Commenting on the psychology of the Sumbanese, he records: 'It has been my experience, however, that when both Christian and non-Christian Sumbanese talk about conversion, they are usually undramatic, rational and rarely touch on emotional questions – in part, a reflection of a general Sumbanese reticence about most forms of emotional expression and lack of language of interiority' (Keane, 2007: 226).

Unsurprisingly, many of the most influential anthropological accounts of conversion have understood these processes as taking place in the context of colonization and decolonization (Hefner, 1993; van der Veer, 1996). The evangelical churches that brought Christianity to Asia and Africa understood their mission in terms of a theology of salvation, namely to bring redemption to the natives. Regardless of their intentions, they brought many other things. Some were intentional, such as technology, education, monogamy, sedentarization and civilization; some were unintentional, such as infectious disease. But however we interpret individual conversion, as a social phenomenon it brought about radical changes in kinship and family, group membership, and patterns of life. Among aboriginal hunter-gatherer communities it often involved a dramatic transition to a settled lifestyle, new dietary arrangements, and above all new patterns of dependency on the state and missions as their traditional economy collapsed. In many colonial societies such as Australia, Christian missions became de facto agencies of the state, operating alongside the local police in imposing law and order in the outback (Schwarz and Dussart, 2010). Conversion in this context always assumed many different levels in terms of its cultural, individual and political meanings and consequences.

Let us take further examples from the recent history of conversion to Christianity in Indonesia, where they are directly influenced in large measure by state intervention in the public sphere. In the early stages of its modern development the official definition of what could count as a religion drove excluded groups (such as the animists) to convert to Christianity in order to obtain public recognition. The second significant change was brought about by the marriage law of 1974 stipulating that couples must share the same religion. This is important because Indonesian citizens have to carry a national identity card, stating their religion, thereby compelling its citizens to opt for one of the recognized religions. However, many modern-day conversions occur as a consequence of inter-faith marriages, when there is also a question about the status of any children born to an inter-faith couple. Because Indonesian law only recognizes marriages between people of the same faith as valid, one of the partners in an inter-faith marriage has to convert to allow the marriage to take place. Thus several legal changes played a major part in shaping the conditions that produced or limited conversions. These included: the presidential decree recognizing a limited number of religions in 1965; the National Marriage Law in 1974; the ministerial decrees on mission activities in 1978; the Law on Pancasila and Social Organization in 1985; and the Indonesian court decision on interreligious marriage in 1989. This legal framework severely constrained open proselytization by traditional evangelical means on the part of Christian churches and guaranteed that inter-faith marriage became the main vehicle for changing religious identities, since only marriage between people of the same faith was recognized in law.

As a consequence of these legal developments the mainstream churches, having abandoned aggressive evangelism, took over social welfare and educational functions for their members and thereby avoided conflict with the secular government and with Muslim communities. They succeed in institutional terms if they abandon evangelism, support the government line and are not exclusive. Over time, the adoption of these strategies means that the mainline churches look increasingly like ordinary secular voluntary associations rather than missionary churches. In summary, conversions on a large scale have taken place in Indonesia as a consequence of the communist crisis and the 1965 *jihad*, when many secular communists converted to Christianity to avoid political persecution. More recently the marriage laws in which couples need to agree on the same religion have resulted in conversions. As a consequence younger generations coming after the 1965 crisis are now converting to Christianity for very different reasons – mainly to satisfy marriage laws.

The sociology of conversion

From a sociological point of view, conversion raises problems of entry and exit from social groups; it is not specifically or necessarily an individual act. We can argue that for any social group to survive it has to address three basic issues. Adapting a model associated with Albert O. Hirschman's *Exit, voice and loyalty* (1970), I will simply call these basic issues of group survival entry, closure and exit. Entry into a religious group raises questions about authenticity and sincerity: is the conversion genuine? By contrast, exit raises obvious questions about loyalty. Because exit can threaten the integrity of a social group, it is normally heavily sanctioned. In Islam, for example, it has given rise to a whole theory of apostasy to account for such events. Conversion is a change in which, if an existing individual casts damaging and critical implications on the validity of Islam, they can be punished. The notion of apostasy in Muslim communities nevertheless remains controversial. 'Closure' refers to processes of securing the loyalty of existing members and converting incoming members to the values of the group. For example, children who are born into a group learn the culture of the group 'at their mother's breast'. For this reason, the regulation and control of women is important for the very survival and continuity of that group. Intermarriage is an acute threat to the integrity of the group, and can only be resolved when and if the children of a 'mixed marriage' are automatically defined as members.

While we can interpret religious conversion within this framework of the sociology of group dynamics, it is not automatically consistent with the theological or ecclesiastical account of conversion. To be more specific, while the liturgical recognition of membership by baptism might be consistent with the idea that entry–closure–exit describes the conditions of any social group (including a church), the sociology of conversion does not sit easily with the intentional model that is present in many narrative accounts of conversion. A persistent problem therefore in the sociology of religion is that the internal ('theological') and external ('sociological') accounts of conversion tend to contradict each other. The majority of sociological and historical accounts of such religious phenomena deny or ignore the actor's accounts. When looking at mass conversions to a religion – such as the movement of Chinese communists of Indonesia to Christianity to avoid persecution – historians unsurprisingly propose materialistic or interested motives for conversion. It appears to be obvious that the Chinese secular communists converted simply to stay alive. There are many examples of such explanations – for example, in the history of conversion within the Ottoman Empire. As a result many social groups were reclassified as Jews or Muslims or Christians as a consequence of changes in the organization of the empire (Baer, 2010).

These accounts while plausible appear to me to be inconsistent with the principles of reflexive sociology as they are described in the work of Pierre Bourdieu (Bourdieu and Wacquant, 1992). Such a sociology requires us to take the intentionality and knowledge of the social actor into account when we as sociologists offer explanations of their behaviour. Social actors cannot be regarded as passive or as mere dupes in the social structure. Nevertheless, in most historical and sociological accounts of conversion, explaining conversion appears to be relatively unproblematic from a secular social science perspective. We need therefore to be careful to distinguish between the 'internal account' and the 'external account', namely how conversion is understood within a religious tradition or from the point of view of the social actor who has been converted, and the sociological social identity resulting from either external compulsion (such as a physical threat or legal constraint) or whether it is a voluntary and individual act driven by self-interest. People convert to a religion for many reasons relating to interest: the church offers welfare and education to converts; conversion promises to improve their social status within a society; or it resolves some ambiguity of social status allowing a person to become fully a member of a society. In the sociological and anthropological literature, conversion is typically seen as driven by self-interest and social considerations relating to social status and material gain. Mass conversions are related, for example, to the role of the state in supporting different religions in a competitive environment, or they are the effect of prior socialization. Conversion then is simply an effect of the nature of competition between groups within the social field.

However, a reflexive sociology of conversion cannot simply ignore the endogenous account. In Christianity the biblical or endogenous account of conversion refers to individual rather than mass conversion. The New Testament account of conversion itself brings into the foreground the vexed question about whether conversions are reliable: are they true and are those who claim to be converted merely disguising their true motives? The life of Jesus suggests quite clearly that those who responded to the call 'Follow me!' often fell by the wayside and that under pressure the disciples abandoned him. The point of these New Testament stories is, we may assume, to illustrate the vulnerability of human beings when confronted by their own sinfulness. In the end the disciples abandoned Jesus to his painful and lonely fate, because they were ordinary rather than exceptional human beings. Obviously the New Testament account of conversion is not interested in missionary work and mass conversions – that is, in the sociology of conversion. It is rather concerned with the quality of faith, devotion on the part of individuals, and the weakness of believers.

Sociologists are of course more interested in mass conversion movements rather than in individual cases. Nevertheless, I draw the conclusion that sociology, especially reflexive sociology, cannot avoid the indigenous problem of the true nature of conversion. As I read the New Testament account of St Paul, conversion is not something an individual voluntarily chooses. A true conversion is one in which the convert is chosen by a power that lies outside the individual. In this regard I follow Talal Asad (1996: 271) when he questioned the role of agency in accounts of conversion: 'Why do we discount the convert's claim that he or she has been "made into" a Christian?' We can all too easily fail to grasp the importance of Protestant individualism for contemporary understanding of conversion as the intense emotional experience of an individual. Asad associates this religious tradition with John Locke's philosophical approach to individualism. He concludes: 'Too often, the assumptions we bring with us when talking about the conversion of people in another epoch or society are the ideological assumptions in and about our own condition' (Asad, 1996: 272). It is difficult to know where Bourdieu's sociology ultimately stands on this issue. Despite the claims about reflexive sociology, he appears reluctant to take into account actors' vocabularies because these are ultimately expressions of positions within a field. However, because he discounts social psychological theories and sociological theories that favour individual choice over social structure, perhaps his sociology of religion could interpret conversion as the effects of a field on the beliefs of individuals. But what if the field was the sacred? What would happen if we thought of the sacred as a religious field in which charisma is the power that shapes individual lives? These competing interpretations would challenge the assumptions about secular rationality that underpin sociology as a whole.

It could be plausibly argued that the internal accounts of conversion – especially the narrative of Paul's conversion – are exactly that – *post hoc* narrative reconstructions of events to demonstrate the authenticity of the experience. Because Paul was not related to Jesus and had not been an early witness, his dramatic conversion was necessary to prove his authority over the early Christian communities. This historical revision does not worry me too much, because it still leaves in place the normative account of authentic conversion: it is an event that happens to an individual often against their will and it cannot be motivated by material objectives. Conversion is something that happens; it is not something that is chosen.

Conclusion: the free will problem

In conclusion we can note a strange parallel between the internal contradictions of Christian theology and the so-called agency and structure
dilemma in sociology. Christian theology has never entirely solved the
problem of human free will – that is, our capacity as moral agents to
choose evil. Similarly, sociological theory has never quite married the
idea that social action implies human intentionality, while the notion of
social structure tends to rule out or minimize the agency of individuals.
For both theology and sociology, it is always both agency and structure.
Is conversion the product of certain 'conditions of existence' – such as
adolescence, the divided self or distressed emotions – or is it the intentions (free will) of the agent that are important? Turning to St Augustine
once more, we can see that he held to several different theories about
what drove individuals to action. In one example he compares habit
and intention by reference to his own dispositions. He spent much of
his life – if we take the *Confessions* to be an accurate statement of his
subjectivity – worried by his own sinfulness, but he often explained the
problem in purely psychological terms. Evil exists and persists because
of the compulsive nature of habit or *consuetudo* which gets its force
from memory. The pleasures we get from our past actions are 'inflicted'
on the memory, and so continue to influence our current behaviour
(Brown, 1989: 142). Memory makes our dispositions not just habitual
but compulsive. For example, Augustine attempted to stamp out the
habit of swearing among his congregation when he became a priest at
Hippo. However, he soon discovered that, although Christian men
wanted to stop swearing, once their tongues had acquired the habit it
was difficult to reform their bad language. While we have initially the
free will to avoid swearing, once we have acquired the habit reform is
almost impossible. Even more problematic, human beings are confronted with the *consuetudo carnalis* – 'a force of habit directed towards
the ways of the flesh' (Brown, 1989: 143). I have chosen this passage
because Augustine's account of human behaviour appears perfectly to
anticipate Bourdieu's 'logic of practice'. For Bourdieu, while we have
the experience of choice or intentionality, when we act we are conditioned by our habitus, which is the ensemble of dispositions we have
acquired from our position in the social structure. Our taste for goods
and services in a modern economy are the outcome of the habitus we
have from whatever class fraction we belong to. Furthermore, the body

becomes involved in these habits in terms of the 'hexis'. Contrary to Kant's theory of aesthetics, our choices are not rational and disinterested, but habitual and interested. Similarly, when our intentions become involved in our conversion – when we freely choose to become a Christian – we also have to recognize the force of hexis and habitus. Bourdieu is frequently defined as a Marxist (Fowler, 2011), but it may be more accurate to say that he was Augustinian.

Conversion in modern Christianity is also taking place in cultures that are typically individualistic and consumerist. In a modern consumer culture, where we are encouraged to think of ourselves as active consumers making choices about commodities and lifestyle, then religious branding adopts consumer sales strategies to promote the idea of religion as a lifestyle choice that brings certain benefits: happiness, success or wealth. This branding of faith is cleverly described by Mara Einstein in *Brands of faith* (2008) in her research on mega-churches which sell religion in a competitive market. This account of commercial religion fits Bourdieu's model of the religious field perfectly well. Do individuals in a commodified world actually choose a religion, or is their religious identity chosen for them by sales techniques that compel them to want Pentecostal services rather as a teenager feels compelled to wear Nike shoes or drink Pepsi? In a consumer society there may be little or no difference between saying 'I am a Gucci person' and 'I am a Mormon'. In both examples the 'choice' of religion comes from outside – in fact, from the structure of the market. The statement 'I choose to be a Mormon' – an act involving agency – is in fact an *illusio* in Bourdieu's terms and may be equivalent simply to the way in which the structure of the religious field has produced a choice, namely a decision to locate myself as a Mormon. Just as the habitus I have acquired from years of preparation makes it difficult for me to give up swearing, so too the dispositions I have in a consumer society make Gucci products or Mormon doctrines highly desirable, and while it appears to me that I am exercising choice, it may be that it is the commodities that are exercising agency.

7 | Religion, state and legitimacy: three dimensions of authority

Introduction: defining terms

Throughout his sociological work Max Weber was pre-eminently concerned with the mechanisms by which power is maintained and legitimized. More precisely, he inquired into the rule (*Herrschaft*) of human beings over human beings, and he saw domination as the central phenomenon of all forms of social organization. Given this obsession – to refer to the exegesis of Wilhelm Hennis (1988: 182) – it is hardly surprising that Weber is often compared to Machiavelli. He was scornful of those political philosophers and historians who wanted to see fellowship or community as the core business of political life. As a pessimistic liberal Weber believed that the main problem of German society was that the political class had failed to exercise leadership, because they had become mere functionaries. It is not surprising therefore that the opening sections of volume I of *Economy and society* (Weber 1978) are preoccupied with questions of power, authority and legitimacy. In these early passages he laid out his now famous definitions of authority in what he called 'the types of legitimate domination' in order to understand 'the bases of legitimacy' which I have already considered in Chapter 2 with special reference to charisma. The early forms of authority included charisma, or the extraordinary powers of personal leadership, and tradition, or the customs and conventions that routinely justify a particular order. These two – charisma and tradition – were oscillating forms of legitimacy in traditional societies. These categories were largely adopted from his friend and colleague Georg Jellinek, who had developed the idea of 'empirical types' to describe the 'religious–theological' and the 'legal–theoretical' modes of legitimacy. Because Weber believed that modern societies are passing through a profound period of rationalization, giving rise to the prevalence of bureaucratic authority, he saw legal rationality as the characteristic mode of contemporary legitimate domination. Weber offered an extensive definition of this type, but the core of this form of legitimacy is the hierarchical organization of offices and the downward flow of commands.

Before proceeding, let us pause briefly to consider some general features of this argument. First, the law is central to Weber's view of modern forms of legitimacy, and the discussion of law dominates both volumes of this posthumous work to such an extent that it could have been more appropriately called *Law and society*. Second, and more specifically, Weber argued that every form of domination requires some degree of voluntary compliance, and hence a theory of legitimacy also requires some notion of obedience. Why do people obey rules, by what mechanisms and according to what justification? Third, he suggested that the grounds of obedience could involve both material interests and affect, but the crucial issue is that every system of legitimate domination 'attempts to establish and to cultivate the belief in its legitimacy' (Weber, 1978, I: 213). No regime can exist indefinitely on the basis of pure force. He went on to assert that the validity of the claims for legitimacy in the case of legal rationality rests on 'a belief in the legality of enacted rules and the right of those elevated to authority under such rules to issue commands (legal authority)'. In *Economy and society* much of volume II is taken up with further developing his theory of law, but the central issue in the actual definition of such institutions is that law is command backed up by coercion of a state enjoying a monopoly of violence or sovereignty within a given territory.

Weber died in 1920, and *Economy and society* was assembled and published by Marianne Weber in 1928. While there has been much dispute about the status of the work, it is undeniably a major statement of his 'interpretive sociology'. It contains an extended account of his theory of legitimate domination. The analytical discussion in volume I does not, however, fully capture Weber's own ambiguity about the basis for legal legitimacy grounded in belief. In volume II Weber (1978, II: 882) brought into question the future continuity of formal legal rationality by noting that occupational differentiation and the demands of commercial and industrial pressure groups had introduced various particularistic laws in which legal experts catered to the particularistic interests of such groups and their sectional interests. Second, the demand for efficiency in legal judgments relating to what he called 'the concrete case' had also undermined legal abstract formalism. He also believed that the class struggle characteristic of advanced capitalism was reshaping the legal order through the emergence of what he called 'the social law', about which he was dismissive, noting that it was based on 'such emotionally colored ethical postulates as "justice" or "human dignity"' (Weber, 1978, II: 874). Claims regarding 'economic duress', for example, are, according to Weber, merely 'amorphous'. Weber made these critical comments because he had attacked natural law alongside other 'metajuristic axioms' (1978, II: 874) as possible foundations of law and morality. Although he recognized that it would 'hardly seem possible to eradicate completely from legal practice all the latent influence of the unacknowledged axioms of natural law', as a consequence of modern rationalism and scepticism, natural law has 'lost all capacity to provide the fundamental basis of a legal system' (Weber, 1978, II: 874). For him, we have already entered a disenchanted world in which appeals to over-arching sources of morality and value are no longer possible.

While critical of natural law traditions, Weber was influenced by Georg Jellinek who, in *The declaration of the rights of man and of citizens* (Jellinek, 2009), had traced the origins of the doctrine of universal and inalienable rights not to the secular principles of the French Revolution, or Roman law, or English common law, but to the Puritan colonialists, who claimed absolute freedom of conscience for all religions, including those of Turks and heathens. Weber had intended to look more closely into legal developments in the time of Oliver Cromwell, and we can assume that he welcomed Jellinek's ideas as compatible with his own treatment of Protestantism in the famous essays of 1904–5 that make up *The Protestant Ethic and the spirit of capitalism* (2002). However, Weber's overriding idea of secularity ruled out the possibility that religion could continue to influence the rights of modern societies dominated by legal rationalism.

Weber feared that the state (*Rechtsstaat*) within a liberal rule of law was being replaced by an administrative or welfare state (the *Sozialstaat*). The political crisis of Germany following the First World War led him to a deeper pessimism about the foundations of the legitimacy of the state. An article from the *Frankfurter Zeitung* from the summer of 1917 was reproduced in volume II of *Economy and society* as 'Parliament and government in a reconstructed Germany', in which he ascribed greater legitimacy to an elected president than to a parliament dominated by party struggles. In his discussion of the crisis of German political institutions Weber talked about the 'minimum consent' required from the ruled, declaring that 'parliaments are today the means of manifesting this minimum consent' (Weber, 1978, II: 1408). The problem with parliamentary systems was that they gave rise to 'negative politics' in which the grievances of citizens are voiced in conflict with the bureaucratic administration of the state, and as such it could never offer any political leadership. This decline of political leadership was manifest in the rise of the *Obrigkeitstaat*, or government by a bureaucracy of anonymous civil servants. Within this discussion of the erosion of formal legal rationality and the growth of a democratic stalemate, it is no longer clear how exactly legal rationality finds its legitimacy.

Carl Schmitt and the crisis of the Weimar regime

These definitions and typologies may appear to be dry, formal and abstract from the standpoint of the twenty-first century, but they have retained a controversial legacy because of their influence on the German legal theorist Carl Schmitt, who became one of the leading legal authorities during the collapse of the Weimar Republic. His analyses of law and sovereignty are associated with the anti-democratic notions of power that fuelled the ideology of the Nazi Party, and he remains influential for his political theory. Born in 1888 to a devout Catholic family, Schmitt witnessed the defeat of Germany and was outraged by the terms of the Treaty of Versailles, which had brought the very existence of the German state into question. In Germany politics had descended into mere struggles between contending parties within a weak state structure. In 1932 he published *The concept of the political* (Schmitt, 1996), and in the following year he joined the Nazi Party. For Schmitt, while politics was a grubby, mundane struggle for influence, the political involved the struggle between friend and foe, and was ultimately what defined the human. In this struggle with a real and concrete enemy, individuals are forced ultimately to take responsibility for themselves and their times. In an emergency people have to make decisions and stick by them. While Schmitt was often thought to have taken the political away from ethical concerns, Leo Strauss in a famous exchange with Schmitt showed that Schmittian political theory was deeply concerned with ethics, precisely because it asserted that the political created the meaningful (Meier, 1995). An earlier work – *Political theology*, which appeared in 1922 (Schmitt, 1985) – also has an ethical and religious dimension. In this early work he famously defined 'sovereignty' as the capacity of a leader to declare a state of emergency. It comes into operation most clearly in terms of undefined emergency powers that fill the gaps in a constitutional order. As such, sovereignty was a limiting concept, because it can only be grasped in an emergency situation when the very existence of the state is in question. In this discussion of the foundations of legitimacy, I am more concerned to discuss his *Legality and legitimacy* (Schmitt, 2004), which first appeared in 1932.

Schmitt's legal philosophy was based on the view that the European states were losing their monopoly of legitimate violence and that political struggles could no longer be understood within existing state-centred theories. Schmitt was deeply influenced by Weber, and argued that the legal system could no longer be understood apart from the substantive politics of class conflict and party struggles. With the rise of National Socialism the distinction between the public and private spheres was losing any meaning. Bourgeois society, which had been the basis of fundamental notions of property, contract and freedom, was being undermined by National Socialism and could no longer be evoked as the basis of political legitimacy.

Schmitt's theories, and his personal career and relationship to Fascism, have been much disputed (Balakrishnan, 2000). We are not concerned directly with these disputes. We simply draw from Schmitt two issues relating to Weber. The first is that Schmitt argued that situating legitimacy in belief was not a secure basis for any enduring authority. If parliaments are institutional expressions of such a belief, then one can have no confidence in belief as a foundation of legitimacy. Parliamentary debates are fickle and subject to external pressures from parties, constituencies, pressure groups and social classes. Second, Schmitt distinguished between legality and legitimacy.

The idea that democratic participation could be a basis for modern legitimacy is largely absent from Weber's political sociology. For Weber democracy was plebiscitary democracy – that is, merely a method of selecting leaders who, after their election, were not directly accountable to the citizenry. Indeed, Weber paid very little attention to the possibility that citizenship and public debate could play a role in modern politics as the foundation of legitimate rule (Lassman, 2000: 96). This discussion of the foundations of legitimacy has unsurprisingly become an issue of considerable importance in political sociology (Mayer, 1998; Mommsen, 1984). For example, Jürgen Habermas in *Between facts and norms* (1996) attempted to show that rational–legal legitimacy was grounded in the participation of citizens in the formulation of legal and constitutional norms rather than simply in belief in such norms.

Following Weber's own secularism, Habermas had to find 'in post-metaphysical conditions' a source of legitimacy in secular citizenship. He argued that 'In justifying the system of rights ... the autonomy of citizens and the legitimacy of the law *refer* to each other. Under post-metaphysical conditions, the only legitimate law is one that emerges from the discursive opinion- and will-formation of equally enfranchised citizens' (Habermas, 1996: 408).

Legality and legitimacy

In these debates legality and legitimacy are often elided in being treated as equivalent – or, in Habermas's terms, they inevitably refer to each other. In Weber's own account the two are not clearly separated. Legal rationality is rule by virtue of legality that is belief in the validity of statutes and the competence by which rules are found and articulated. In my analysis of the problems of legitimacy in modern societies I propose to treat legality and legitimacy as in principle analytically distinct. Let me then formulate the distinction between these two dimensions more precisely before attempting to apply them to modern political regimes.

These two dimensions can be defined for purposes of abstract formulation as independent dimensions of domination, although in empirical reality they may be combined in various ways. As analytical criteria they allow us to construct a two-by-two table in which some governments may in principle be legal but not legitimate, while others might be legitimate but not legal. This distinction had real force in Germany in the 1930s and 1940s around the question: was the Nazi regime of Adolf Hitler legal but not legitimate? One answer was that the Reich's chancellorship was legal, but the coercive suppression of public debate and the violent expulsion and destruction of various minorities rendered the regime illegitimate. The charismatic authority of Hitler did not overcome this basic lack of legitimacy.

Following Habermas, we will treat legitimacy as a component of a democratic order in that facilitating will formation and belief formation requires meaningful elections, the formation of political parties, the recognition of legitimate opposition, the free circulation of ideas by the mass media and so forth. These components of modern legitimacy are not particularly contentious, despite the sceptical views of both Weber and Schmitt that public opinion can often be fickle and contrived. These democratic components of legitimacy also ensure the regular and transparent transition of elected governments and their leaders. By contrast, tribalism, patriarchal authority and hereditary monarchy in contemporary societies may be regarded as possible criteria to define rulership as illegitimate.

By legality, I appeal to liberal theory that recognizes the rule of law, habeas corpus and due process as fundamental to a decent society. Legality is, however, in one important respect different from legitimacy in the sense that it has an important coercive aspect. Whether or not I believe in the law of the land is irrelevant, because as a citizen I cannot choose to obey the law or not to obey the law. I can vote against a government, but I cannot decide to ignore the laws that are enforced by the courts. Habermas (1996: 121) recognized this issue when he observed that

Legitimate law is compatible only with a mode of legal coercion that does not destroy the rational motives for obeying the law: it must remain possible for everyone to obey legal norms on the basis of insight. In spite of its coercive character, therefore, law must not *compel* its addressees but must offer them the option, in each case, of foregoing [*sic*] the exercise of their communicative freedom and not taking a position on the legitimacy claim of law, that is, the option of giving up the performative attitude to law in a particular case in favour of the objectifying attitude of an actor who freely decides on the basis of utility calculations.

Finally, we should remind ourselves that for Weber every order of legitimate domination also addresses the question: why should I comply with these norms? A third dimension of authority might be drawn from utilitarianism, namely that any government that can satisfy the basic needs for life and security of its citizens can be regarded as legitimate in terms of 'utility calculations'. Any state (regardless of its legality and legitimacy) that satisfies basic needs and offers me a modicum of security may gain my compliance, even when the state may act against some minority. There may be a situation in which I believe that my interests (to obtain a job, to raise a mortgage and to acquire a pension) are threatened by an exceptional wave of immigration. I might decide as an Australian citizen that it is not in my interests to allow boat people to enter the country without due process, and hence decide to support a party that wants to contain or stop illegal entry into the land. Although towing boats back to Indonesia might be incompatible with international law on the treatment of undocumented immigrants, I may prefer to support utilitarian considerations of personal interest. Habermas

(1996: 512) discusses the possibility that such utilitarian considerations might justify significant restrictions on immigration on the grounds that limits on immigration might avoid civil conflict and violence against existing migrant minorities. His response is ultimately to ground legitimacy in citizenship not as an exclusive but inclusive right that points finally towards a world citizenship in which we would recognize a range of mutual obligations between communities of free individuals: 'Only a democratic citizenship that does not close itself off in a particularistic fashion can pave the way for a *world citizenship*, which is already taking shape today in worldwide political communications' (Habermas, 1996: 514). This idea of world citizenship may find its legal counterpart in the notion of 'community necessity' in which through international law citizens of separate states can recognize their duties towards others.

However, this question of utilitarian justification of government cannot be easily contained within the basic dichotomy of legality and legitimacy. I contend that there is indeed a third dimension of the conditions of compliance, which we will call the performative principle. It is not hard to imagine a state that is neither fully legitimate nor completely legal, in which the basic conditions of existence are satisfied at least for the majority of citizens, who in turn give their consent to soft authoritarianism. By contrast, one can imagine a government that is legal and legitimate but incompetent, and which no longer has the support of the majority. The idea of 'performance legitimacy' has in fact often been used to contrast the West with those societies in Asia that have been deeply influenced by Confucianism in which there was an expectation that a good ruler was one that provided the people with rice and with security. This attitude was also an aspect of communist rule, and today the Communist Party, by raising millions of Chinese out of poverty, has performative legitimacy (at least for citizens living in urban areas who have prospered in the era of Deng Xiaoping). Because communist ideology no longer provides a convincing belief system, the party has embraced a combination of Neo-Confucianism, nationalism and pragmatism. However, the principal emphasis is on the capacity of the political elite to deliver continuous growth (Bell, 2008).

One might observe that the dilemma of many European governments, especially in Greece and Spain, in the economic downturn after the crisis of 2007–12 is the problem of implementing austerity packages in the face of public opposition and their inability to construct policies that promise, let alone deliver, economic growth. In contemporary secular politics the unemployment rate in Western economies is probably the key test of the performative legitimacy of an elected government. We also know that unemployment has become a stubborn problem of the modern economy in which a variety of changes – technological efficiency, outsourcing, and the decline of both agricultural production and heavy industry – have presented governments with almost impossible limitations on performance. Can we conclude therefore that religion no longer has any role in the legitimacy of the modern state?

On civil religion

Peter Lassman argues that Weber did not intend his three ideal types of authority to suggest any evolutionary model of social change. However, these types 'possess an implicit historical as well as a more systematic dimension' (Lassman, 2000: 90). In this chapter we can reasonably interpret these categories of domination as spelling out a theory of secularization in the sense that charismatic leadership (by prophets, for example) gives way, through a long process of rationalization, to rule by bureaucrats or *Fachmenschen*, namely the experts and technicians who run modern governments and their bureaucracies (Stauth and Turner, 1986). One can agree with Weber in the sense that modern politicians are celebrities rather than charismatics in so far as their personal 'charm' is engineered by fashion consultants and media experts rather than through divine inspiration.

We have already seen that Weber dismissed or neglected any discussion of democracy as the most obvious form of political legitimacy in secular societies. He followed Robert Michels (1962) who in *Political parties* in 1911 had argued that the modern party system would result inevitably in 'the iron law of oligarchy', namely the bureaucratization of political representation in which the party bosses would determine election outcomes. I regard this account of politics as a component of his general ideas about secularity, since he does not consider religion as an important aspect of modern legitimacy. We have already seen that he was influenced here by Jellinek, who had suggested that modern notions of freedom, especially the idea of freedom of conscience and the autonomy of the individual in the emergence of human rights, were the direct legacy of the Reformation rather than modern liberalism (Hennis, 1988: 169). Weber's view that European societies were now secular and could no longer appeal to religion as a platform for legitimacy might not have any obvious validity in the United States. Weber had considered the possibility that America might avoid the 'iron cage' (Offe, 2005). Could it therefore draw upon religion as a basis for the justification of rule? One possible candidate here is indeed the notion of a 'civil religion'.

The idea of religious freedom – that is, freedom of conscience – is a basic assumption of theories of civil liberties and tolerance. The purpose of civil society was to provide security for its citizens, leaving religion to the individual, and hence the sovereign in a secular constitution was obliged to respect religious freedom. By the end of the seventeenth century the religious conflicts of the English Civil War had been settled by the Glorious Revolution, by the union of Scotland and England, and by new ideas about tolerance as illustrated by the political theories of John Locke (1946) in 1667 and by Samuel Pufendorf (2002) in 1687. The assumption of Lockean secularism was that religion is a personal matter of private conscience and should not impinge on the public domain. Of course Locke in 'A letter on tolerance' in 1667 was mainly concerned to bring an end to the intolerance between Catholics and Protestants, and equally between Puritan sects. Another aspect of seventeenth-century tolerance was the growing openness of societies that were engaged in long-term trade and colonization. These principles of tolerance and the separation of religion and state were fundamental to the American constitution, but the consequence has been to create a free market of religions which has not always favoured the institutional dominance of Christianity, and has in effect opened up a cultural space for a civil religion.

In a plural, diverse and multicultural society, social diversity could perhaps be contained within the broad umbrella of a 'civil religion'. Separate and different religious traditions must be tolerated in a liberal environment in the hope that they might somehow contribute to a more general 'civil religion'. This notion had its origin in Rousseau's political and educational theories. In *The social contract* (1973) he argued that Christian belief in a supernatural world was inimical to social life on this earth. In *The creed of a priest of Savoy* Rousseau (1956), rejecting the Christian view of the sinful nature of humankind, insisted that all humans need religion as a bulwark against despair. It was deism that gave full recognition to the emotions and the social role of religion in sustaining civil society. However, this religion was to be fabricated by a lawgiver operating in defence of a republic. In the

French Revolution Rousseau's *Social contract* was translated into the 'administrative reality' of the state, and provided intellectuals with a 'new perspective of redemption through political power' (Nisbet, 1990: 141). Robespierre in 1794 drew up the doctrine of the Religion of the Supreme Being, and the idea of France as a singular and undivided state corresponded perfectly with the organization of the Terror, and with Rousseau's understanding of the submersion of the individual in the state.

For Robert Nisbet religion operated, as Tocqueville said it would, in the form of the local and autonomous congregation, and the separation of religion and politics protected the emerging democracy from the clutches of an established church. While the Protestant Ethic was seen by Nisbet as fundamental to the development of American associational democracy, he was ambivalent about Protestantism. The Reformation had destroyed much of the communal life of the Middle Ages, rendering the guilds suspect and casting doubt on the bonds of kinship, and the principal elements of the Reformed Church were 'the lone individual, an omnipotent, distant God, and divine grace' (Nisbet, 1990: 84). By contrast, he argued that Roman Catholicism 'was the last real stronghold of the kind of authority that lies in religious institutions, in ritual and in sacrament' (Nisbet, 1975: 89). While Protestantism had succumbed to the 'acid' effects of modernity and as a result had lost all sense of genuine community, Catholicism retained a vivid and vital sense of ritual practice. However, the 'greatest religious event of our age' was the transformation of Catholicism as a result of the changes brought about by the Vatican Council in 1960 under Pope John XXIII, and he feared that the result of these changes would be an eventual secularization of Catholicism. The danger was that reformed Catholicism would go the same way as Protestantism.

An American tradition of authentic Christianity had been, in Nisbet's view, corrupted by the youth revolts of the 1960s. In widespread post-war alienation, people looked for community in 'easy religion', but the result was 'a vulgarization of Christianity' (Nisbet, 1990: 27). Consequently the manifestation of religion in the student movements was a significant departure from the religious legacy of the foundations of American civilization, and his language was mildly scornful of what he called 'the astonishing recrudescence of religion – at least the trappings of religion – among those elements of society (chiefly college youth at the present time, but the ranks are spreading)' (Nisbet, 1975: 82).

He lamented the growth of 'fundamentalist or Pentecostalist religions' at the expense of mainstream Christianity (Nisbet, 1986: 44). He was not alone in recognizing how the post-war student population was spear-heading a revolution in culture, including religious culture. Talcott Parsons (1974) called this an 'expressive revolution' in which the pre-dominance of cognitive rationalism was being displaced by an expressive and emotional culture that celebrated the right of individuals to have 'experience'. Similarly, Daniel Bell (1976) recognized the cultural contra-dictions of capitalism in terms of a struggle between traditional forms of asceticism and discipline and new forms of leisure and hedonism arising with post-industrial society. These trends have continued and intensified with consumerism and the emergence of an online society. The spread of Facebook and Twitter is perhaps the perfect modern example of this, and in the religious sphere these cultural developments are to be found in a post-institutional, individualized and hybrid religiosity that sociologists have called 'spirituality'. The new religious forms typically take place outside any organized group and definitely outside organized religion, involving, in the words of Grace Davie (1994), 'believing with-out belonging'. This phrase perhaps perfectly captures Nisbet's notion of the erosion of community in modern societies.

Nisbet's criticisms of the idea of civil religion contrast sharply with Robert Bellah's famous *Daedalus* article, 'Civil religion in America' (1967). Against the notion of secularization, Bellah argued that there was a religious tradition in America that is separate from but connected to Christianity. This civil religion incorporated the historical sense of America as the First New Nation, the City on a Hill and the Israel of the New World. It was a history of sacrifice and suffering but eventual redemption. It was also a history of tragedy from the Civil War to Vietnam, it contained symbols of national injury and deliverance such as the Arlington Memorial, and it was reinforced and revivified by periodic festivals such as Thanksgiving. Bellah, insisting that it was not a perverted or degraded version of Christianity, also speculated that civil religion was the natural companion to a republican form of government, and in this regard he implicitly followed Rousseau in believing that Christianity had no necessary connection with secular government.

In a subsequent reflection on the debate about his article, Bellah adop-ted a language that sounds in some respects like a version of Rousseau's notion of a republic. He wrote (1978: 18):

A republic will have republican customs – public participation in the exercise of power, political equality of citizens, a wide distribution of small and medium property with few very rich or very poor – customs that will lead to a public spiritedness, a willingness of the citizen to sacrifice his own interests for the common good, in a word a citizen motivated by republican virtue.

In Bellah's account of republican America and its civil religion there is little or no reference to intermediate associations. Rather, the citizen is connected to the state via the beliefs, values and rituals of the civil religion. He went on to recognize that this republican ideal was vastly different from the liberalism of Adam Smith, because it did not assume that the self-interest of the individual in the marketplace would ever produce an orderly and coherent society. He concluded his article on the legitimacy of the republic with recognition that consumerism and 'naked self interest' had undermined the institutions that are the vehicles of the civil religion. He asked:

Have not the churches along with the schools and the family – what I have called the soft structures that deal primarily with human motivation – suffered more in the great upheavals through which our society has recently gone than any other of our institutions, suffered so much that their capacity to transmit patterns of conscience and ethical values has been seriously impaired? (Bellah, 1978: 23)

There is some possibility here of a convergence between Bellah and Nisbet around the idea of patriotic virtues – but these are not specifically Christian, and Bellah's view (like that of Rousseau) that Christianity and republicanism are not compatible does not sit easily with Nisbet's critical response to the notion of a civil religion. Bellah has perceptively argued that from Washington to more recent American presidents there is an acknowledgement that God as the Supreme Being stands over the nation, but in official discourse there is rarely any reference to Jesus Christ, precisely because in a multifaith society any acknowledgement of Jesus as Saviour would be divisive. The idea that the nation is guided by a Supreme Being is in fact very close to Rousseau's idea that in a republic religion needs such a Being, but it does not need the theological baggage of a religion of salvation. The question is: how much of Bellah's version of civil religion, whose principal historical spokesman was Abraham Lincoln and whose core value is republican virtue, survives in modern politics and religion?

Conclusion: the erosion of legitimacy

Sociologists are perhaps prone to 'cry wolf' whenever there is a problem about the legitimacy of capitalist societies. Nevertheless, there does appear to be a systematic problem about the basis of the legitimacy of the modern state. For various reasons, I have argued following Weber that neither tradition nor charisma appears to be an effective source of authority, and legal rationality has been compromised in so far as the law serves the interests of the dominant elite rather than the people as a whole. This argument leads us to the conclusion that only performance can guarantee legitimacy. The prospects for performative legitimacy rest on economic achievement, and if we take employment as a crucial measure of performance, then democratic governments face an enduring problem. One's position will depend greatly on whether one regards unemployment as cyclical or structural. Cyclical unemployment would simply follow the business cycle, but many economists have argued that unemployment is a structural problem of late capitalism in which greater efficiency, computerization, and the decline of manufacturing with post-industrialism have created a permanent problem of unemployment and declining incomes.

In response to the financial and economic crisis from 2008 onwards, the austerity packages in Europe that are designed to reduce the burden of debt have so far done nothing to improve unemployment, which has in Greece and Spain risen to alarming levels. In the United States it has been argued that the modest rise in employment in 2011–12 was not a consequence of 'quantitative easing' but produced rather by people permanently leaving the labour market. In many European societies the electorate, most notably in France, has responded by voting out those governments that have been identified with austerity strategies. The other response has been through various levels of civil disobedience. These developments indicate that governments are having difficulty satisfying the performance criterion of modern governments, and hence their legitimacy has become questionable.

It is not clear how the Christian Churches will respond to this crisis. On the one hand, they are deeply embedded in modern capitalism, especially through the prosperity gospel and the rise of the mega-church. On the other hand, religious leaders have also spoken out forcefully in condemning the growth in social inequality and the rampant greed of consumer societies. Rowan Williams, the Archbishop of Canterbury, in a sermon commemorating the Golden Jubilee in the United Kingdom, criticized the culture of greed, hostility to strangers and lack of responsibility to society. There has also been support for Occupy Wall Street from the Churches, which have also criticized the irresponsibility of a greedy society. These developments, including the rise of populism in the form of the Tea Party movement in the United States, suggest a significant legitimacy deficit in modern societies.

When thinking about legitimacy deficits we need to keep in mind one important transformation of the state, especially in Western Europe, namely the reduction of state activity. Between the 1930s and 1960s there was an extraordinary expansion of social security in the United States, the National Health Service in the United Kingdom, and the Scandinavian state welfare systems. From the 1970s onwards these systems were slowly cut back, undermined and then abandoned in favour of market solutions and private provision. As a result, we can argue that the state has reduced expectations about its performance. The mood in contemporary America is to demolish Big Government, while the austerity model in Europe may have the same effect by reducing the tax basis of the state. Consequently performance as the basis of legitimacy in the contemporary world is modest by comparison with the mid-twentieth century. Privatization has been a key strategy in the last three decades, because 'in an age of budgetary constraints, privatization appears to save money. If the state owns an efficient factory or costly service – a waterworks, say, or a railway – it offloads it onto private buyers. ... What we have been watching is the steady shift of public responsibility onto the private sector with no discernible collective advantage' (Judt, 2010: 107–8). These developments have also taken place alongside the modern intensification of globalization. Because more and more services are outsourced and production units are transported overseas, it is increasingly difficult for citizens and their governments in the West to exercise control over vital utilities and resources. One consequence of these developments is that the state is held responsible for less, and so the field of legitimacy shrinks.

PART III

Comparative and historical studies

8 | Buddhism and the political: the sangha and the state

Introduction: Max Weber's *The religion of India*

Contemporary scholars of religion are often deeply suspicious of the use of such expressions as 'the religion of India' or more generally 'the religions of Asia', or worse still 'the Asian religions'. The anthropological argument, which we came across in Chapter 6, is that in trying to generalize about religions we are often unwittingly working with a Western – or, more specifically, a Protestant – view of what counts as 'religion'. This implicit Protestant view in emphasizing correct belief over ritual practice and community raises problems about how we regard ritual traditions that are associated with 'other religions'. This raises difficulties about what belongs to culture and what to religion (Asad, 1993; Keane, 2007). Is 'Hinduism', which is an umbrella term for a cluster of diverse beliefs and practices, a 'religion', or is it simply the 'culture' of South Asia? To some extent 'Hinduism', as simply the religion of the 'Hindu', was a creation of British administrative policies in India and the efforts of Christian missionaries in translating Christian ideas into Indian culture (Viswanathan, 1996).

A modern approach to defining 'Hinduism' attempts to capture the diversity of an evolving tradition by noting that 'It is a cumulative collection of communities, faiths, beliefs, and practices that have come together over the centuries, although its ancient roots are traditionally seen in the cultures of the Indus Valley, Saraswati River civilization, and Indo-European people' (Narayanan, 2005: 15). In defence of Weber, he appeared to be aware of these difficulties, observing:

> It may well be concluded that Hinduism is simply not a 'religion' in our sense of the word. ... What the Occidental conceives as 'religion' is closer to the Hindu concept of *sampradaya*. By this the Hindu understands communities into which one is not born ... but to which one belongs by virtue of a common religious aspiration and common sacred paths. (Weber, 1958: 23)

For Weber these communities (or *theophratries*) include, among others, both Jainism and Buddhism. I will return later to the problem of Buddhism as a religion, but to conclude these opening remarks we might also keep in mind that Weber in the companion volume *The religion of China* notes similar difficulties with the idea of Confucianism as a religion. He declared that 'Confucianism exclusively represented an inner-worldly morality of laymen. Confucianism meant adjustment to the world, to its orders and conventions' (Weber, 1951: 152). In Weber's sociology a religion has to be distinct from and in some degree of tension with 'the world' of politics and economics. This tension gave rise to two orientations to the world: asceticism, on the one hand, and mysticism, on the other. This meant either active engagement with or against the world through ascetic discipline or adjustment to or flight from the world in terms of a mystical retreat. This model was the basis of the famous essay translated as 'Religious rejections of the world and their directions' in *From Max Weber* (Gerth and Mills, 2009).

We must deal with one more preliminary problem, namely Weber's association of Hinduism with caste. He correctly saw the rise of Buddhism in South Asia against the background of a diffuse spiritual tradition known subsequently as Hinduism, which he described as a religion associated with notions of ritual pollution and castes. In fact it would be more accurate to argue that we cannot understand Buddhism without a prior grasp of the history of the religious traditions in ancient India that were organized around the values of the Brahmins. Furthermore, we cannot understand this early Vedic tradition without understanding the idea of caste. Ancient India was created by endless incursions by peoples from Afghanistan and Central Asia through the north-west passages. This procession of 'Aryan conquests' over the centuries created a large number of petty kingdoms and ruling princes. In this hierarchical system, incoming guest workers were eventually consigned to a lowly caste or pariah group that undertook menial tasks, often considered to be polluting. These diverse religious ideas and institutions operated at a village level, and Weber argued at the very beginning of his study that India was a system of villages in which membership was defined by birth. It is not surprising therefore that *The religion of India* starts with an account of caste in relation to Hinduism. Weber boldly asserted that caste is 'the ritual rights and duties it imposes, and the position of the Brahmans, is the fundamental institution of Hinduism. Before everything else, without caste there is no Hindu' (Weber, 1958: 29). Indian caste hierarchy was based on the four *varna*s: the Brahmin, the warrior (*ksatriya*), the people (*vis*), and the servants (*sudra*). This hierarchical division of society by basic functions cut across the differentiation of the society into tribes and lineages. These castes were inherited positions, and therefore the most prestigious of the Brahmins were defined by several generations of ritual purity. Brahmins had control of major rituals and were guardians of the written tradition. While the Brahmins were ritually separate, they also encompassed or completed the social system, whereas lower castes were ontologically incomplete. One important feature of this system was that ritual authority (the Brahmins) was separate from the system of economic and political power (the *ksatriya* caste). In Weber's terms, the symbolic power of the Brahminical caste did not necessarily translate into political power.

Generally speaking, anthropologists of Indian society have been sceptical about the value of the notion of a caste system that had so dominated early writing about India. Modern reinterpretations of caste probably start with the work of Mysore Srinivas (1989), who identified a pattern of social mobility, known as 'Sanskritization', in which lower castes, in imitating the ritual behaviour of higher castes, could move up the social ladder. In short, the caste system was more fluid than conventional views allowed. More recently anthropologists have argued that the so-called caste system was a good deal more porous, fluid and fragmented, and that the real core of the system was the *jati*, the hereditary endogamous group often associated with occupational specialization. These terms and their implications remain a contested field, but what cannot be disputed is that in the India before the Buddha social inequality existed in terms of a system of hereditary and hierarchical distinctions in which the Brahmins were at the pinnacle of rules defining and controlling pollution. The *varna* system, to use Durkheim's terminology, was a form of primitive classification that was both cosmological and sociological in providing legitimacy for the secular distribution of power (Smith, 1994).

Scholars normally read *The religion of India* as a contribution to his comparative sociology of economic ethics, but his account of India has as much to do with politics as it does with economics. We can read the book as an account of why citizenship, as it was known in the West, did not emerge in South Asia, and his answer was couched in terms of the role of caste, the segregation of various sectors of the population by norms of pollution, and the conservatism of village life. But we can also read the work as an account of the relations between religion and politics – or, in the case of Buddhism, between the monarchy and the monastic community or *sangha*. I contend that this reading of Weber brings into focus the forms of state legitimacy in Asia, and the complex relations between the monarchy, the Buddhist monastic elite and the laity.

The transformation of Buddhism in Weber's great work is understood by reference to the emergence of Mahayana and the inclusion of the laity into Buddhism as a religion and not simply as the spiritual technique of celibate monks. As a result, some Buddhist traditions offer greater scope for lay participation in meditation and ascetic discipline. In Japan various Buddhist movements developed that rejected the monastic order in its entirety. For example the great religious leader Shinran (1173–1262) creatively developed a version of the Pure Land teaching when he was exiled and forced to live in the provinces away from the conventional institutions of the capital. His teachings, which had become influential in Tokyo by the time of his death, emphasized the community of equal members, rejecting initiation, state support and monasticism. Spiritual enlightenment was available to the laity via yielding through a spontaneous religious experience to Amida Buddha (Amstutz, 1997). In much of Asia the traditional Buddhist pattern of legitimacy began to break down with the arrival of British colonialism, and more recently the relationship between Buddhist monasticism and the state has changed once more with the spread of democratic ideas and the rise of a middle class. Only in contemporary Thailand can we find the traditional pattern of a Buddhist king who protects the Buddhist tradition and a *sangha* that in return gives him legitimacy through the system of merit making.

Weber's characterization of early Buddhism

Rather than concentrating on the factors that inhibited capitalism, Weber claimed with reference to Hinduism that 'legitimation by a recognized religion has always been decisive for an alliance between politically and socially dominant classes and the priesthood' (Weber, 1958: 16). But did the same apply to Buddhism? Before attempting to evaluate Weber's sociology of Buddhism in the light of contemporary research, we need to spell out the argument in *The religion of India* (Weber, 1958). The decisive feature of early Buddhism for Weber was that it promulgated spirituality for monks to the exclusion of the laity. What Weber referred to as 'Ancient Buddhism' is a 'specifically unpolitical and anti-political status religion, more precisely, a religious "technology" of wandering and intellectually-schooled mendicant monks. Like all Indian philosophy and theology it is a "salvation religion", if one is to use the name "religion" for an ethical movement without a deity and without a cult' (Weber, 1958: 206). More precisely, he argued, Buddhist philosophy is indifferent to questions about divinity, because it is a spiritual technology that aims to release the individual from suffering in order eventually to achieve a state of nothingness or *nirvana*. The crucial issue here is the exclusion of the laity from complete fulfilment of Buddhist practice, because lay engagement in the everyday world of production and reproduction meant that they could never complete the comprehensive discipline of the Eightfold Path. He argued in *The religion of China* that, in the historical development of Buddhism and its eventual spread to Japan, Buddhism had become a 'folk religion' with distinctively magical elements. Thus 'Buddhism in its imported form was no longer the redemptory religion of early Indian Buddhism, but had become the magical and mystagogical practice of a monastic organization' (Weber, 1951: 225). One consequence of these developments was that there were no religious communities for the laity, and individual lay people went to the monks for magical services to restore their health or to bring them comfort. Buddhism did not develop a strong congregational structure, which was characteristic of the Abrahamic religions. Hence Buddhism was thus, in Weber's eyes, an essentially spiritual technology.

Whereas Islam is often seen by Western critics as heavily involved with the political (as in the expression 'political Islam'), Buddhism is by contrast seen to be associated with pacifism, or at least seen as fundamentally an apolitical spirituality. Buddhist doctrines of suffering, mindfulness and release from this world through self-discipline appear to be far removed from the history of Christian Crusades or the Islamic *jihad*. Among academic sociologists this understanding of Buddhism may well have been fostered by the legacy of Weber's sociology of religion. For example, he was particularly interested in the early carriers of religion, arguing that the carrier of Islam was a warrior class, that Confucianism was the ethical system of cultured prebendaries with a literary education based on secular rationalism, and that the social carriers of the primitive Church in early Christianity were artisans. In terms of early Buddhism, the carrier of mindfulness was the forest-dwelling mendicant monk. For Weber these early carriers of religion had a long-term impact on their values and institutions. In *Weber and Islam* (Turner, 1974) I criticized his account of Islam, pointing out, among other issues, that the carriers of Islam from the African coast to the city-ports of Southeast Asia were Sufi traders, who were members of brotherhoods with international connections. It was trade rather than the sword that brought the message of the Prophet to Southeast Asia. Has Weber's view of early Buddhism and its world-rejecting spirituality survived the test of recent scholarship?

Weber frequently made use of Ernst Troeltsch's church–sect typology, but he also adopted his own notion of religious virtuosity to describe the religious lifestyle of individuals whose religious capacities were extra-ordinary. Such individuals were endowed with charisma. Thus in *The sociology of religion* (1966b) he introduced the idea of a religious hierarchy or stratification of individuals in terms of their religious capacities or talent. Their capacities may be innate, but he also stressed the importance of discipline in the pursuit of a heroic religious life. He noted (2009c: 287) that the 'sacred values that have been most cherished, the ecstatic and visionary capacities of shamans, sorcerers, ascetics and pneumatics of all sorts, could not be obtained by everyone'. These forms of 'intensive religiosity' give rise to 'a sort of status stratification in accordance with differences in charismatic qualifications'. These virtuosi as a result often came into conflict with the religious establishment, because the officials of an institution that bestows grace through its own formal hierarchy will resist a challenge from such charismatics. But tensions with the everyday world are more significant, and it was to these problems that Weber drew particular attention. We might reasonably argue that the basic tensions with the everyday world are overproduction (such as labour in order to produce food) and reproduction (such as the establishment of families in order to raise children).

With respect to the world, there are two primary religious orientations, the mystical–orgiastic escape and the ascetic–active engagement in order to control the world, and, as we know, Weber famously saw the roots of Western rationalization in the ascetic–active orientation that took the discipline of the monastery out into the everyday world with long-term consequences for the rise of Western rationalism. Given his focus on Protestant asceticism, there has been less interest among sociologists of religion in the contemplative–mystical–ethical dimensions of virtuosity, for example in the lives of saints. Weber never completed his sociology of religion with a study of Roman Catholicism, concentrating instead on the history of pietism and the Protestant sects. There is therefore little attention paid to Catholic piety in relation to his famous dichotomy of mysticism and asceticism. In the Asian context Weber regarded the separation of the virtuosi and the mass in stark terms. While the elite were focused on contemplation and mastery of scripture, 'the virtuosos allowed the masses to remain stuck in magical tradition' (Weber, 2009c: 288). As a result, the social world was not subject to the processes of rationalization that Weber saw as the unintended consequence of Protestant asceticism.

In *Religion and social theory* (Turner, 1991) I conceptualized Weber's virtuoso–mass typology in terms of an unequal exchange between the religious elite and the mass. In order to fly from the world the religious elite must abstain from production and reproduction, and hence they become dependent on alms, donations, charitable provisions and gifts of all varieties. In return, the elite offer the layman a blessing in terms of the distribution of charisma through prayer, the laying on of hands, and through the administration of religious rituals. Typically in Asia, the mendicant monks beg for rice from the laity in exchange for the transfer of charisma, and through this exchange the lay person can acquire merit. However, because the laity demands health and wealth from such a religious exchange, organized religion will be under pressure to satisfy these demands from the laity, and hence there is always pressure for compromise. Thus he argued (Weber, 1966b: 103–4) that 'all religions and religious ethics have had to reintroduce cults of saints, heroes or functional gods in order to accommodate themselves to the needs of the masses. ... Islam and Catholicism were compelled to accept local, functional gods as saints, the veneration of which constituted the real religion of the masses in everyday life.' The history of Buddhism appears fully to endorse Weber's sociology of the mystical–contemplative orientation.

In contemporary research there are important objections to Weber's view of early Buddhism and my interpretation of Weber, for example in Ilana Silber's *Virtuosity, charisma and social order* (1995). Against my 'materialistic interpretation' of the interaction between Buddhist monastic elites and the laity, Silber argued that the exchange relationship between them is more accurately understood as a gift relationship in the framework of Marcel Mauss's anthropology of the gift. He argued in *The gift* (Mauss, 1976), first published in 1924, that gift exchange had to be understood as a total social phenomenon with multiple legal, social and economic aspects. Silber claimed that in Buddhism there was always a complex combination of interest and disinterest in the relationships between monks and lay people in terms of gift-giving through lay donations. The gift has, on the one hand, to be free of any interest on the part of the lay person and has, on the other, to create solidarity between monks and laity. Lay donations were an important foundation of Buddhist monasticism, but they cannot be fully understood as simply 'payment' for soteriological services. From the perspective of the laity, to emphasize the social services of the monks to the laity would compromise their spiritual vocations. Thus she proposed (Silber, 1995: 213) that a more adequate interpretation of these donations 'is that they contribute to mediating between two otherwise polarized and even antagonistic sectors, between a religious elite exemplifying certain ideals, and lay believers willing to acknowledge the same ideals but unable or unwilling to commit themselves to their fullest enactment'. The donation mediates between the total commitment of the monk and the worldly involvement of the laity, and the religious gift in this context is a materialization of trust rather than competition between elite and laity. In Asian societies before the development of either markets or banking institutions the Buddhist monasteries 'came to constitute the most reliable channels for the conservation, fructification, and display of wealth' (Silber, 1995: 215), and their very continuity over time was a major aspect of social solidarity, binding elites and laity together.

Silber's analysis provides a valuable understanding of the complex interaction between ideological and economic aspects of the gift in supporting monastic institutions and the ascetic lifestyle of monks. While her analysis contributes to a more subtle and complex analysis of lay donations in the reciprocity between monks and lay people than my emphasis on simple economic exchange in my *Religion and social theory*, she may have underestimated the political role of Buddhism and its historical connections to monarchy. Contemporary scholarship has drawn attention to the inevitable and necessary connections between Buddhism and politics as a correction to Weber's analysis of monks as forest-dwelling, apolitical ascetics. Thus, while the aim of followers of the Buddha was to seek ultimate overcoming of the world through meditation and other techniques, the Path was always to take place within the world, and hence Buddhists are forced to engage with politics rather than to avoid it. In his research on early Buddhist kingship Balkrishna Gokhale (1966) notes that in the teachings of the Buddha there was a theory of politics in which there was a clear distinction between 'the wheel of law', which is the teaching of the *sangha*, and 'the wheel of command', which is the work of the state. In this interpretive framework the state is necessary for maintaining the social order and for defending Buddhist institutions.

These early Buddhist principles, in which the evils of war were criticized but the state was accepted as a necessary institution, are often illustrated by the history of King Ashoka (268–239 BCE), whose empire extended over much of India. From his capital in modern-day Patna, Ashoka made a public conversion to Buddhism, and through the idea of 'righteous conquest' he extended Buddhist values in his kingdom and beyond. Repenting of the violence of his early conquests, he promulgated a version of the *dharma* consisting of moral virtues, and his reign is celebrated in various legends that are known as the *Ashokavandana*. In these narratives Ashoka became the symbol of authoritative Buddhist rulership, combining compassion and power to establish a stable and peaceful society.

By the twelfth century CE Buddhism had all but disappeared from India, partly under pressure from the spread of Islam and partly as a consequence of the growth of Hinduism. Buddhism had, however, spread to Tibet, China and Japan. During Buddhist expansion outside India the Asokan model of kingship remained significant as a normative framework for the intersection of religion and politics, and was adopted in Sri Lanka and Southeast Asia. As Buddhism developed outside India, Theravada Buddhism also became a popular religion as it spread through villages and Buddhist teaching was translated into vernacular literature. Despite these changes at the local level, the principles of Asokan rulership remained in the sense that the Theravada kings were not given legitimacy on the basis of descent but on the basis that they represented the *dharma* and were hence *dharmaraja*s. Their charisma came from behaviour in their past lives, and their political legitimacy was based on their patronage of the *sangha*. The early Buddhist kingdoms have been described by Tambiah (1976) as 'galactic polities' in which the cosmic order was reflected in the social order. A powerful centre under the control of a *dharma* king was surrounded by dependent principalities, and the authority of the king guaranteed the expansion of his rule and the defence of Buddhist institutions.

These religio-political structures were remarkably resilient and enduring, but they were eventually disrupted by the arrival of French and British colonialism from 1815 to the end of French Indo-China in 1954.

The British East India Company sent agents to Burma in 1612, but they were resisted. The Anglo-Burmese War (1824–6) and subsequent wars allowed the Company to establish control over the whole of Burma. It was annexed to India in 1886, eventually becoming a separate colony in 1937. Under British colonial rule in Sri Lanka (British Ceylon) and colonial Burma the two principles, or Wheels, of religious and political authority were abandoned, and the British abolished traditional monarchies and broke the tradition whereby the *sangha* was supported by donations and displaced the Asokan norms of good government. Siam avoided direct colonial control, but in response to external threats it evolved as an absolutist monarchy with a powerful internal bureaucracy. State building in Siam is often attributed to two remarkable modernizing rulers – King Mongkut (r. 1851–68) and King Chulalongkorn (r. 1868–1910) – who steered Siam away from the clutches of Western imperialism. However, an alternative interpretation is that their rule was conditioned by the expansion of Western capitalism in Asia and that the centralization of power in Siam was in response to an emerging world economy (Mead, 2004). Siam's involvement in the world economy was consolidated by the Bowring Treaty of 1855, an agreement between Britain and Siam to liberalize foreign trade with Siam. It specifically allowed free trade by foreigners in Bangkok, opened a British consulate and allowed the British to buy land in Siam. This trade agreement stimulated exchange between China, Singapore and Bangkok, and as a result Siam became a key factor in the production of rice for global consumption under British control. The rice-producing plains of Siam were connected to the world economy, while other areas of the country went into decline. These economic connections also had ideological and political consequences as the absolutist monarchies attempted to introduce Western ideas about science and modernization in which the Siamese elite came to accept the need for Western civilization. Chulalongkorn undertook the modernization of the labour force, created a Council of State in 1874, introduced fiscal reforms and reduced the power of the nobles by creating an absolutist monarchy. He also modernized military training and worked towards the reform of education. These absolutist developments in Siam came to an end in 1932.

British colonial governments were not seen as legitimate, mainly because they were foreign and they did not support Buddhism. French colonialism permitted the appearance of continuity with the old order by maintaining monarchies and support for the *sangha*, but French colonialists were clearly not Buddhist. Siam remained a Buddhist monarchy, but its absolutist rulers undermined or abolished autonomous centres such as Chiang Mai and Na. The Siam government also centralized authority in Buddhism, by placing all monks under a single institution. Furthermore, the state ideology was nationalist rather than Buddhist, especially after King Vajiravudh (1881–1925) came to the throne in 1910. His main objective was to use nationalism to buttress the monarchy in a period when there was agitation against royal absolutism. He undertook a number of major works including building a railway system, but the national debt forced the government to take out a large loan from Britain. His taxation system also produced discontent such as the insurgency in Pattani in 1922. By 1925, when Prince Prajathipok came to the throne, the monarchy was at its lowest point, and was seen to be corrupted by favouritism and by a royal family that was a bastion of the elite whose Western education and lifestyle cut them off from the people. Throughout the region there was opposition to colonial rule, often in terms of millenarian movements and charismatic monks (Keyes, 1976). When these millenarian protests failed, they were by the 1920s replaced by Buddhist-inspired nationalist movements, for example in Burma (Maung Maung, 1991). These movements laid the foundation for opposition to colonial and post-colonial governments. In Vietnam the self-immolation of Thich Quang Duc in June 1963 was a major turning point in opposition to the Republic of Vietnam and its American ally. However, Buddhism was subjected to severe and frequently violent control by communist governments after the unification of Vietnam in 1976. In China the Cultural Revolution (1966–76) and the Khmer Rouge regime of Pol Pot (1975–9) in Cambodia resulted in the systematic destruction of Buddhist culture. In Thailand social unrest and military regimes have fragmented the Buddhist *sangha*, but the state succeeded in controlling Buddhism to its own ends (Keyes, 1971). Furthermore, the conflict with Muslims in the southern provinces has underlined the identification of Thailand with Buddhism, virtually making it a state religion. The Chinese invasion of Tibet has also caused a significant dislocation of Buddhism, especially with the exile of the Dalai Lama. While some Tibetan monks have actively resisted Chinese control, His Holiness has so far been opposed to violent opposition. The Tibetan situation raises in an acute form the traditional question of the legitimacy of Buddhist involvement in politics, and thus in violence. From this brief historical sketch it is obvious that the integrity and influence of Buddhism were severely shaken by various colonial interventions, civil conflict and colonial wars.

Weber on acosmic love: Krishna, Arjuna and the Buddha

In a lecture given in 1997 and later reprinted in *The Robert Bellah reader* (Bellah, 1999), Robert Bellah offered an analysis of Weber's notion of *Liebesakosmismus*, which is often translated as simply 'acosmistic love'. Bellah suggested that it is better translated as 'world-denying love', and connected the concept with Weber's ideas about an ethic of brotherly love that Weber saw as the fundamental ethic of the great prophetic religions. In some respects these ideas about world-denying love anticipated the discussion of the religions of the axial age that was the topic of Karl Jaspers' *The origin and goal of history* (1953) and later of S. N. Eisenstadt's *The origins and diversity of axial age civilizations* (1986). The basic idea of a world-denying religion found its expression in the so-called *Zwischenbetrachtung* or 'Intermediate reflections' (Weber, 2009b) that came between *The religion of China* and *The religion of India*.

The core of Weber's definition of an axial religion is that it exists in a tension with 'the world'. These prophetic or axial religions have or present a universal message, thereby breaking with the loyalties of locality, kith and kin. They are salvational religions, because they offer a solution or resolution of this generic tension, and in his ideal typical model they are either ascetic and inner-worldly or mystical and other-worldly. These religions are contrasted with magic or magical religions, which offer material benefits by magical practices, and which are thus fully accommodated to worldly society. The literature on Weber's sociology has concentrated largely on the inner-worldly asceticism of the Protestant sects, but Bellah, in drawing attention to the idea of world-denying love, offered an alternative version of Weber's sociology of religion, namely the rationalization and routinization of acosmistic love. The end result of these transformative processes is the production of a 'social organic ethic' – that is, an ethics that have become compromised by and integrated into the dominant institutions and values of secular society. While asceticism was treated by Weber and his followers as the most radical and challenging of religious orientations, Bellah raised the issue that acosmistic love appears to be closer to mysticism than to asceticism, and thus closer to saviours than to prophets.

Following Weber, Bellah started this account of the euphoria of a world-denying brotherly love with ancient India, and in particular with the idea of Buddhism as the religion of a renouncer. He argued that the core meaning of religious renunciation in the Indian context was to leave the household, typically becoming a mendicant. To give up the role of the householder was to free oneself from the necessary round of work and reproduction. The Brahminical system incorporated the idea of leaving home into a concept of the life cycle that is divided into four stages: studentship; householder; forest-dweller; and finally the renouncer. Bellah claimed that in Vedic ideology only a married householder could undertake the two crucial activities sustaining society as a whole, namely offering sacrifices and procreating children. There remained therefore an unresolved tension or contradiction between these two roles of the householder and the renouncer. While he believed that Weber's virtuoso–mass distinction is extreme, the conclusion was that 'without householders there would be no one to feed the renouncers' (Bellah, 2011: 529).

In Bellah's attempt to revive evolutionary theory for the sociology of religion, one can say that through his analysis of the axial religions he is seeking to establish the conditions that gave rise to ethical universalism, the ethical and religious systems that broke out of the concentration of kinship loyalties to proclaim that all humans are brothers. The crucial point about Buddhism is that it launched the axial age in South Asia by an 'ethicization of the world' (Gombrich, 1996). Buddhism declares an ethical system of radical non-violence, and undermines the tradition of the Brahmins by rejecting their hereditary status, along with the four *varna*s. Only a person who in following the Eightfold Path attains enlightenment can be regarded as a true Brahmin. The end of the path of renunciation and adherence to the *dharma* is *nirvana*, the ultimate end of earthly desire. The *dharma* – the teaching of the Buddha – is available to everybody regardless of any inherited social status. We must be careful, however, to avoid thinking that Buddhism and Brahminism have enjoyed separate and independent histories in South Asia. For one thing, Brahminism (and later what we now call Hinduism) reacted to the rise of Buddhism and in many ways absorbed Buddhist teaching. Buddhists had in any case to use Sanskrit to compete with Brahmins to defend their interests at court. By the middle of the first millennium the Brahminical vision of society and politics had become dominant, and Buddhism created a version of this vision by developing the notion of the king as a *bodhisattva* (Bronkhorst, 2011). Modern-day Hinduism has also changed significantly, especially in the diaspora, where its architecture, practice and teaching has evolved to meet the needs of urban middle-class Indians living in the West (Waghorne, 2004).

Conclusion: the political as a calling

One central issue in these commentaries on Buddhism from Charles Keyes to Robert Bellah via Richard Gombrich is that the Buddhist monk, *contra* Max Weber, lives in society in close interaction with the laity, and that the *sangha* was deeply embedded in the secular social structure. As we have seen in the ideal typical example of King Ashoka, there is an important and necessary connection between the king as world conqueror and the monk as world renouncer. This symbiosis is also somewhat tragic, because eventually it calls into question the practical viability of the very act of renunciation. Any society requires an order, and this requirement inevitably means the necessity of the political. The political creation and maintenance of a social order has to be able to draw upon violent means to suppress opposition and to protect borders. All societies attempt to control and regulate violence, but it must be held in readiness to defend the social order against external attack and internal collapse. The continuity of the *sangha* ultimately depends on the sword of the king.

Bellah beautifully illustrated this dilemma in South Asian traditions through the story of Krishna and Arjuna in the narrative of the Indian epic the *Mahabharata*. This famous episode is known as the *Bhagavadgita* ('The song of the Lord'), and for many devoted followers the epic spells out the essence of Hinduism as offering different but valid and universal pathways to salvation. This poem in many ways expresses the core of Hindu spirituality in establishing the intimate relationship between humans and God. It involves the famous story of the struggle between the descendants of King Bharata, whose name can be interpreted as 'India'. The main part of the narrative deals with the conflicts between two families – the Pandavas and the Kauravas – in which the Kauravas try to cheat the Pandavas in order to gain the kingdom. Before the battle of Kurukshetta begins a dialogue takes place between Krishna, who is the incarnation of Vishnu, and Arjuna, one of the Pandava brothers, regarding the necessity and inevitability of violence and the obligations of Arjuna as a warrior. Sitting in their chariot, Arjuna is depressed by the prospect of human suffering and by the fact that he may be forced to kill some of his own relatives. In response to his dejection, Krishna outlines the three paths to salvation. Fundamental to this model of religious virtue is the *dharma*, or the obligations and responsibilities associated with his particular status in society. Unless people fulfil these duties the social order would crumble. In Arjuna's case, his duty as a warrior is to engage in conflict. *Dharma* here implies more than a collection of mundane duties. It is the way of life of perfection involving legal, political and religious duties. These duties must be carried out in a spirit of non-attachment in which Arjuna fulfils his obligations without any sense of personal gain or glory. The role of the warrior is a selfless calling. Thus the poem spells out the three modes of being – devotion, selfless action and knowledge – and in the conclusion of the poem Arjuna is granted a vision of God through his devotion.

The *Mahabharata*, an epic poem of some 90,000 stanzas, was composed between the second century BCE and the first century CE. Originally a martial ballad, the poem was preserved and transmitted by the Brahmin caste, and came to describe the ethical duties of different sections of Indian society. Although the *Bhagavadgita* contains a message of supreme spiritual insight, it is also the case that Krishna, the avatar of Vishnu, instructs Arjuna in the duties that are appropriate to his *varna* as a warrior (*ksatriya*). The implication is that Hinduism, regardless of its evolution over time, is not a pacifist doctrine. We have seen that Buddhism, which teaches absolute non-violence, challenged the idea that Brahminical piety could be guaranteed by birth and inheritance. But Buddhism could not escape the conundrum presented by the need for a political order to protect the *sangha* and to periodically cleanse it of corruption. The monastic tradition required a righteous king who would guard the *dharma* from decay. The religious and the political were always woven into the pathways to salvation. Arjuna recognizes that no being lives in this world without killing; even the ascetics living in the forest cannot fully escape from this world of violence. In this sense the *Mahabharata* is a tragic tale of the inevitability of human violence, because *dharma* or righteousness exists in the same world with power. When Arjuna kills in defence of the community, he will incur no sin.

Max Weber's sociology of religion is also in one sense a tragic account of the rationalization of religious pathways to salvation. But the salvation offered by either saviours or prophets is no longer available to us.

The secular world is dominated by the economic market and the bureaucratic state, and these are not institutional arenas within which the ethic of brotherly love has any place. The various spheres of life in the modern world function independently of religion, and at best some of these spheres, such as the aesthetic and the erotic, might offer some compensation for the loss of a meaningful world.

Perhaps the darkest aspect of Weber's sociology appeared in the two lectures at the end of his life on 'politics as a vocation', which he gave in January 1919 to a student audience in Munich, and 'science as a vocation', in September 1919. One could argue that in these two lectures Weber appeared as the modern Brahmin attempting to outline the duties and responsibilities of a person who chooses science or politics for their station in life, their modern secular *varna*. In the end neither choice provides a satisfactory mode of life. In both lectures he considered the problem of religion in a secular society that lacks both ethical and spiritual clarity. He was clearly influenced by his reading of the *Bhagavadgita* in his understanding of Hinduism, and in the lecture on politics observed that one 'will find war integrated into the totality of life-spheres in the *Bhagavadgita*, in the conversation between Krishna and Arjuna. "Do what must be done", i.e. do the work, which, according to the Dharma of the warrior caste and its rules, is obligatory and which is objectively necessary. Hinduism believes that such conduct does not damage religious salvation, but, rather, promotes it' (Weber, 2009a: 123). Both lectures are far removed from the standard interpretation of Weber's sociology as the standard-bearer of value neutrality (Lassman and Velody, 1989).

Let us look more closely therefore at 'politics as a vocation'. Dieter Conrad (1986) has suggested that in his study of Indian *dharma* Weber outlined an ethical position that resembled his own view of modernity in which the various spheres of life are separate and autonomous. The caste system endorsed a form of ethical relativism, because the righteousness of one caste had no necessary consequences for some other caste. In the modern world the differentiation of spheres has also for Weber created a form of ethical polytheism, namely a world of competing 'gods' without any ultimate source of authority. In secular politics there are two fundamental choices: an ethic of responsibility and an ethic of conviction. Joachim Radkau (2009: 514) argues that, while these are often seen as alternatives, in fact Weber suggested that they can be combined. However, in the context of the lecture Weber, in his description of the ethic of conviction, probably had German pacifists in mind, whose politics were based on passions, ideals and unshakeable values. By contrast, the ethic of responsibility suggests that we should carefully consider the consequences of political actions and pragmatically weigh the means necessary to achieve political ends. The point of these descriptions of ethics was to suggest that politics, rather than being a career involving base motives, was a calling with its own ethical requirements. The motives of a political calling were passion, a sense of responsibility and judgement.

For Weber both the nationalists who wanted revenge through a protracted war and the pacifists who wanted peace at any cost lacked sound judgement. In making these assessments Weber returned to the theme of the inevitability of violence as contrasted with the ethical demands of religion. In Christianity the message of Jesus was constantly compromised by the necessity of institutional survival. While 'the Sermon on the Mount, an acosmic ethic of ultimate ends, implied a natural law of absolute imperatives based upon religion' (Weber, 2009a: 124), the Church recognized that force was necessary to suppress heretical views. Luther safeguarded the righteous from acts of violence by accepting the role of secular authorities in the conduct of war, and Calvinism also accepted the necessity of violence in defence of the faith. The inescapable feature of political life is violence (Weber, 2009a: 121), and hence anybody who becomes involved in politics must recognize these 'ethical paradoxes' (Weber, 2009a: 125). The ethical dilemma for people of conviction, in concentrating on their motives and ideals, is that they do not consider carefully the consequences of their actions. The actual day-to-day exercise of politics requires both passion and perspective, but ethical compromise is inescapable for those people who take responsibility for their actions.

9 | *Confucianism as state ideology: China*

Introduction: Max Weber on *The religion of China*

In the West there is a long tradition of scholarly interest in the uniqueness of China. For example, in the seventeenth century Gottfried W. Leibniz (1646–1716) devoted considerable attention to the question of Chinese distinctiveness as an aspect of his understanding of the plenitude of reality in his concept of theodicy. He thought that God had created a world of infinite variety, and that the diversity of cultures was simply one aspect of this enriching multiplicity. In this specific sense he argued that we live in the best of all possible worlds. His ambition was to create a 'commerce of light' to match the exchange of commodities that already existed between Europe and Asia (Perkins, 2004). Despite this early flowering of cosmopolitanism, by contrast in the nineteenth and early twentieth centuries, debates about the Orient were more inclined to see China as moribund and despotic. In 1859 John Stuart Mill (1989: 72) in *On liberty*, while praising the 'wisdom' and 'good customs' of the Chinese, claimed that they 'have become stationary – have remained so for thousands of years; and if they are ever to be farther improved, it must be by foreigners'. Western attitudes towards Chinese bureaucratic administration were often a strange mixture of admiration and criticism. Georg W. F. Hegel in *The philosophy of history* (1956) had praised the stability and regularity of Chinese administration. Taking his lead from Karl Marx's notion of an 'Asiatic Mode of Production', Karl Wittfogel (1957) in *Oriental despotism* argued that Asiatic despotism had its origins in the large-scale irrigation works that required centralized management to co-ordinate seasonal flooding of arable land. He suggested that political despotism in Stalinist Russia was simply a continuation of this long-standing political and economic system of centralized control. The static and despotic character of China followed a similar pattern in which centralized power stifled economic innovation and political liberty. The turning point in modern approaches to Asia has been the result of a more sophisticated appreciation of the problematic nature of

Western assumptions about the Orient. Edward Said's *Orientalism* (1978) is a good example of this development. More recently Andre Gunder Frank (1998) has done much to 're-orient' our understanding of the 'Asian Age', and more popular works such as Martin Jacques's (2009) *When China rules the world* have begun to recognize the growing influence of modern China in economic and military terms. In this evolution of twentieth-century thought about China, Max Weber's *The religion of China: Confucianism and Taoism* (1951) has remained a constant source of reference.

Weber's examination of Chinese civilization was his first large-scale study of religion outside the West, and was designed as a volume within the much larger project on the economic teachings of the world religions. His analysis of China concentrated on the powerful role of the literati and their control over the centralized bureaucracy, the traditionalism of Confucian teaching, and the conservative effects of family and kinship. Although the book is overtly about orthodox Confucianism and Taoism as heterodoxy, over half is devoted to an analysis of the social structure of traditional China. There is also the substantial chapter on the literati which Weber's biographer Joachim Radkau (2009: 474) claimed was uppermost in Weber's mind, because at the time he was engaged in a bitter political fight with the German bureaucrats or literati. Following the way in which Weber's argument unfolds, he starts with the analysis of money, claiming that China failed to develop an integrated and effective monetary system, and this failure produced a significant brake on the development of rationalism in monetary exchange. Second, and following his thesis in *The city* (Weber, 1966a), Weber noted that autonomous and vibrant cities were absent, and hence there was so to speak no space in the social structure for a genuine bourgeois culture to emerge. He did recognize that guilds were widespread in Chinese society, but they did not enjoy adequate legal protection. Instead, China was characterized by a top-heavy centralized bureaucracy, which was run by the Confucian literati. In short, China represented a clear example of what Weber described as a 'patrimonial bureaucracy', the centralization of which meant that state officials had little connection with local culture at the village level. He was also interested in the geography of China and its system of land ownership. He believed that Chinese history had been characterized by recurrent attempts at land and taxation reform, but these official policies had been forcefully resisted by the peasantry, which had a deep suspicion of state interference. Weber blamed much of the ineffective approach to land reform and the 'largely irrational conditions of landownership' on 'fiscal policies which alternated between arbitrary interventions and complete laissez-faire' (Weber, 1951: 80). In the absence of primogeniture and with a growing population, there was a tendency for the land to be divided up into holdings of ever decreasing size, and as a result large-scale capitalist agriculture failed to develop. Finally, he noted that the local organization of kin groups meant that the villages were highly traditional and resistant to change. Having discussed the social structure, Weber concluded the study of China with the famous discussion of Confucianism as an ethical system and Taoism as a magical heterodoxy in which he argued that the notion of *tao* in emphasizing stability and tranquillity never offered a radical challenge to the secular world. In short, the 'Chinese "soul" has never been revolutionized by a prophet' (Weber, 1951: 142).

Much of the critical literature on Weber's thesis has been edited by Wolfgang Schluchter (1984). This literature is, unsurprisingly, focused on the causes of the failure of capitalism in China. However, in my view John Love (2000: 173) correctly suggested that *The religion of China* should not be seen simply or narrowly as an addendum to the famous 'Protestant Ethic Thesis' about the religious inspiration of rational capitalism. The grand theme of the final stages of Weber's sociology was the rationalization of culture in the West and its consequences. We might further specify the emerging theme as involving a deeper analysis of the nature of religion as such around the contrast between inner-worldly asceticism and mysticism, between religion as a 'cultural instrument' to reshape the world or as an experience in which the human subject becomes a 'vessel' of grace. One of the central issues in Weber's work on China is the simple but profound underlying question: is Confucianism a religion?

Weber's answer was quite explicit. First, the Chinese language, he asserted, has no distinctive word for 'religion', but 'there was first: "doctrine" – of a school of literati; second – "rites" – without distinguishing whether they were religious or conventional in nature. The official Chinese name for Confucianism was "doctrine of the Literati" (*ju chiao*)' (Weber, 1951: 144). He concluded that 'Confucianism, like Buddhism, consisted only of ethics and in this *Tao* corresponds to the Indian *Dharma*' (Weber, 1951: 152). The point of this argument becomes more obvious if we turn to chapter 6 on the sociology of religion in volume I of *Economy and society* (Weber, 1978), where Weber gave a more explicit account of the differences between oriental and occidental religion. While recognizing that the distinction between asceticism and mysticism is fluid, he proposed that the Occident was dominated by an ascetic drive to confront the world, while in the Orient there was a greater emphasis on contemplative mysticism. There were in addition important organizational differences around law, congregations and priesthood. It was significant, he claimed, that in the Orient the 'Asiatic salvation religions' were produced and promoted 'as pure religions of intellectuals who never abandoned the "meaningfulness" of the empirical world' (Weber, 1978, I: 553). In the Occident asceticism took the discipline of the monastery into the everyday world of the laity, and this creation of inner-worldly ascetic Protestantism led to rational control over sexuality, family life and economic activity. The outcome was the man of vocation and 'its unique result was the rational organization of social relationships' (Weber, 1978, I: 556). Thus Weber's sociology involved not so much the narrow study of the social conditions that favoured capitalism, but rather the life disciplines or 'life orders' that produced particular personality forms, especially the historical eruption of the men of vocation or *Berufsmensch* (Stauth and Turner, 1986).

In this chapter, following Weber's sociology of world religions, I will concentrate primarily on debates about Confucianism in order to illustrate the complex interaction between state and religion. In this book as a whole I treat the relationship between state and church as primarily a relationship of conflict. However, with respect to China it is important to keep two issues in mind when thinking about the modern context. First, the relations between state and religion involve both conflict and competition, and occasionally cooperation. In these changing relationships the state and religion are mutually constitutive. Second, China, as with other Asian societies, has a number of distinctive religious traditions, including the revival of popular religion such as the Black Dragon King Temple (Ashiwa and Wank, 2009). Confucianism nevertheless colours all manifestations of religious activity.

Confucianism as secular piety

In *Religion and modern society* (Turner, 2011c) I argued that Max Weber's sociology of religion could be understood as a comparative sociology of piety. In this respect I followed Wilhelm Hennis (1988) in claiming that Weber's sociology as a whole could be seen through the framework of 'personality and life orders'. This approach directs us to examine how ethical systems formulate practices (or more narrowly rituals) that shape dominant personality systems. I went on to argue more explicitly that these religious rituals are directed towards the human body. The constant – indeed, lifelong – adherence to religious rituals determines the habitus of individuals and social groups, and in turn conditions the personalities associated with different social strata. In Chapter 8 of this volume we saw how Brahminical religion had prescribed various practices to certain social strata, consistent with the personalities that were deemed appropriate to them. In this chapter I propose to offer the same treatment to Confucianism as an ethical system that is as a long-enduring 'life order' or habitus giving rise to the Confucian personality. I note that in *The religion of China* Weber (1951: 157) offered this account of honour and piety, not as a contrast but as a different accent: 'Feudalism rested on honor as the cardinal virtue, patrimonialism on piety. The reliability of the vassal's allegiance was based on the former; the subordination of the lord's servant and official was based upon the latter.' The formative nature of piety (*hsiao*) can be seen in the traditionalism of patrimonial bureaucracies and in the Confucian hostility to any signs of insubordination. The subordination of women to men, peasantry to lords, and society to emperor guaranteed the tranquillity and stability of the system as a whole. This approach offers a Weberian route to a deeper understanding of whether and in what sense Confucianism is a religion.

To return once more to Robert Bellah's *Religion in human evolution*, his aim was to show that Confucianism is a 'world religion' and a product of the axial age, and as such developed universalistic notions of transcendence. Although my approach to the idea of a secular piety is consistent with much of Bellah's interpretation of Confucianism (and surrounding systems such as Taoism), I argue that Bellah does not pay sufficient attention to the political dimensions of Confucian ethics. He also gives insufficient attention to filial piety and its legacy as a profoundly conservative aspect of Confucian ethics. I claim that transcendent world religions tend to clash with familial and kinship systems as components of 'the world'. Let us turn now to his careful and insightful analysis of Confucianism.

Bellah's aim was to defend the idea that Confucianism was a product of the axial age, and is in this sense a world religion with its own notions of transcendence and spirituality, and that Confucius (551–479 BCE) stands in the ranks of the famous philosophers and prophets of that revolutionary age. Bellah, drawing upon modern interpretations of Confucius's *Analects*, debated the importance of the two central concepts of Confucianism: the virtue *ren* (humaneness) and *li* (ritual). Rejecting earlier interpretations of *ren* as 'humanity', he embraced the argument in Herbert Fingarette's *Confucius: the secular as sacred* that *ren* underlines the universalism of Confucian doctrine, namely that 'society is men treating each other as men' (Fingarette, 1972: 77). Turning to the idea of *li* as ritual or mere convention, Bellah claimed that the term embraces the idea that if only human beings could behave properly according to ethical discipline there would be no need for punishment in society or violence in warlike activity. Confucius established a pattern of self-cultivation by which character could be developed to live this life of humaneness. It is within the shelter of these shared rituals and customs that humans can become truly human, and hence the *Analects* express a universal ethic that transcends the merely local.

Having established the claim that Confucianism is a universalistic ethical system and that we should use the word 'religion' to describe it, he turned finally to Weber's account which he described as 'extraordinarily brilliant and influential', but he wanted to challenge the idea that salvation in Confucianism is simply political. He suggested that as a political ideology Confucianism could not have survived as a powerful cultural and religious force in Chinese history. The lasting influence of Confucianism in the realm of politics depended on 'its ability to uphold a normative standard with which to judge existing reality and never to compromise that standard completely' (Bellah, 2011: 477).

Bellah made a powerful argument to regard Confucianism as both a religious and an ethical doctrine that did not merely adapt to social conditions, but offered reasons against accepting the rule of the unjust. While he also admitted that it was 'harder for Confucians to imagine disobeying a parent' (Bellah, 2011: 479) than a ruler throughout Chinese history, I do not think he paid enough attention to questions of gender inequality in his observations about religious universalism in which the basis of Confucian humanism was to treat all people as human beings. The issue behind 'acosmitic world-denying love' is to recognize the humanity of every person regardless of ethnicity, race and culture, and yet the Abrahamic religions did not in practice recognize gender equality. St Paul's message about there being neither male nor female has to be read alongside his diatribe against sexual desire, his defence of celibacy and his recognition of marriage as the final barrier to eroticism. Similar issues arise in both Buddhism and Confucianism. I am suggesting that religious universalism is typically compromised around the issue of gender equality. Religious universalism has to recognize that for example the disciples of Jesus had to abandon family and kinship in order to devote themselves wholly to Jesus Christ as Lord. Kinship was fundamental to the religious traditions of China, where ancestor worship 'has been the very warp of a high culture throughout millennia' (Thompson, 1996: 31). These issues relating to kinship and ancestors provide a significant constraint on any universalistic impulse in Confucian values. In the case of Confucianism, Bellah did not fully recognize the traditional role of filial piety as the bedrock of Confucian conservatism. By contrast, Weber was far more explicitly critical of filial piety. He claimed that 'Confucianism placed a tremendous stress on familial piety, a stress which was motivated by belief in magic, in view of the importance of the family spirits. This familial piety was cultivated in practice by a patriarchal and patrimonial-bureaucratic political organization' (Weber, 1978, I: 579). It is primarily within congregational religions that co-religionists could replace kinfolk, because the notion of brotherly love could not breathe within the confines of an exclusive kinship network.

Following a distinction in classical Greek political theory, we can conclude this discussion of Confucianism by making a distinction between soul-craft and state-craft. The first involves the discipline of the self; the second, the discipline of society. Both are necessary to secure political order and social harmony. The Confucian *Analects* appear to be a complete and complex statement of this balance between the government of the soul and state command over society. In particular filial piety was, as Weber recognized, the necessary partner of patrimonial bureaucracy. Many writers, including Robert Bellah, have argued that the most striking feature of Chinese history is its continuity. To what extent does Confucianism and centralized power continue to dominate Chinese politics and culture? How are these cultural continuities shaping official Chinese Communist Party (CCP) responses to freedom of religion and to human rights more generally?

The shortage economy of religion

When we use the word 'state' we should keep in mind that the state in China had some exceptional qualities (Jacques, 2009). China may be more appropriately described as a 'civilization-state' whose structure and culture – especially its sense of superiority and commitment to social and political unity – are the product of political evolution over thousands of years. China, unlike other Asian societies such as Japan, Singapore or South Korea, is not the product of recent post-colonial nation-building exercises. Although China has been radically disrupted at various stages in its modern history – the 1911 Revolution, the 1949 Revolution and the Cultural Revolution (1966–76) – contemporary China has the borders it acquired in the Qin Dynasty (221–206 BCE). This historical continuity 'surely puts China in a class by itself' (Bellah, 2011: 248). The centralized state remains pivotal to society, and its Confucian culture is all pervasive. In its contemporary attempt at eradicating its 'century of humiliation', its present and future will be deeply conditioned by its past.

The Chinese polity is unique in that historically there was never any sense that it was obliged to share power with any other institution. Despite Bellah's attempt to recognize Confucianism as a religion, China has never had an organized religion. Confucianism and Taoism had no centralized authority such as a pope or priesthood or anything like a congregational religion. As we have seen, loyalty to family and state were important aspects of Confucianism, and it was only under extreme circumstances such as famine or civil war when popular unrest might result in a widespread belief that the emperor had lost 'the mandate from heaven'. There was never any notion that the common people could enjoy inalienable rights, and the Western notion of citizenship has been slow to evolve in China; the CCP has been suspicious of Western attempts to impose human rights conditions over China.

Much of the contemporary official resistance to human rights and human rights movements is associated with the fact that the CCP regards human rights norms as an aspect of Western globalization and as an unwarranted intrusion into its internal political affairs. The CCP has been conscious of the role of rights talk in the fall of the Soviet system in 1991–2, including the role of Solidarity and the Catholic Church in the transformation of Eastern Europe. The conflict between the CCP and the Roman Catholic Church goes back to the foundation of the People's Republic in 1949, when Pope Pius XII forbade Catholics to co-operate with the Communists, resulting in a shortage of bishops and priests. The CCP retaliated by attempting to create a parallel and official Catholicism in the China Catholic Laypeople Patriotic Association in 1957, and eventually identified five bishops who were willing to participate in the new Association. Nevertheless, there is a thriving underground Catholic Church, including an underground Catholic Bishops Conference, and it is estimated that China now has a Catholic population of twelve million members (Marsden, 2003). The CCP has remained deeply suspicious of Catholicism, being aware of the role of the Church in the fall of Polish Communism, and media images of the fall of the Berlin Wall in 1989 were significant in demonstrating the impact of such social movements. Human rights criticism of Chinese politics was particularly important in the aftermath of the crisis of Tiananmen Square in 1989. The so-called June 4 Movement played an important role in shaping official fear of political opposition. The international erosion of communism in the wider world has often reinforced the determination of the CCP to remain loyal, at least officially, to Marxist-Leninism. Contemporary Western pressure on the Party to liberalize its policies is often seen within the framework of Chinese history as simply further evidence of foreign meddling in Chinese society. The West is assumed to manipulate opposition movements in China through sponsorship of 'heretical sects' to cause embarrassment to the CCP. Suspicion about the disruptive potential of sects and cults has a long history in Chinese politics, thereby explaining the current hostility to Falun Gong.

In a recent sociology of religion, Fenggang Yang (2012) has explained the character of religion in China via the so-called economic or market model of religious growth which had been developed originally to explain the vitality of religion in the United States. The theory suggests that open religious markets in which religious groups (or 'firms') are relatively free to compete for followers ('customers') produces a dynamic environment in which religions can grow and prosper. By contrast, restricted markets, where the state seeks to suppress or regulate religion, produce black or grey markets in which illegal or semi-legal groups attempt to provide religious 'products' to a limited market. The more restricted the market, the more we can expect a sizeable grey market to evolve. The theory also assumes that individuals in restricted markets will face high costs in 'buying' and 'consuming' religious goods and services. The model has obviously a *prima facie* relevance in comparing China and America in the twentieth century. Whereas America has had, in the absence of an established church, a robust religious market producing a diversity of suppliers, China is the classic example of what Yang (2012: 123–58) calls the 'shortage economy of religion'. In the struggle to modernize China, both Communist China and the Nationalists embraced secularization as their dominant approach to traditional religions, which were regarded as mere superstitions (Nedostup, 2010). The outcome was a sudden reduction in the supply of religious goods, services and personnel.

The CCP, embracing radical atheism as its preferred ideology, set out to remove religion from Chinese society, and during the Cultural Revolution the atheist movement against all forms of religion was further intensified. However, following the death of Mao Zedong in 1976, Deng Xiaoping launched economic reforms and open-door policies in 1978, and by 1982 adopted a more liberal policy towards religion in the famous Document No. 19, which recognized past mistakes in official policies towards religion. The Document acknowledged the complexity of religion and the fact that in China religion is seamlessly interwoven with culture, ethnicity and national traditions. The new approach allowed academics to study religion as 'culture' and at the same time permitted lay people to engage in religion under the umbrella of cultural activities. While Western observers have often seen this development as a sea change, Yang draws attention to the fact that there are still significant restrictions on the practice of religion, including practices that claim to be purely cultural.

Falun Gong ('Wheel of law') has become a notorious illustration of continuing restrictions. Its founder, Li Hongzhi, was born in 1952 and embraced the teachings of *qigong* at an early age. He established his own school of traditional healing in 1992, and initially gained political approval for these practices. It combines Buddhist–Taoist beliefs and traditional exercises, and claimed the right to assemble to practise healing exercises in public spaces. Falun Gong appealed to the powerless and the dispossessed. When the movement was banned by the Ministry of Civil Affairs in 1999, the leadership responded with acts of civil disobedience. The authorities have replied with a mixture of extra-judicial measures that amount to administrative discipline: hard labour for re-education, 'custody for repatriation', detention for 'further investigation', loss of jobs and so forth. These measures are described by Ronald Keith and Zhiqiu Lin (2006: 61) as examples of 'recidivist state instrumentalism'. The CCP has defined various 'cults' as crimes and employed state institutions to reinforce 'socialist spiritual civilization' against 'feudal superstition'. On 12 July 2006 it was reported in *Embassy*, the Canadian foreign policy newsletter, that the Canadian government announced its intention to investigate allegations that Falun Gong prisoners in Chinese jails were being murdered and their organs sold to transplant patients. One piece of evidence is that prior to 1999 when Falun Gong was banned, the state was harvesting organs from 1,600 prisoners executed each year. Since 1999 there has been a rapid increase in organ transplants, and it is estimated that some 41,500 organ donors in that period are unaccounted for. If these allegations prove to be true, the removal of prisoners' organs without consent will give 'extra-judicial procedures' a new and sinister meaning. Falun Gong is however simply one illustration of the many *qigong* groups that have emerged in China to offer health services that combine religious beliefs, scientific theories of health and physical culture.

Consequently China's religious policies are deeply ambiguous. The CCP continues to embrace atheism as its ideology, but it also encourages religion as culture in order to attract overseas Chinese to participate in religious sites and practices. In the 1990s the Party encouraged the rebuilding of Buddhist temples as an aspect of its tourism policy to attract overseas Chinese back to China. This strategy is known as 'Build the religious stage to sing the economic opera' (Yang, 2012: 110). At the same time the CCP attempts to suppress Protestant evangelism and the re-emergence of an independent Catholic Church, and it has been brutal in its response to 'evil cults'. The result, according to Yang, is the creation of a tripartite market in which the red market is the legal space for religion, the black market is the illegal provision of services, and finally there is a large grey market where both legal and illegal suppliers provide a bewildering mixture of religious activities.

Fenggang Yang's economic or market model of Chinese religion provides important insights into contemporary developments, and he carefully analyses the contradictions and complexities of official policies in which continuing restrictions on religious practice inevitably fuel a large grey market of religious services. Yang's study inevitably raises questions about what a religious revival is. Are *qigong* groups simply urban health movements or examples of religious revival? The situation is complicated because many leaders of such movements claim they are not religious in order to avoid official punishment. On this issue the economic model does not provide much guidance. It is essentially an account of the efficiency of a religious market in terms of supply side. The model does not look at demand-side issues, because it takes demand as a constant. It is focused on the efficiency of supply in both open and closed markets, and it does not attend to the quality of the product, only its quantity. As Yang (2012: 21) admits, the economic model 'concerns only the process of exchange, not the nature of the religious "products"'. However, when I buy a car I am not only interested in the price, but in the quality of the product. Is it beautiful and does it work? One might speculate, from the standpoint of an economic model, as to whether inflationary pressures inside an overheated market in America have produced low-quality religious products. If we accept the model, we might reasonably ask of these religious manifestations (such as state-sponsored Buddhist temples for tourism): is this the real thing? One way into this question is to ask whether there is any continuity of Confucianism in modern China that has survived as the underlying bedrock of Chinese religions. Yang's excellent study of China pays very little attention to Confucianism, to which there are only two references.

Where, however, is the real dynamism of the religious market? Western observers have been looking towards the introduction of evangelical Protestantism and charismatic Pentecostalism from outside China as the principal lever of religious revival. According to Lian Xi (2010), much of the vitality of Protestant evangelical Christianity is its ability to draw on the past. Indigenous popular Christianity, deriving support from the working class, was emotional and irrational, and it concentrated on individual conversion rather than on social problems. More importantly, indigenous preachers were often critical of foreign ministers of religion. In retrospect, popular religion was the most important development of Christianity in China; its membership grew from under one million in 1949 to around fifty million today. This indigenous stream of popular Christianity is very different from the type of religion that has been promoted by disciplined, puritanical and rational Protestantism, especially in the urban areas. Indigenous Christianity, which Lian Xi dates to the Taiping Heavenly Kingdom, gained its strength from its resonance with traditional Chinese religious culture. While rejecting the traditional Chinese gods, popular Christianity affirmed many of the basic features of traditional belief and practice including millenarian beliefs, the ecstatic visions of the future, and the malevolent intervention of demons in everyday life. In the context of the social and political turmoil of twentieth-century China, the millenarian aspirations of popular Chinese religious belief appear more relevant to reality than the restrained, disciplined and rational optimism of liberal Protestant theology.

Despite the continuing prominence of secular Marxist-Leninism as the official political discourse, it is difficult to understand Chinese culture and politics outside the framework of Confucian political philosophy of good government and peace in civil society. The main point of Chinese opposition to 'evil cults' is to avoid social unrest. We might call this Confucian legacy a politics of virtue. While constitutional lawyers and dissident groups internally and human rights lobbyists externally are attempting to impose the rule of law, we might better understand Chinese domestic politics as a rule of virtue. As we have seen, the traditional legal arrangements of imperial China were based on Confucian values and can be described as a system of moral 'familialism'. This system involved unconditional filial piety, the welfare of the dominant status group over the individual and reverence for seniority. There was also a 'Confucianization of the law', which meant that both judge and ruler drew directly from morality, especially where strictly juridical guidelines were absent or ambiguous. This traditional system promoted the idea of rule of law as the rule of virtue. In many respects the criminal law was the cornerstone of this juridical–moral system, because it was the basis of social control. This system broke down during the Cultural Revolution, and one can interpret the post-Cultural Revolution period of institution building and law reform as an attempt to prevent any relapse into the excesses of class struggle and generational conflict. The 1999 national plan for managing public order sought to contain the growth of criminal gangs, the production of fake agricultural goods, the proliferation of 'evil cults' and a rise in juvenile delinquency, and to manage the massive internal migration of peasants to the cities. With these reforms there has been a political emphasis on the need to promote the rule of virtue. As an antidote to 'blind Westernization', Chinese citizens are called upon to embrace Confucian virtue in the form of the 'four beautiful virtues' (*si mei*), of beautiful thought, language, behaviour and environment, and the 'four haves' (*si you*), of consciousness, morality, culture and discipline (Bell and Chaibong, 2003).

The growth of rights in China is not just a consequence of external forces, but depends on internal and independent movements for citizenship. There is ample evidence for these developments from significant academic publications, the struggles of intellectuals, the resistance of peasants to changes in the use of the land, and the protests of workers against exploitative and degrading work conditions. We can summarize these diverse movements as an attempt to move from the rule of man (warlordism, Mao or the Gang of Four) to the rule of law, in which there is proper respect for legal procedure and less dependence on legal flexibility to solve social problems. After the Cultural Revolution and

the removal of the Gang of Four, China's legal reforms and modernization after Deng Xiaoping opened up China. These reforms are in many
respects a reassertion of traditional Confucian norms of respect, duty
and stability. As we have seen, this feature of traditional rule and the
failures of China's criminal law institutions are perhaps nowhere better
illustrated than in the CCP's response to the Falun Gong problem. Thus
the official response to Falun Gong displays the worst aspects of legal
flexibility in which pragmatic policy needs replace legal procedures.
The ethos of 'state instrumentalism' and the use of the notion of 'social
harm' give rise to opportunities for considerable human rights avoid-
ance and abuse. The worst features of state instrumentalism include
detention without trial, extra-legal detention and indefinite custody for
investigation. These procedures are enforced on the basis of the extra-
judicial authority of public agencies.

What are the prospects of liberal change in support of human rights?
One important modern development which the Party cannot easily
control is the growth of the Internet as a means of mobilizing political
opinion, developing political education and sustaining critical evalua-
tion of state activities. China's new computer users are primarily a post-
1989 generation and they are recruited from urban, educated youth
who use computers and the Internet to criticize party policies and to
promote social and political reform. They are known as China's 'cyber-
dissidents'. The Internet created a virtual public space which the CCP
sought to control by regulations, censorship, filtering and site blocks,
but connections could always be routed by proxy servers in Hong Kong,
Europe and the United States. Dissidents such as Huang Qi have nevertheless been attacked by the Party, and in July 2002 a Declaration of
Citizens' Rights for the Internet was circulated as an expression of the
civil rights in the UN Declaration. According to Reporters without
Borders in 2004, China jailed more Internet users for their expression
of social and political views than the rest of the world put together.
Within the context of domestic politics in China, the Internet is probably the most promising prerequisite of democratization, but it also
provides opportunities for a significant expansion of online religion.

Conclusion: the rise and fall of civilizations

Comparative sociological studies often mask underlying assumptions
of superiority and distinctiveness. Weber's studies of world religions

were initially motivated by an interest in the causes of capitalism and why it was a distinctive feature of European and then American history. Contemporary studies of China often carry the same underlying civilizational assumptions. Fenggang Yang (2012: 6), for example, claims that in the post-war period theories of secularization 'served as the theoretical justification for the political ideology of secularization'. In other words, sociological theories of the secular were themselves a secular ideology. However, one might argue the same about market or economic models of religious growth. When Rodney Stark and Roger Finke (2000) describe the success of the American religious market in *Acts of faith*, they are also celebrating American culture as one that encourages innovation and experimentation, and at the same time defends and promotes the rights of individuals to choose their own religions without interference from the state or an established church. The American Dream is a narrative about the escape of the early settlers from the limitations that were imposed by an established church and the state. The notion that religion cannot flourish in Europe until the chains of the established religion are broken is parallel to the argument that the secular economy cannot flourish until 'Washington' and 'Big Government' are brought under control and cut down to size. Secular entrepreneurship and religious entrepreneurship are simply opposite sides of the same coin.

The evangelical churches in the West see the reforms of the era of Deng Xiaoping that opened up the Chinese economy to Western companies and commodities as a god-given opportunity to open up China to the Christian message. Christian Chinese businessmen returning to China bring both the good news of the Bible and Western technology to Chinese society. The American colonies were seen by Christian leaders such as John Wesley as a parish for the conversion of souls, and modern-day China is also a new frontier for Christian endeavour. These opportunities for trade and mission have of course also raised questions – not just about the rise of China, but the corresponding decline of the West. This mirror-image situation of rise and fall has brought public intellectuals such as Niall Ferguson (2012) to re-think many of Weber's observations about the rise and possible fall of Europe in relation to the rise of American capitalism. In thinking about the conditions that produce, not just capitalism, but civilization as such, Ferguson offers a comprehensive list of causes, including competition, work ethic and science, for the rise of the West that echoes Weber's sociology of the Protestant Ethic. Just as Weber wrote his comparative study of religion in the context of the crisis of Germany and the rise of America, so contemporary work on China is written in the context of the crisis of Europe and the 'unravelling' of America. Henry Kissinger (2011: 546) in *On China* perhaps inevitably connects the 'rise of China' with the decline of America, noting that China's success is not a military one but rather 'reflects importantly a declining American competitive position, expressed by obsolescent infrastructure, inadequate attention to research and development and a seemingly dysfunctional governmental process'. Fareed Zakaria (2008) in *The post-American world* has also had an important impact on the public sense of an American crisis. Much of the contemporary popular intellectual writing on China can therefore be read as an attempt to recapture and revitalize the notion of 'the American century' that was made popular by Henry R. Luce in February 1941 when he declared that the bill of rights, the American constitution and the American way of life should be shared with all people (Luce, 1941). Weber's view of religion and economic vitality is the often hidden but irrepressible basis of these debates in which China has emerged as principal criterion for judging the rise and fall of the West.

10 | *Religion, state and Japanese exceptionalism*: nihonjinron

Introduction: Japanese uniqueness

In this volume I have deliberately and self-consciously referred to the work of Max Weber in virtually every chapter as a starting point from which to launch a study of politics and religion within a comparative perspective. In the case of Japan we cannot employ the same strategy, because he had little to say about Japanese society. However, he concluded *The religion of China* (1951: 248) with the observation that the 'Chinese in all probability would be quite capable, probably more capable than the Japanese, of assimilating capitalism which has technically and economically been fully developed in the modern cultural area'. For Weber, China and Japan were different in one crucial respect. Whereas in China the literati had been the dominant status group, in the case of Japan he observed that the samurai had despised 'the pen-pushers' of the imperial bureaucracy (Weber, 1951: 120). Japan obviously presents a challenge to Weber's views regarding the social conditions that contributed to the rise of capitalism, given the impressive success of Japan as an industrial society.

Weber commented on the organization of religion, specifically Buddhism, in Japan in *The religion of India*, and we might speculate therefore about what Weber might have written about Japan had he written *The religion of Japan*. First, there is a well-established tradition of folk religion in Japan that was local and closely related to agricultural production and seasons. Mountains have been an important part of Japanese religion and symbols of national specificity. Weber noted (1958: 281) that the religiosity of the ordinary people 'approximated general Asiatic and ancient conditions insofar as Shinto, Confucian, Taoist and Buddhist deities and redeemers were called upon according to function and occasion'. Second, Buddhism was closely connected to the Japanese system of power, and noble families were interrelated to the hierarchy of monastic authority. Among the samurai elite, Zen

186

Buddhism with its stern discipline and hard training was attractive to the samurai lifestyle. Weber (1958: 278) in a discussion of the various Buddhist sects observed that the samurai 'cherished the exercises as a means of hardening and discipline for their vocation'. However, Buddhism over time lost much of its religious vitality and 'for the great majority of the villagers, who made up most of the population it was closely intermingled with folk religion that pieced together ancestor worship, portents, directions, and concerns with a beneficent though capricious nature'. In the late Tokugawa days much of this assembly of belief and practice became structured into something that we recognize as Shinto, but 'it was long in getting out from under the wide, though porous, umbrella of Buddhism' (Jansen, 2000: 217). Buddhism and Shinto were merged into a common ritual system, and most Buddhist temples included a Shinto shrine.

Third, Shinto was to a large extent the creation of the Meiji Restoration, which refashioned existing religious beliefs and practices to create a unified nation-state under the overarching authority of a divine emperor. To solidify the relationship between state and religion, an Office of Rites was created in 1868, and there was a campaign to remove Buddhist elements from Shinto in order to render Shinto a state religion. Buddhist temples were abolished and Buddhist sutras were destroyed. As a state religion Shinto only came to an end when Emperor Hirohito disavowed his divinity on 1 January 1946, and post-war democratization cancelled state support for Shinto shrines. However, church and state were never separate in Japanese development and Robert Bellah (2006: 359) argued that 'this archaic substratum has never completely disappeared'.

Fourth, Christianity had little success in penetrating Japanese society. From the late sixteenth century Christian missionaries were periodically persecuted, while they struggled to find a foothold in Japanese society, and under the Meiji Restoration Christianity, which was inevitably associated with barbarian civilization, was banned. The official approach to Christianity was eventually relaxed under foreign pressure and in 1873 the ban was lifted, and for a time Protestant educational institutions had some success. In the post war period Christianity came to enjoy more widespread appeal, possibly because it had no significant connection with the emperor system. Weber noted some analogies between specific Buddhist sects and Protestantism. For example, the 'Shin sect, founded at the beginning of the thirteenth century, in sharp contrast to the Zen sects, may be compared to occidental Protestantism, at least insofar as it rejected sanctification by good works and upheld, rather, the sole significance to the faithful devotion to the Buddha Amida' (Weber, 1958: 278).

Finally, Confucianism, which was imported from the seventh century onwards, played an ambiguous role in Japanese society. On the one hand, it was associated with scholarship and education and had high esteem among Japanese intellectuals, but on the other, its association with China was often a problem for the nationalist sentiments of the Japanese. China regarded itself as the 'Central Country' whose dynasties were always Great Dynasties, and these ideas did not sit easily with the Japanese sense of cultural superiority. Thus regardless of 'the attractions of Confucianism for its rulers and educators, it was not equipped to be a state ideology. Moreover, there was a consistent anti-intellectualism in warrior society, and loyalty and valour received higher marks than book learning and benevolence' (Jansen, 2000: 201). Weber, writing on Confucianism in Japan, was dismissive: 'Confucianism in Japan was a rather literary hobby of individual circles' (Weber, 1958: 282). What then of the Weber thesis?

In *Tokugawa religion* Robert Bellah (1957: 195–6) identified an important development of inner-worldly asceticism in Shin Buddhism, writing that its 'obligation to hard work, selfless labor and to the restraint of one's own desires for compensation is closely linked to the obligations to sacred and semisacred superiors who are so stressed in Japanese religion, as also to that state of profound identification with ultimate nature'. Shin intellectuals reconciled greed, selfishness and the pragmatic need for profit by means of the *jiri-rita* doctrine of 'benefit self, benefit others'. The basic theme of Bellah's study of the Tokugawa period was that Japanese culture demanded loyalty to the group rather than to any abstract theological or ethical principles. In a later article (Bellah, 1963) he speculated on the more general features of Weber's argument in Asia. It appears that there is not much support for the idea that inner-worldly asceticism contributed to the rise of Japanese capitalism (Davis, 1989). However, in this study of religion and politics I am more concerned to understand how religion is interwoven with modernity, and second, whether religion presents any significant challenge to the political. As we will see in a discussion of the Meiji Restoration, Japan experienced a classic top-down, state-driven road to modernity in which the various religions, with the possible exception of Confucianism, were subordinated to politics. Buddhism offered no challenge to Japanese political institutions, and whereas Japan in its quest for modernization embraced Shinto as the state religion, by contrast China and Turkey took on radical versions of (Western) secularization as the dominant ideological framework of nation building. Against these interpretations, we have to take seriously the view that Western social science concepts are often irrelevant in the case of Japan, especially when it comes to the study of 'religion' (Amstutz, 1997: 120).

In this respect Japan presents a challenge not just to Weberian sociology, but to Western scholarship generally, because Japanese culture typically presents itself to the world as historically exceptional. Japan has a mythical sense of its divine origin, and hence of the uniqueness of its culture and society. While Western scholars are often criticized for their Orientalism, their Japanese counterparts might equally be criticized for their Occidentalism in believing that their culture was superior to their neighbours, and thus scholars such as Hirata Atsutane (1776–1843) proposed that the Japanese differed from and were superior to the Chinese, and indeed to all other cultures, because it is the homeland of the gods. In Shinto belief the world was created by two heavenly deities, Izanagi and Izanami, who gave birth to many powerful spirits including the sun goddess Amaterasu. Her descendant Jimmu Tenno became the first emperor of Japan. The Japanese term for spirits is *kami*, which is often translated as 'god' or 'deity', but in fact *kami* included a wide range of beings, many of whom have distinctively human characteristics. Many of these beings, who were imported from Buddhism and Taoism, were benign, while others had demonic and violent natures. Buddhist spirits or enlightened beings are known as *butsu* and *bosatsu*. The three most significant divine beings were Amida, Kannon and Jizo. Amida, who rules over the Pure Land or Western Paradise, played a major role in the evolution of Buddhism in Japan. The spirits of dead ancestors also joined the ranks of the *kami*, and hence Shinto as a religion was closely tied to localities and to kinship structures. The public functions of Shinto became a controversial issue in modern Japanese history, because of the problematic status of Emperor Hirohito and the role of the Yasukuni shrine in Tokyo, which is dedicated to the *kami* of Japanese dead from the creation of the Japanese Imperial Army in 1871 to the victims of the Second World War. The emperor, who enjoyed divine status, was also a focus of Shinto religion. Whereas in China the emperor could be criticized and in principle could lose the Mandate of Heaven, the emperor in Japan was the embodiment of the gods and had direct contact with heaven. He could not be held accountable for his actions, and loyalty to him was unshakeable. Despite the radical changes that took place in Japan during the twentieth century, the continuity of the emperor and his family can be taken as evidence of the depth of Shinto beliefs in Japanese culture. Shinto is thus deeply embedded in the Japanese sense of uniqueness, partly because Shinto is so closely connected to the Yamato region of Honshu, the principal island where the shrine of Amaterasu is at Ise.

The Amaterasu myth had its origins in Shinto beliefs, but it was not confined to Shinto. The Confucian scholar Aizawa Seishisai (1781–1863), the leader of a samurai reform party, who wrote the great political text *Shinron* in 1825, regarded Japan as a universal standard for other nations. This sense of difference and superiority was greatly accentuated by Japanese isolation and, when Western powers arrived in the second half of the nineteenth century with their superior military capability and vastly different ideas, the threat of these barbarians created a crisis in Japan. Gradually Japan became encircled by nations that were beginning to industrialize and to explore trading opportunities in East Asia and the Pacific. From the late eighteenth century Russia began to probe the islands of the northern Pacific, and Britain, having established trading centres in India, began to push into Southeast Asia and then into the coastal cities of China. The Opium Wars (1839–42 and 1856–60) were major turning points in Asia when the British, having acquired Hong Kong, began to show an interest in Japanese waters. America, having achieved independence from Britain, was also emerging with trade and military interests in the Pacific.

The threat of barbarian penetration was eventually and dramatically realized by the arrival of Commodore Perry, whose plans for an expedition to Japan were first reported in Edo in 1852. Perry had received instructions from the American president not to disturb the tranquillity of Japanese society, but by the time he arrived with two sailing vessels in July 1853 he was determined to circumvent any Japanese attempts to thwart his mission to open Japan to trade, and, having delivered his official documents to the governor of Uraga, he received a promise of a definite response by the spring of 1854. Perry duly returned in the following spring with a greater display of naval power, and reached agreement with the Japanese to open two ports for American trade through a treaty signed in March 1854. On completing the treaty arrangements, Perry announced that Japan was open to the West and that the conclusion of the treaty demonstrated that the Japanese were a compliant and adaptive people. Perry was followed by Townsend Harris, who became American consul in 1856 and pressed the Japanese negotiator, Hotta Masayoshi, to open five ports to American trade. During the protracted negotiations Harris was residing at Shimoda, and this choice of residence caused further outrage because of its strategic position in Edo Bay.

The treaty with America provoked an extensive and controversial debate in Japan about how to manage the disaster that threatened to overtake them. Recognizing the need to comprehend the nature of the Western threat, the Japanese established the Bansho Shirabesho or Institute for the Study of Barbarian Books, and the first opportunity to study abroad came with a mission to the United States in 1860 to ratify the Townsend Harris treaty. The Japanese leadership was only too aware of the impact of Western intervention in China and was anxious to avoid a similar fate. Aizawa Seishisai's *Shinron* ('New proposals') played an important part in shaping the Japanese response to the Western barbarians. Faced with stark and unattractive options, the Japanese leadership could prepare for war and adopt a policy of *joi* ('expel the barbarians'), but in the short term they did not have the military capacity to drive them out. They could attempt to absorb the alien culture in order to prepare in the long run for such an expulsion, but such a policy could be self-defeating. The policy would require the Japanese to appease the foreigners by giving them access to Japanese ports. The Japanese would themselves, through absorbing Western influences, have to become barbarians. The loyalist position came to be expressed in the slogan 'honour the emperor, expel the barbarian', and the loyalist strategy would require Japan to modernize its army, undertake political reform, and promote loyalty to the emperor by supporting the legacy of Shinto as a state religion. In ideological terms Japan's march towards modernity involved a union between a divine emperor, the land of the gods and its people.

The Meiji Restoration and modernization

The so-called Meiji Restoration occurred in January 1868 as a coup d'état in Kyoto at the imperial court by men from feudal princedoms in the west and south-west of Japan. As an outcome of this political coup, a decree was issued to end the hereditary office of the Tokugawa shogun, and at the same time to re-establish the emperor's direct personal responsibility for government. The ambiguity of the event is that it was less a restoration than a renovation, since the men who carried out the coup were heavily involved in the creation of a centralized bureaucracy, a modern army and industrialization. Renovation rather than restoration had propelled Japan into the capitalist age by welcoming 'men of spirit' who had the talent to change Japan and to take Japanese society out of the hands of the samurai, whose power rested on status not merit. The slogan 'honour the emperor, expel the barbarian' thus provided a platform for a new class alliance that was able to dismantle much of the feudal structure of Tokugawa Japan by land reform in 1871. This coup in effect created modern Japanese citizenship through tax reform, which provided the state with revenue, and conscription, which provided the army with men. Educational reform was designed to create a civic culture within which a new type of virtue, consistent with the new Japan, could flourish. These reforms were driven by fear of external invasion and occupation by Western powers, and to avoid this fate Japan's transformation was rapid and profound. Although the Meiji Restoration, in abandoning feudalism, brought about a radical change in culture and society, 'Japanese group life continued to thrive. Tightly organized all-embracing groups demanded the complete loyalty and devoted service of its members' (Bellah, 2003: 187). In other words, a deeply conservative social substratum served modernization.

In his comprehensive assessment of Japanese history in *The Meiji Restoration*, W. G. Beasley (1973) said that the modern Western historian of Japan had to ask three questions. The first is to weigh up the external and internal causes of social change, and to keep a balance between them. In other words, it would be wrong to see social change as simply a response to Western imperialism. Second, the historian has to assess the long-term impact of historical development before the Restoration against the changes that took place after the coup. Did controversy over foreign policy provide the means by which socio-economic factors could become causally significant, or was it these socio-economic conditions that contributed to the manner in which the political consequences of foreign policy could be worked out? Finally, he asked whether the debate about politics and economics among Japanese historians had led to a 'relative neglect of ideas *qua* ideas' and whether it is important for example to take the idea of loyalty seriously as one of the driving forces of social change (Beasley, 1973: 12). The Meiji Restoration involved the creation of a new ethics that were addressed to the issue of modernizing

Japan and creating a new civilization. These 'ethics of spirit' which concerned self-cultivation were part of the concern of the state to exclude both individualism and socialism, and to build a harmonious and coherent society (Reitan, 2010; Sawada, 2004). Let us turn to the issue of ideas, especially religious ideas.

In Chapter 9 I provided a defence of Weber's analysis of Confucianism as an ethical system of government that played an important role in the legitimacy of a bureaucratic state. I was critical of Robert Bellah's conclusions about China, in part because I think he neglected the conservative significance of filial piety and gender inequality in Chinese Confucianism. Japan has been significantly and continuously influenced by Chinese culture, and especially by religions from China, but whereas Confucianism played a conservative role, both cultural and political, in Chinese society, in Japan it assumed on occasion a far more creative if not radical function. During the Tokugawa period the principal aim of the shogunate was to achieve the subordination of the peasantry to the samurai, and the authority of the major feudal lords or daimyo over the samurai. The ideological counterpart of this hierarchical system was a patriarchal notion in which political subordination to the emperor found its counterpart in filial piety which required loyalty of the household to the senior male. The Tokugawa regime was based on the notion that birth was essential to authority. Confucianism was to introduce a new element into this tradition by setting a 'new role of the samurai in Japanese society, that of government rather than war; or to put it another way, substituting ethical leadership for naked military force' (Beasley, 1973: 35). The point about Chinese Confucianism was that in principle it was based on merit through educational achievement rather than on birth. In China the civil service examinations provided an opening for young men of talent, and in Korea too, although entry into the bureaucracy was increasingly confined to men of social rank, the examination system rewarded talent. In Japan the rigid status system did not initially or easily conform to this Confucian ideal.

In late Tokugawa society and in Meiji Japan there was a growing demand for men of talent. By the late nineteenth century the policy of encouraging talent was made a reality through an education system that was designed to create a Japanese meritocracy, and the new political leadership came to believe that the success of the education system would be measured in terms of its promotion of achievement over inherited status. These social changes were associated with the growing irrelevance of the grand samurai, who were no longer a powerful feudal class and not uniformly members of the salaried bureaucratic elite. The reforms of 1868–73 undermined their monopoly of office in both the civil and military arenas. The Japanese leadership of the Meiji Restoration, which was drawn from the middle and lower strata of the samurai class, were pragmatists and realist–bureaucrat politicians who believed that the defence of Japan could only succeed if it was based on national unity. In all of their policies they were 'samurai-bureaucrats trained in Confucian ideas', and in this leadership role they oversaw Japan's successful transition from 'the "centralized feudalism" of Tokugawa days to a similarly centralized form of capitalism' (Beasley, 1973: 421–2). The Japanese process of modernization was neither a bourgeois nor proletarian revolution, but it might be appropriately called a nationalist revolution.

The Meiji revolution created the foundation for Japanese industrialization, but it was also the foundation of militarism. Japanese imperialism, its role in the war in the Pacific and its final defeat in the Second World War catapulted Japan into world politics, and eventually into the world economy. Military defeat and occupation had devastating consequences not only for society and economy but for deeply held beliefs. After military defeat the Japanese public had difficulty in coming to believe that their leaders were accountable, and even more difficulty in imagining any institutional checks on the authority of the emperor (Eisenstadt, 1996: 252). During the American occupation General Douglas MacArthur came to the conclusion, on expert advice, that it was advisable not to humiliate or punish Emperor Hirohito publicly, because completely removing him from office would cause further disruption and uncertainty in the public mind. Nevertheless, military defeat and the large-scale destruction of Japanese cities represented a major shock to Japanese tradition and psychology, and new religions and cults promising worldly success and otherworldly comfort proliferated. American occupation did not end until 1957, and the 'revolution from above' brought about dramatic changes, including dismantling the 'emperor system'.

American confidence that the defeat of Japanese 'fascism' demonstrated the superiority of the American way of life was nowhere better illustrated than in the figure of MacArthur himself as the Supreme Commander for the Allied Powers (SCAP). Apart from punishing its military leaders, the American programme of reform was aimed at a political democratization of Japanese society, which involved undermining the remaining feudal hierarchy, creating a civil code to transform the samurai model of the family, creating workers' rights, promoting strong trade union organizations, and bringing an end to male primogeniture. The reforms also brought to an end financial support for Shinto shrines, and as state support for religion came to an end there was an explosion of new religions. In the post-war period, and with a constitution that proclaimed freedom of religion, over three thousand new religions claimed a membership of thirty to forty million believers. While the majority of these religions 'coalesced around the search for harmony and emphasized the core values of Japanese rural civilization like loyalty and sincerity' (Jansen, 2000: 712), some cults such as Aum Shinrikyo, which was responsible for the attack on the Tokyo underground in 1995, were associated with alienated youth rebelling against the regulated lifestyle and conformity of corporate post-war Japan.

The irony of the post-war 'revolution from above' is that it 'encouraged a visible political shift to the left' (Duus, 1998: 268), because the main opposition to the emperor system before and during the war had come from Marxists, trade unionists and socialist intellectuals. While SCAP was concerned to democratize Japan, the more conservative businessmen argued that democracy was a product of affluence, and affluence a consequence of rapid economic development. The outbreak of the Korean War in June 1950 provided an important economic stimulus in East Asia, but it was also a warning to America and its allies that communism was a serious threat in global terms. The American occupying forces were increasingly less willing to see the promotion of the left in Japanese politics. If the military security of Japan could be left to the American forces, Japanese capitalism could thrive under the American umbrella. Unfortunately cultural conflicts around American military bases, which often provided opportunities for the growth of tawdry bars, prostitution and petty crime, fuelled the resentment and motivation for anti-American demonstrations. These local tensions were often combined with the peace movement against nuclear power, and Nagasaki and Hiroshima became global symbols of a vibrant anti-nuclear movement. These tensions and conflicts gave conservative politicians and businessmen ample ammunition against the 'excesses' and 'injustices' of the occupation. With the appointment of Yoshida Shigeru to serve as prime minister for five terms between 1946 and 1954 Japan was able to begin the conservative 'reverse course' which meant the restoration of pre-war public rituals: the imperial garden party, patriotic songs, and visits to the Yasukuni shrine. More importantly, it involved stronger opposition to left-wing groups, reversal of the anti-trust laws permitting the creation of economic cartels, and the re-centralization of the police force (Duus, 1998: 280). There were also important changes to the organization of industry in which, for the restoration of managerial privileges, the system of 'lifetime employment' and factory loyalty was created. Eventually the economic miracle of the 1960s laid the foundation for the 'new conservatism' of the late 1970s and 1980s with the appointment of Prime Minister Nakasone Yasuhiro in which Japanese political leaders took their inspiration from Ronald Reagan and Margaret Thatcher.

As a consequence of these post-war developments the Japanese leadership wanted to forge a new role for Japan as a prosperous middle-class society on the international scene – that is, to engage with economic globalization. However, despite Japan's economic involvement in globalization it has not abandoned its deeply conservative traditions, and in some specific ways it has preserved its isolation. One illustration of the continuing cultural conservatism is the gender division of labour, which remains strong in Japan. Although women were drawn into the labour market during Japan's economic boom, the ideology of 'good wife, wise mother' remained a popular slogan, and indeed as household incomes increased, women's participation in the workforce declined in the 1960s. Although housewives went back to work following Japan's economic stagnation, the idea of the housewife as the norm remained. The obstacles to female employment have included the idea that women should put family values and house (*ie*) before work. The paternalistic attitude of both corporate and union leadership in believing that women had to be protected meant that employment was reserved for men, and industrialists assumed that women might be employed prior to parenthood but not afterwards. However, the main reason for this cultural conservatism is the absence of large-scale migration to support its labour market, and consequently there is little evidence of the social diversity that follows from migration and multiculturalism. We can regard this cultural isolation as the preservation of a Japanese aesthetic, the roots of which are unambiguously religious. These contradictions between cultural conservatism and economic globalization in modern Japan raise more general questions about theories of globalization and cultural cosmopolitanism.

Globalization theory

For many sociologists globalization has become the dominant paradigm of contemporary sociology, generating new concepts relating to mobilities, glocalization, globalophilia, cosmopolitanism, mondialization and 'the second modernization' (Beck, 2000). There are a set of related issues about cosmopolitanism, national epistemologies and multiple modernities that require our attention. In this discussion I briefly consider three issues that are especially pertinent. First, much globalization theory is historically superficial, and to overcome this problem a distinction between early and late globalization is useful. Second, there is an implicit tendency to treat globalization from a narrow, Western standpoint. Finally, in mainstream globalization theory there is often an unfortunate neglect of religion, mainly because globalization theory, like modernization theory in the past, has placed considerable emphasis on the secular nature of these developments. Given the emphasis on economic globalization, the role of religion has been neglected despite the fact that religious globalization pre-dated contemporary secular forms by many centuries. In fact, early contributions to the globalization debate emerged out of the sociology of religion and religious studies, especially in terms of the traditional interest in 'world religions' and more recently through the comparative and historical study of religions. Indeed, the whole notion of 'world religions' pre-dates the contemporary interest in globalization by at least a century. Religion and globalization were explored in the early work of Roland Robertson on inter-civilizational analysis, human rights and religions (Robertson, 1982; Robertson with Chirico, 1985), culminating eventually in the influential volume *Globalization* (Robertson, 1992). His work is important because, among other issues, it clearly recognized the historical significance of religion in globalization. More recent work on globalization theory has not treated religion and related cultural dimensions as particularly relevant to our understanding of contemporary globalization. In this regard, I have in mind the work of Ulrich Beck, Anthony Giddens, David Harvey, George Ritzer and Saskia Sassen, which contain little reference to religion. By contrast, my interest in Japan in this chapter is based on the assumption that one cannot understand Japan's place in global modernity without reference to its religious traditions and their relationship to enduring group loyalties.

One problem with the work of contemporary sociologists is that their theories have ignored the early stages of globalization in order to make the argument, in the sociology of Ulrich Beck, for a 'second modernization'. If we take pre-modern forms of globalization seriously, then one obvious Asian example can be seen in the history of the silk routes, which lasted for some three thousand years. These intercontinental trade routes connected ancient China and the Mediterranean. Designated as the Silk Road (*Seidenstrasse*) by the German geographer Ferdinand von Richthofen in 1877, these trade routes played a major role in the transmission of Buddhism to China in the first century CE and later to the growing importance of Islam in Central Asia in the seventh century. Islamic Sufi orders in connection with South Asian trade played a major role in connecting the Middle East with South and Southeast Asia long before the modern period. Early globalization had strong connections with the missionary activity of the major religions, and the cultural landscape of Asia was subject to globalization processes centuries before the impact of capitalist trade or in the twentieth century by the invention of the Internet.

But were these early religious movements and social networks genuinely examples of what we now want to call 'globalization'? It is important to demonstrate, in addition to the existence of extensive trade and cultural networks, the emergence of what we might call a 'world-open consciousness' in the pre-modern period as the precursor of modern cosmopolitanism. There is ample historical evidence about interconnectedness through trade, cultural exchange and religious conversion in the past, but we need in addition to demonstrate the emergence of cultural openness to the outside world. Robert Holton (2009: 101) is surely correct to insist that 'to qualify as cosmopolitan, such inter-personal milieux need to exhibit some sense of inter-cultural openness'. Travel, pilgrimage and internal trade do not automatically produce a global consciousness such as cosmopolitanism.

In the history of religious conflict and co-operation, a traditional consciousness emerged around the question of alterity and consequently one can detect an early reflection on religio-cultural differences that created the beginning of an ecumenical consciousness. It may however be an exaggeration to call these early responses to the problem of otherness an example of 'reflexive cosmopolitanism'. These early forms of awareness of the Other were for one thing not epistemologically critical and open; they were based more on the assumption that other traditions were either defective or false. Thus tolerance of difference has had a slow, fragile and uncertain development, and as we have already seen Leibniz, in his curiosity about Chinese civilization, was perhaps the first Western philosopher to give a plausible philosophical justification for taking other beliefs seriously (Turner, 2005). In this regard, we should reject the assumption that the growth of cosmopolitanism and the emergence of a cosmopolitan consciousness are recent phenomena.

The conditions that favour reflexive traditionalism include geographical mobility and economic exchange, but it also requires an evangelical religious culture that undermines the idea that a religious community (church, *sangha* or *umma*) is fundamentally an extension of kinship relations. In other words, and following the arguments of Badiou and Bellah, some degree of universalism was required for the emergence of inter-cultural reflexivity. However, reflexive traditionalism did not automatically generate what we might call a 'vernacular hermeneutics of doubt' – that is, a systematic questioning of the roots of normative justification of cultural superiority. In religious traditions that are grounded in locality and the importance of kinship there can be little scope for recognition of otherness and difference. An unquestioned notion of revealed Truth that is embedded in the ethnic community must have exclusionary consequences. My argument is that from the Meiji Restoration onwards Japan developed a reflexive traditionalism in its attempts to understand and come to terms with the West, but these encounters with the Other did not produce a cosmopolitan openness, because the Other was, in the early stages of Japan's encounter with the West, clearly barbaric. As a consequence of American occupation, industrialization and entry into the global market, Japan imported many Western ideas and institutions, but it has only a limited vernacular cosmopolitanism. To understand this continuing sense of isolation in Japanese culture we must turn to the '*nihonjinron* literature'.

Cultural conservatism and *nihonjinron* literature

In postmodern social theory, while cultural hybridity is typically associated with postmodernism, postmodern culture is regarded as an offshoot of globalization. It is reasonable to ask whether Japanese society is culturally hybrid and therefore to consider whether globalization is also leading to the development of Japanese cosmopolitanism. To simplify the argument somewhat, hybridity in the West is primarily a product of labour migration, involving waves of legal and illegal migration drawn into the labour market by global demand over the last

century. The result has been the creation of layers of diasporic communities and cultures that have transformed life in the West.

As we have seen through much of its early history, Japan was cut off
from the outside world, apart from its exposure to Chinese culture, which
brought both Confucianism and Buddhism to Japan. Modern-day Japan
has not, however, been exposed to any significant inflow of foreign
migrants. In post-war Japan, from 1945 to 1949, there was a period of
repatriation, and these 'repatriates' (*hikiagesha*) were marked as distinct
from Japanese citizens; Koreans, Chinese and Taiwanese became foreigners or Third Country Nations (*sangokujin*). Further repatriation of
women and children occurred in the 1980s, but these migrants were also
regarded as culturally Chinese (Watt, 2009). Japanese people returning
from South America have also been confronted by major obstacles in
their attempts to assimilate culturally (Roth, 2002). In 2010 there were
some 230,552 Brazilians living in Japan, of mainly Japanese descent,
out of a total of 2,134,151 foreigners. In recent sociological literature it
is common for migrants to Japan to be regarded as carriers of a new
multicultural Japan (Goodman, Peach, Takenaka and White, 2003), and
there is a widespread view among cultural sociologists that migrant
communities are beginning to change Japanese society, resulting in a
more open and less conservative culture. In fact three groups –
Koreans, Chinese and Brazilians – constitute around 70 per cent of all
foreigners living in Japan. Naturalization rates are also low at around
15,000 per annum. As a result, major Japanese cities are not multicultural and diverse, and they are not characterized by the presence of
migrant ghettos. In fact, Japan has in recent years been resisting external
labour immigration, apart from a small trickle of Korean, Chinese and
Vietnamese short-term migrants. Japan, which currently has around two
million migrants, or less than 2 per cent of its population, is thus unique
in the industrial world in not having experienced any significant inflow of
international migrants. This resistance to foreign influence is associated
with the notion of Japanese exceptionalism or the discourse on *nihonjinron* which has promoted (if not created) the notion of Japan as a
distinct and homogeneous society.

Nihonjinron, or literally 'theories about the Japanese', covers a vast
array of writing about the peculiarities and uniqueness of Japanese
culture and society. The nationalistic ideologies of race and difference
that emerged in the eighteenth and nineteenth centuries laid the foundation for contemporary views about the uniqueness of identity and

national character. These writings assert that the Japanese are racially unique, that their island culture has been historically resistant to external influences, that their language has a unique grammatical structure, and that there is a distinctive Japanese psychology that distinguishes them from foreigners. *Nihonjinron* also includes the reflection of Western writers on Japanese uniqueness, and these two bodies of writing, by insiders and outsiders, have mutually reinforced this sense of national uniqueness. Writers often assume that this literature is modern, and Shmuel Eisenstadt (1996: 104) talks about how 'the *Nihonjinron* literature burgeoned' after the Second World War, giving the impression of an integrated society. However, many aspects of this literature can be traced back to the Tokugawa period, and after the treaties with the United States in the middle of the nineteenth century the problems of defining the nation acquired a new urgency. Of course this discourse has changed over time, and currently there is an attempt to adjust *nihonjinron* to the presence of more foreigners in modern day Japan. With economic growth, the literature on Japanese identity has become more positive, confident and assertive. The notion of *kokusaika* emerged in the 1970s to express the internationalization of Japan through global trade, but it expressed not so much an opening up of Japan as a defensive attempt to control outsiders (Itoh, 1995). The strategy of *kokusaika* would ensure that Japanese national culture and interests were defended in an international arena. A second element in this strategy was 'inward' (*uchi naru kokusaika*), namely the domestication of the foreign to conform to Japanese standards of behaviour. These cultural strategies would work to preserve the notion that Japan is a nation-state constituted only by Japanese citizens (Pak, 2000). Of course, there were some changes in the post-war *nihonjinron*, because it was no longer possible to refer to the emperor as a divine figure of unquestionable authority, and the pre-war themes of imperialism had also become problematic. The new national discourse therefore played an important role in post-war Japan, as it did in other Asian societies that were seeking to re-establish their identities after achieving national independence (Clammer, 2000). The top-down modernization of Korea, Taiwan and Japan has produced a pattern of cultural homogenization. These Asian societies were 'developmental states', unlike the 'regulatory state' of more advanced societies such as the United States. Their developmental model involved intense state involvement resulting in 'compressed modernization' (Chang, 2010).

Modernization in Japan involved the management of ethnic minorities such as the Ainu, Burakumin, Koreans and Okinawans who fell outside the mainstream during Japan's industrialization project after the Meiji Restoration (Weiner, 1997). They were culturally backward and did not fit easily into Japan's strategy of rapid modernization. In their struggle against the United States, the importance of a unifying national essence became even greater. The Japanese essence had been created by the Meiji oligarchs who used state rituals, civic ceremonies and military involvement to promote the idea that the Japanese imperial line was unbroken. As we have seen, it was not until MacArthur issued the 'Civil Liberties' directive that criticism of the emperor was permitted at least in principle, women were formally emancipated, trade unions were permitted and the sun flag (*hinomaru*) was banned. As a result of these social changes the system of *kokutai* – variously translated as 'sovereign', 'native land' or 'family state' – began to collapse (Bix, 2000). With the end of American occupation, Japan returned to its traditional social structures based on loyalty, respect and hierarchy. The post-war Japanese political and intellectual leadership began to assert its identity outside the American model of a democratic capitalist system and, more importantly, outside American culture. In the 1980s senior politicians such as Prime Minister Nakasone Yasuhiro returned to the theme of the purity of the Japanese nation and criticized America for its racially mixed population. Intellectuals such as Shoichi Watanabe argued that the racial purity of Japan should be celebrated and respected. The economic boom appeared to encourage a return to ethnocentric nationalism based on the idea that Japan was unique as a result of geography, history and specific cultural features such as language and grammar (Dale, 1986).

Sociologists of modern Japanese society however often claimed that the notion of Japanese uniqueness has been abandoned, or at least modified, by young Japanese; because they are exposed to foreign culture in the media they readily consume foreign commodities and they are interested in foreign travel, unlike their parents. The notion that Japan is now culturally diverse is defended by Yoshio Sugimoto in *Introduction to Japanese culture* (Sugimoto, 2010), where he shows how in public discourse there is much greater recognition of Japan's internal differences. Hence Japanese culture is seen by cultural sociologists as fluid, mutable and unsettled. These arguments focus on what I would regard as surface changes in Japanese popular culture, which are not convincing evidence of deeper and more radical changes. Perhaps there is some degree of cultural experimentation among young Japanese, but they are not thereby exposed to any cultural challenge in their own societies. What happens when young Japanese people travel overseas? In *Cultural migrants from Japan*, Yuiko Fujita (2009) shows how young Japanese migrants often start with a romantic or idealized view of the West, which is quickly shattered when they arrive in cities such as New York or London. Their experience of racial prejudice and stereotypes in the West does not result in an emergent transnational identity or cosmopolitan conscious-ness, but rather travel forces them to renegotiate or even deepen their Japanese national identity. The central premise of *nihonjinron*, that Japan is culturally homogeneous and unique, remains intact.

The fact of cultural insularity can be further illustrated by an exami-nation of the attitude of corporate Japan to recruitment strategies, which are not especially favourable towards Japanese applicants with degrees from Western universities. By contrast, they prefer 'home-grown' Japanese recruits with degrees from Japanese universities who have the appropriate deferential attitudes towards senior management (Tabuchi, 2012). While the annual number of university students enrolled in Japanese colleges has remained constant at around 3 million, the number studying abroad has declined from a peak of nearly 83,000 in 2004 to less than 60,000 in 2009, according to the Organisation of Economic Co-operation and Development. The contrast with the globa-lization of South Korea is striking. Whereas in 2011 South Korea with half Japan's population sent 73,350 students to American universities, the number of Japanese students was only 21,290. Japanese students who have acquired Western values and interpersonal habits are thought to be incompatible with the management style of modern Japanese companies. These recruitment strategies are a testament to the surviving inwardness of Japanese culture.

We might ask therefore what Japanese hybridity and postmodernism is. The sociological answer is relatively simple. It is essentially the rise of a post-war consumer society in which foreign commodities and services such as Western fast-food outlets are widely available. These foreign consumer goods and services produce a veneer of culture hybridity, but they are absorbed and wrapped up in an envelope of Japaneseness. In other words, this absorption of global consumerism falls under the category of *uchi naru kokusaika*. If South Korea has experienced a compressed modernity, Japanese society, with its late and restrained cultural globalization, has yet to experience what Zygmunt Bauman (2000) has called liquid modernity, let alone postmodernism. Perhaps the most obvious illustrations of my argument are the low level of international marriages in Japan, the absence of large waves of migration and equally limited emigration, and the severe restrictions on naturalization, whereby foreigners are excluded from Japanese citizenship. When official Japanese discourse does refer to coexistence with foreigners, it is on the assumption of a social and cultural hierarchy, and in this official language foreigners are classified as an undifferentiated mass.

Conclusion: shrinking population and declining religion

The real problem in Japan in relation to migration, multiculturalism and the religious foundations of national continuity is demography. It is well known that Japan has a low fertility rate and a rapidly ageing population. In the 1880s life expectancy for men at birth in Japan was 42.4 years, and a century later it was over 75. By 2008 the average life expectancy for Japanese women was 85 years, and this is predicted to rise to 97 by 2050. It is also predicted that by 2021 the proportion of the population over the age of 65 years will have risen to 23.6 per cent. Okinawa has the highest density of centenarians in the world, with currently some 600 people out of a population of 1.3 million over 100 years. Japan's population peaked around 128 million in 2008, but its population will decline by around 1 million per year in the coming decades. By 2060 Japan will have a population of 87 million and more than 40 per cent of the population will be older than 65. There has also in recent decades been limited emigration, with some 75,000 Japanese living permanently overseas.

With a declining workforce of young people and a rapidly rising population of old people, Japan faces stark choices. It can attempt to resist dependence on migration to renew its labour force by developing labour-saving technology; it can encourage the return of overseas Japanese; it can adopt welfare and employment policies to promote fertility by giving tax support to young couples; it can eliminate retirement and increase the efficiency of older workers through re-education; and finally, it can and has increased short-term visas to temporary workers. In the area of welfare provision, Japan may also encourage non-profit organizations and promote volunteerism, but these non-government agencies cannot provide significant solutions (Ogawa, 2009). Policies to increase fertility are unlikely to succeed. Similar strategies in Singapore have failed, and there is no reason to think that a dramatic reversal of low fertility rates is at all possible. The Japanese population will continue to decline alongside its stagnating economy unless it can abandon the ideology of uniqueness and 'racial purity', resigning itself to a multicultural and multifaith future. The remarkable resilience and continuity of Japanese religion and social structure may be finally undermined by the Malthusian logic of its declining fertility and ageing population. Cultural and religious diversity will be the inevitable outcome of any dependence on migration to solve its population problem, and the result will probably be the end of *nihonjinron*.

11 | *State and Turkish secularism: the case of the Diyanet*

WITH BERNA ZENGIN ARSLAN

Introduction

In this chapter we examine the case of Turkey, which has been regarded, in both academic and political circles, as a model of successful secularization from the time of Mustafa Kemal Atatürk. In contesting this common and simplistic assumption, we concentrate on the history and role of the Diyanet, which is, we argue, yet another illustration of the management of religion by the state. As a result we develop an argument against the conventional view of republican Turkey as a deeply and uniformly secular society. Turkish secularism has been considered an interesting case by both academic and political observers, because it represents a 'working example' of Muslim secularism. The Ottoman reforms from the early nineteenth century and those of the new Republic were designed to bring about modernization, and eventually Turkey was launched as a secular nation-state on the model of French secularism. Among the various reforms conducted during the Early Republican Period (1923–38) it is possible to consider the regulations and reforms enacted in the early 1920s as building blocks of the secular system. A raft of legislative changes transformed the institutional structures of the Ottoman Empire into the secular arrangements of the Turkish nation-state. An important example of these institutional reforms was the abolition of the existing Ministry of Islamic Law and Charitable Foundations (Şeriye ve Evkaf Vekaleti), which was founded in 1920, and the creation of the Diyanet İşleri Başkanlığı (Directorate of Religious Affairs) in 1924 to manage religious services for the Sunni majority.

The Turkish experiment with and experience of secular modernity has thus been celebrated by a large number of liberal scholars for successfully secularizing a Muslim-majority country with a long and persistent history of robust Islamic traditions, and for producing modern Muslims who were able to come to terms harmoniously and comfortably with liberal democracy. Today this perspective has been enthusiastically incorporated into scholarly debates emerging from the aftermath of the

Arab Spring, in which Turkish secularism has been held up as the principal model for building democracy in the Middle East and beyond. However, opinion about Turkish secularism is in fact divided. Liberal scholars have interpreted these institutional developments as constituting the successful creation of a modern and liberal Islam. Other critics have seen the Turkish experience as a failed attempt to create secularism, namely the separation of state and religion. Critical scholars have remained sceptical about the use of the term *laiklik*, which was favoured by the elite of the Kemalist regime to suggest that it was equivalent to the French concept of *laïcité*. The sceptical response is based on the belief that Turkish secularism is an exception or a deviation from the standard notion of secularism as the separation of church and state. An examination of Turkish religious groups and institutions in civil society suggests that religion does not function as an autonomous sphere outside the state's control. For example, the state has not been neutral in its relationship with minority religions, as the case of the Alevis illustrates. The Turkish state has not taken a neutral position with respect to religion, and hence there is no disinterested level playing field when it comes to social policy. Consequently Turkish secularism is frequently framed as incomplete (Parla and Davison, 2008), or as a specific form of secularism where the state controls religion (Gözaydın, 2008: 224; Gözaydın, 2009: 15 and 272), or as a deviation from the original model of French *laïcité*. Thus, Turkish secularism has come to be regarded as an exception in comparison with other Muslim-majority countries, where presumably the coexistence of Islam and democracy has failed, and in the West, where in principle the state is separated from religion.

Diyanet İşleri Başkanlığı plays an important role in shaping secularism as well as the general religious domain in Turkey. In contemporary debates about the form of Turkish secularism, the Diyanet is represented as an institution, which demonstrates Turkey's deviance from the French model of secularism. Founded in 1924 as a state-funded institution, the Diyanet's duties were wide-ranging, such as assisting in religious services, employing *imam*s (as well as preachers and *mufti*s), funding mosques and issuing *fatwa*s. The Diyanet's major role is defined as 'enlightening society about religion' (Gözaydın, 2008: 216). The Diyanet is an example of the departure of the Kemalist state from a basic notion of secularization as separating the affairs of the state and the religion. Similarly, the state-funded *imam* and preachers' schools that have been created for the education of Sunni Hanafi *imam*s, compulsory religion classes from the level of primary to high school levels and publicly funded theology departments can also be recognized as examples of the overlap between religion and the state, and thus examples of where Turkish secularism exhibits its limits. From this perspective, these institutions and their practices are explained as the compromise of the secularist People's Republican Party (CHP) with influential religious groups on its way to the formation of a secular state during the Early Republican Period (1923–38) and after.

However, the practice of secularism in Turkey in which the modern state intervenes in the sphere of religion is, we would argue, not an exception or deviation, but in fact the rule. The management of religion is the common practice of the modern state, even a building principle of secularism. To put it differently, we suggest that the Turkish state's engagement with the field of religion has not been a case of flawed secularism, but on the contrary an example that fulfilled the basic practice of the secular nation-state – that is, to manage or govern religion in the name of national security and social unity. In this sense the Diyanet is far from being an exception; it is an effective institution of the secular state. Therefore, in our approach, secularism is a political doctrine that is not based on the separation of the fields of religion and the state with clear boundaries, but rather secularism involves the oversight and regulation of religion by the state. In other words, rather than originally intending to refrain from engaging with the sphere of religion, the modern nation-state manages, regulates and governs religion by demarcating it as a separate field from law, education, science, health and economy, and by constantly redefining the boundaries that separate religion from other fields (Asad, 2003). Our approach recognizes that the secular and the religious are historically constructed and mutually constitutive fields. The argument is therefore critical of the assumption regarding the neutrality of the secular nation-state towards religion. The example of Turkey also presents a significant case in terms of relations between the religion of the majority and the religions of the minorities, in which the secular state comes to represent the majority religion: in our example, to represent Sunni Islam.

From this perspective it is possible to argue that the Diyanet since its foundation has been one of the most significant institutions of the secular Turkish state in promoting, managing and governing religion. It has become an important site of the state in defining what lies within and outside the borders of acceptable practices of religion, specifically

Sunni Islam. Through various mechanisms, such as providing financial support, human capital and the institutional and bureaucratic foundations, the Diyanet creates a social foundation and a discourse for the type of Islam that the Turkish state wants to promote. It works on constructing a modern and secular notion of 'religion' (Hassan, 2011: 455), which claims to be rational, moderate and national. Claiming to 'unify the diversity of religions' in a moderate and peaceful manner, the Diyanet defines limits and forms of Islam that can take place in public life.

Since 2002, when the Justice and Development Party (or Adalet ve Kalkınma Partisi, hereafter AKP) came to power in Turkey, the Diyanet has gone through a number of changes. First of all, it acquired more economic power, and with the increase in the number of its employees (such as *imam*s, preachers, *mufti*s and teachers of Qur'an courses) it grew in size, becoming a much larger institution than before. From 2002 to 2010 the Diyanet's budget increased fivefold, and its personnel almost doubled, from 74,000 to 117,000. More recently, through new projects such as the foundation of the Bureau of Religious Guidance for Families (Aile İrşat ve Rehberlik Bürosu) at the *mufti*s' offices in various towns and cities and the Religious Services Development Project (Din Hizmetleri Gelişim Projesi) – or the Project of Family Imams, as it is popularly known – the Diyanet has been working on 'moving *imam*s out of mosques' and having them engage more actively with the community to provide guidance 'under the light of Qur'an and Sunna, based on morality centered knowledge'. Thus, the Diyanet started working actively on integrating children, women and the elderly into its religious services in Turkey (see www.istanbulmuftulugu.gov.tr/aile-irsat-ve-rehberlik-burosu/tanitim.html). At the same time, it increased its influence in Europe through mosques over which it had gained control (Çitak, 2010; Yurdakul and Yükleyen, 2009). It started employing many more female officers (Hassan, 2011), working and using new technologies and marketing strategies more effectively for these purposes. In 2012 the Diyanet TV channel started broadcasting, targeting children and women in particular. Thus, while aiming to reach a larger and more diverse audience, the Diyanet began playing a more active role in assisting state politics and developing activities that would make it, and the religious and moral perspective it represents, more deeply embedded in everyday life. In the next section of the chapter we will comment on the role of the Diyanet in Turkish secularism under the

AKP administration, and question whether this is an erosion of secularism or a shift in its practice.

Turkish secularism and the Diyanet's role

The history of secularism in Turkey can be traced back to the Ottoman Empire in the nineteenth century. The development of the empire found a parallel in many similar political transformations across the globe, including integration into the capitalist market economy, restructuring of the bureaucracy, and reorganization of social life. In fact, parallel transformations were taking place in Japan after the Meiji Restoration, as we have seen in Chapter 10. These changes were made possible as a consequence of the implementation of secularizing policies during the Tanzimat period (1839–76), especially in the areas of law, education and state administration. In this period the elite aimed at 'creating a centralized state which was not a part of the Islamic tradition' (Mardin, 2006: 107). In order to integrate itself more effectively into European markets the Ottoman state was obliged to introduce reforms and adopt European commercial codes (Mardin, 2006: 263). The codification of *shari'a* (*Mecelle*) in an attempt to modernize legislation was also a project of the late nineteenth-century Ottoman state. The centralization and bureaucratization of the Ottoman state obviously contributed to the process of secularization, and, as part of the modernization of the empire, secular schools were opened up, giving rise to an important stratum of secularly educated bureaucrats. As Şerif Mardin (2006: 260–1) notes, since the early stages of the Tanzimat reform, the *ulema* 'gradually relinquished their status' and 'in the era preceding reform, *ulema* had occupied positions as magistrates, jurists, professors, historians, agents of government, librarians, astrologists and – often – members of mystic (Sufi) orders that were centers of reunion for religious discussion but also crossroads of political networks'. During the Tanzimat period most of the official positions that had in the past been normally occupied by the *ulema* were gradually taken over by secular employees of the state. The Tanzimat reforms introduced a structural and functional transformation of bureaucratic positions, which were increasingly occupied by members of the new secular elite. The foundation of the Diyanet represented a continuation of rather than departure from this secularizing approach, namely the replacement of traditionally educated religious men by new secularly educated bureaucrats of religion.

Secularism and modernization were the founding principles of the new Republican nation-state that was founded in 1923 by Mustafa Kemal Atatürk. Kemalism, the ideology of the state of the early Republican period, promoted a Western and national model of modernity that required a top-down transformation of the society by the state. Although as we have observed secularization had started during the late Ottoman period, an overall cultural, social and institutional disconnection from the Ottoman heritage – conceived and constructed as both backward and Islamic – was the central theme of this formation of the secular Turkish state. The change in language and alphabet from Arabic to Latin established clear boundaries between the Islamic past and the secular present. This state-led secularization of the Republic has been understood in terms of the individualization (Gözaydın, 2008: 217) and privatization of religion, where religion was removed from the public sphere and reduced 'to a matter of faith and practice of the individual' (Gözaydın, 2008: 217). This development required both 'wiping out the visibility ... of all religious signs and practices from the public domain' and 'a radical reorganization of the public realm' (Yeğenoğlu, 2011: 226–7). As an aspect of this secularization, public employees were forbidden to wear headscarves and turbans in the workplace. An exception was made for the president of the Diyanet and for *imam*s and preachers working at mosques, who were allowed to wear turbans and religious gowns while providing religious services. Concomitantly, Turkish secularization created an 'enlightened' version of Islam, which promoted a 'progressive' and modern interpretation of religion that would be based on reason and science rather than on 'superstition' such as pilgrimage to tombs and other 'archaic practices' such as following a sheikh. The Diyanet became one of the institutional bases of this ideology, which 'continues to entail an existentially secular definition of "religion" that consigns Islam to its secularly "appropriate" places' (Hassan, 2011: 454–5).

As Istar Gözaydın (2008: 217) notes, 'religion was to remain in the personal domain and only requires state intervention to the extent that it concerns and objectifies the social order'. From an 'Enlightenment Secularist' perspective, 'separating religion and state to ensure dangerous religious passions and "superstitions" be confined to the private sphere' is an important development (Gözaydın, 2008: 217). It defines the public representations and presence of Islam as political and dangerous. The Diyanet, which enjoys a monopoly over the public representation of

Islam for the secular state, has played an important role in creating expressions of national unity in the religious domain. Social unity is emphasized, while different traditions and interpretations of Islam, as well as private institutional forms, are seen as a threat to national unity. While Sunni Islam has been constructed as an important component of Turkish national identity (Yıldız, 2001), the institution of the Diyanet has been the site of the production and representation of a nationalized Islam, and this official or national Islam is praised by the state for being apolitical and neutral. In short, official Islam is recognized as moderate and harmless, and valuable in the promotion of a peaceful society.

Ali Bardakoğlu, the president of the Diyanet between 2003 and 2010, has explained its role as a state institution in terms of maintaining social order in Turkey through the promotion of moderate Islam which is based on rationality and 'sound knowledge' and not 'superstition' and 'sentimental religiosity'. He considered this version of Islam as a public framework that embraces the diverse religions in the country:

The position of the *Diyanet* within the state organization is not in contradiction with secularism, according to the following principles that are upheld in Turkey: (a) religions should not be dominant or effective agents in state affairs; (b) the provision of unrestricted freedom for the religious beliefs of individuals and religious liberty are under constitutional protection; (c) the prevention of the misuse and exploitation of religion is essential for the protection of the public interest; (d) the state has authority to ensure the provision of religious rights and freedoms as the protector of public order and rights.

What we see here is the protection of religious liberties on the one hand, while at the same time there is a mechanism to control the expression of religious demands that might threaten social order. (Bardakoğlu, 2004: 369)

The *Diyanet* pursues stable ideas and experiences, which ensure social peace and trust. It promotes such aspects of religious experience; it does not promote extreme ideas. (Bardakoğlu, 2004: 370)

Sound knowledge helps in fighting superstitions, ignorance, false ideas, misuses of religion and abuses in the name of religion. In Islamic history, Muslim scholars took responsibility for fighting superstitions, ignorance and fanaticism. They took this responsibility because religious knowledge requires, by its very nature, such a struggle. The *Diyanet* gives priority to providing healthy and sound religious knowledge to society. The intention in doing this is to educate people and to promote the tolerance of various religious trends in society. The *Diyanet* promotes a religiosity based on scholarship, sound knowledge and interpretation. Sentimental religiosity is introverted, and closed to the external world. Sentimental religiosity may lead to total self closure, and for such people it will be difficult to open their minds to critical thinking. (Bardakoğlu, 2004: 371)

The *Diyanet* acknowledges this diversity and promotes a moderate, tolerant and embracing perception of Islam. (Bardakoğlu, 2004: 372)

The Diyanet, Directorate of Religious Affairs

The Diyanet has been one of the strongest institutions of the secular state in Turkey, through which it not only managed religion, but also created and promoted a specific form of modern Islam that affirmed the ideology of the nation-state. It is important to note that the Diyanet was founded on 3 March 1924, the same day that the *Shari'a* Courts were closed down, the Caliphate and the Office of the Şeyhülislam were abolished, the Ottoman dynasty was expelled and the Unity of Education Law (Tevhid-i Tedrisat Kanunu) was enacted. These were the foundation reforms of the Turkish secular state. They brought to a conclusion the old regime's administrative mentality and institutional structure, creating the basic institutions and grounds of secularism for the new nation-state. The Unity of Education Law brought about the closure of the *medrese*s that had traditionally provided religious education, and collected the various educational institutions under a single educational authority in the Ministry of Education, which was founded on premises of modernism and secularism. Also in 1924 the *imam*s and preachers' schools were opened to provide some degree of continuity in religious education, but this time under the supervision of the state. The abolition of the Caliphate, like other founding reforms of the Republic, was without doubt the most significant step in providing legitimacy for the new state on the basis of a national identity that was seen to be above religion (Berkes, 1998; Kadıoğlu, 2010: 492). Similarly, by expelling the last remnants of dynastic rule the new Republic was clearly determined to end the Ottoman regime and the Islamic past.

The foundation of the Diyanet as the Directorate of Religious Affairs on the same day was a continuation of the legislative process, which abolished the Office of the Şeyhülislam and founded the Ministry of Islamic Law and Charitable Foundations in 1920. The *şeyhülislam*, who was the highest-ranked *mufti* in the Ottoman state, the chair of the *fatwa* institution and the leader of *ulema*, was responsible for juridical, educational, religious and administrative affairs. The Ministry of Islamic

Law and Charitable Foundations was founded as a 'ministry to organize religious affairs and the *waqfs*' (charities) and incorporated the institutions of the Office of the Şeyhülislam (Gözaydın, 2009: 16). After a brief period of time following the foundation of the new Republic and the acceptance of secularism as one of its basic principles, this ministry was replaced by the Diyanet, which in fact had a lesser status, being founded as an administrative unit under the office of the prime minister. It is important to note that in this institutional reform process for modernization and secularization, the Office of the Şeyhülislam lost all its functions apart from those relating to religion. Similarly, this process ended the influence of the *ulema*, while the Ministry of Islamic Law and Charitable Foundations provided an institutional ground for their presence. After their salaries were cut, the last move to end the *ulema*'s presence was the closure of this ministry in 1924 and the foundation of the Diyanet in its place (Mardin, 2011: 162). It was during this period that the *ulema* first lost their influence over a range of different fields in addition to religion, before being replaced by the new men of religion – that is, by the bureaucrats of the modern state's institution of the Diyanet. It is worth noting that

the term *diyanet* was carefully chosen in legislative discussions to express 'religious affairs' in the sense of 'matters of personal piety' over its potential alternative *diniye*, which could have implied the new institution's religious responsibilities in the fields of economy, society, policing and education, which are intentionally distributed to other branches of government. (Hassan, 2011: 454)

Therefore, the foundation of the Diyanet not only more narrowly defined 'religion' as worship (*ibadet*) and belief (*itikat*), but also opened up a space within the state for the representation of a 'true' Islam. A modernized form of Sunni Islam that is distanced from the fields of law, education and science is defined by the state as an acceptable form of religion, while excluding other sites and practices of Islam such as the *tekke*s and Sufi lodges. However, in 1965 the scope of the Diyanet's services was extended to include not only worship and belief but also morality. For example, the current legislation defines the duties of the office of the *mufti* as 'conducting affairs of the religion of Islam that are related with the principles of belief, worship and morality; enlightening the society on religious questions with activities such as conferences and preaching, and answering religious questions'.

Because the Diyanet is protected by the constitution, a constitutional change would be required to change or to close it. The rules and regulations of the Diyanet are explained in the legislation prepared by the office of prime minister, which organizes the duties of *imam*s, *mufti*s and preachers (*vaiz*), defines the hierarchy between them, determines the content of *khutba*s (Friday sermons), and regulates the dress codes on the basis of the general dress codes of public offices. Thus, the intention is to create uniformity and homogeneity across the mosques in Turkey. The central organization of the activities of the Diyanet was consolidated after 28 February 1997, when the office of the prime minister began to determine the content of the sermons for the Friday prayer as well as the morning prayers of Ramadan and the Feast of the Sacrifice.

It is reasonable to argue that the Diyanet has covered the financing and regulation of the field of religion not only in Turkey, but increasingly across Europe wherever there are Turkish migrants. Although Islamic communities and Sufi orders in Turkey, such as the Gülen community and the İsmailağa order, which have rapidly grown in recent decades, and Milli Görüş (National Outlook) in Europe, have their own networks and independent financial resources, it is the Turkish state that predominantly provides resources to religion and regulates this field. Probably more important is the growth of functionaries, who are employed in the various ranks of the Diyanet and who regulate its perspective towards Islam. The influence of the statist and modernist perspective of Islamic groups is clearly visible in contemporary Turkey. Two examples are Fethullah Gülen, the spiritual leader of the Gülen community, who used to be a preacher employed by the Diyanet, and Prime Minister Tayyip Erdoğan, who came from a Milli Görüş background, and who is a graduate of a public school for the education of *imam*s and preachers.

As we have seen with the formation of the Turkish nation-state, the French notion of *laïcité* is commonly accepted as the key model of Turkish secularism in terms of its emphasis on the separation of the fields of state and religion, and as the principle by which all religious symbols are removed from the public sphere. As in France, the state in Turkey does not allow for an official or established religion. The article that was added in 1924 to the Constitution of 1921 recognizing Islam as the religion of the state (Devletin dini din-i İslamdır of 20 April 1924) was abolished in 1928. Thus, Turkey differs from many other modern states in Europe that have an official religion, such as Greece (the Greek

Orthodox Church), Finland and Norway (the Lutheran Churches) and the United Kingdom (the Church of England). Having been based originally on French *laïcité*, the Turkish experience of secularization has acquired its own specific characteristics. For example, unlike France, where the state only provides help to religious groups for the foundation of their places of worship, in Turkey the state itself funds Islamic buildings, their operation and the employees of the mosques. Similarly, in Turkey the syllabus of religious instruction is based on the Sunni Islamic tradition and is mandatory from primary schools onwards, but in France there is no mandatory religious education, and when religion is taught it appears as religious history in the history syllabus (Akay, 2011). There is one significant difference. The secular state in Turkey provides services to the Sunni Muslim majority, and unsurprisingly this provision has been criticized for departing from its stated policy of religious neutrality. Although it is argued that state and religion are separate, the state is deeply engaged with religious affairs.

Religious minorities in Turkey and the Alevi community

The religious groups that are not represented in the Diyanet can be easily identified as not conforming to moderate Sunni Hanafi Islam. The Diyanet does not therefore provide religious services to minorities such as the Alevis, and it is difficult to claim that religious communities fully enjoy their rights to organize freely (Akay, 2011). The official perception that they represent a threat to social unity creates various bureaucratic and political obstructions against their legal recognition. In Turkey the Lausanne Treaty of 1923, which among other provisions allowed for a significant transfer of populations between Greece and Turkey, has been interpreted in such a way that only the Jewish, Greek and Armenian communities are officially recognized as religious minorities. Minorities other than these official categories do not enjoy the rights given by the Lausanne Treaty. For example, there is no provision for their religious education. Only the Armenian, Orthodox Christian and Jewish minorities gained the right to have their own religious education and instruction in their own languages according to the Lausanne Treaty. It is estimated that the Kurdish population of modern Turkey is about 12 to 15 million, while the Alevis are the largest religious minority with an estimated population of 12 million, of whom some 3 million are Kurds. The Arab population is 1 million, the Armenians number around

55,000 to 66,000, the Jewish population is 25,000 and the Greek population is 2,000. The Diyanet, with its huge budget, serves almost none of these minorities.

Sufi lodges have been suppressed and banned in Turkey. Throughout the history of the Republic these religious brotherhoods have continued underground. With the abolition of Sufi lodges, the Alevi *dergah*s or lodges had to end their activities, and they were forced to conduct their religious rituals secretly. Historically, the state has attempted to deal with the Alevis through a process of what we might call 'Sunnification'. The most obvious physical manifestation of this strategy is the construction of mosques in areas where the Alevis live. Although Alevis do not accept these mosques as their places of worship their number has steadily increased in Alevi regions, especially after the 1980 military coup. The most striking example is Tunceli, where in 1986 there were only 18 mosques, but by 2009 there were 116 (Akay, 2011, Özcan, 1990. 19). Thus it is possible to claim that by defining the religious traditions of the Alevis in a certain way, the state has tried to make it an acceptable manifestation of religion in a secular society.

Let us dwell briefly on the place of the Alevi community in modern Turkish history. From the foundation of the Turkish Republic the Alevis, who represented around 20 to 25 per cent of the total population, were enthusiastic supporters of secularization because they assumed it would protect them from persecution by the majority. They embraced secular citizenship without difficulty, becoming loyal supporters of the state. Their commitment to the state has been expressed by their willingness to join the army and to act as civil servants. They nevertheless retained their separate religious traditions and before the 1960s lived in regions and villages that typically isolated them from the Sunni majority. The Alevis are a distinctive tradition, believing that there is a sacred hierarchy of authority, and their mystical and esoteric beliefs are unlike modernized Sunni Islam. The core of their ritual tradition is known as *cem*, and this tradition is guarded and organized by religious leaders called *dede*. The Alevis are associated with Shi'ism because they believe in the twelve *imam*s of Shi'ism and recall the martyrdom of Hasan and Huseyin. As a result, the Sunni majority often believe that the Alevis are Shi'ite Iranians, but the Alevis reject this accusation. They also believe in the equality of men and women, whereas Sunni Islam keeps men and women apart in the mosques and assumes that women are separate from men and require protection. In their prayers and ritual life they favour the Turkish language over Arabic. Despite the radical changes taking place in modern Turkey, the Alevis have remained committed to the secular Republican tradition because they have seen secularism as an important system protecting their religion and way of life. They therefore tend to venerate Atatürk and adhere to more left-wing secular politics. It is unsurprising therefore that they have become increasingly ambivalent about contemporary political life, which has seen a growth in the influence of Sunni Islam within the state. The original republican tradition, which as we have seen supported 'religion' (*din*) in general as necessary for social unity, has come to mean in practice support for an orthodox and 'official' version of Sunni Islam (Shankland, 2003: 159–60).

The Diyanet in contemporary Turkey

We can observe a number of significant changes in the Diyanet after the AKP came to power in 2002, such as the significant rise in its budget, its increasing presence in Europe, the introduction of new technologies and marketing approaches into its activities, and the increase in female employees (Hassan, 2011). The Diyanet's budget increased almost five times, from 553,364,200 YTL in 2002 to 2,650,530,000 YTL in 2010. Although the Diyanet is not a ministry as such, its 2010 budget is higher than the budgets of most other ministries, including the Ministry of Interior, Ministry of Exterior and the former Ministry of Industry and Trade. It is more than the total of the Culture and Tourism Ministry and Ministry of Transport, and close to the Ministry of Justice.

The Diyanet began sending religious representatives abroad in 1971 in order to prevent Turkish migrants living in these countries from employing religious personnel in informal ways and to insulate them from dangerous political ideas (Gözaydın, 2009: 136). The regulations that were made in 1984 defined the duty of the Diyanet abroad as 'enlightening our citizens living abroad on religion', providing religious services, organizing religious–scientific educational seminars and conferences, and examining and monitoring the influence of social life in these countries on Turkish citizens (Gözaydın, 2009: 138). In addition to spreading peace and tolerance, it was charged with fighting against 'destructive and divisive currents targeting' Turkish citizens (Gözaydın, 2009: 146). Thus the Diyanet is as concerned with maintaining national unity in its activities abroad as it is within the country. In Germany it represents Islam 'as the cultural component of being Turkish' (Yurdakul and Yükleyen, 2009: 223).

Since 1984 the Diyanet has become an influential institution in Europe, where the mosques it operates and the delegates elected to the boards of major organizations represent Muslims in European countries. In her analysis of the Diyanet's activities in France, Zana Çitak describes it as 'a foreign-policy instrument of the Turkish government' abroad (Çitak, 2010: 625). Conceived as a 'neutral' institution and as representing the Turkish state abroad, the Diyanet mosques in France have become appealing not only to the Turkish immigrants living there but also to Muslims from other ethnic groups. The result is that the Diyanet competes with other Turkish Islamic groups in attracting followers to its mosques and also for places at the administrative boards of Islamic organizations in Europe.

Similar results of the Diyanet's activities in Germany have been reported. The Diyanet İşleri Turkish Islamic Unity (DITIB) was founded in 1983 in Germany, and has been in competition with the Milli Görüş association (Islamische Gemeinschaft Milli Görüs), which has been politically active in the country since the 1970s. Thus

Diyanet Isleri controls 800 mosques alone, and Milli Gorus controls 514 mosques in Europe, most of which are located in Germany. Both have established a social service network over several decades in Germany; both have women's and youth groups, Koran reading courses, and funeral funds; and both try to attract the same Muslim clientele – second-generation Muslims in Germany. (Yurdakul and Yükleyen, 2009: 218)

The Diyanet employees (*imam*s and *ateşe*s) represent themselves as 'non-political' or neutral, unlike the followers of the Milli Görüş movement, who, they argue, have a political agenda in their religious activities. On the other hand, from the perspective of the members of Milli Görüş the Diyanet is not a neutral institution but rather a representative of the secularist state's policies abroad. A member of Milli Görüş states that the Diyanet was founded in Europe 'after Evren's coup d'état ... against the rising Islamic trends in Europe' (Yurdakul and Yükleyen, 2009: 220).

In 2011 the Diyanet was discussed in the national media in response to a new project it planned, which the media referred to as the 'Family Imams Project'. The Diyanet publicly rejected this label, and referred instead to a project targeting village *imam*s (www.haberturk. com/yasam/haber/609264-diyanet-islerinden-aile-imamligi-aciklamasi,

www.cnnturk.com/2011/turkiye/03/09/simdi.de.aile.imamligi.uygu
lamasi.geliyor/609423.0/index.html). This project, which was called
the Religious Services Development Project (Din Hizmetleri Gelisim
Projesi) by the Diyanet, was designed to expand religious services beyond
the mosques by visiting 'citizens ... in their houses and workplaces' and
providing them with information on various subjects such as education,
health, ecological balance and staying away from 'bad habits' (such as
alcohol consumption, gambling and smoking). The Diyanet claims that
this project, which expands the duties and role of *imam*s – 'not merely
leading the prayer and ... call to prayer but listening to the community's
problems' – aims at 'developing and spreading a social-morality centered
piety' and – using the current language of the market economy –
'increasing the effectiveness and efficiency of religious services' (www.
cnnturk.com/2011/turkiye/03/09/simdi.de.aile.imamligi.uygulamasi.
geliyor/609423.0/index.html). In this way the Diyanet came to be
diffused more broadly into the everyday life of the communities.

In 2012 the Diyanet developed its own television channel which
addresses children through special children's programmes. The Diyanet's
concern to reach children could also be seen in its 'I love my mosque'
(www.diyanet.gov.tr/turkish/camiyiseviyorum/index.html) campaign.
The Diyanet aimed this project specifically at children, encouraging them
to identify with and attend the mosques. Identifying mosques as 'a symbol
representing cultural codes', the current president of the Diyanet, Mehmet
Görmez, says that they have an important role in the spiritual education of
children. He states that for the children to 'learn the values of their society'
and 'perhaps more importantly to discover feelings of unity and collectivity' they should be introduced to the mosque (www.diyanet.gov.tr/turkish/
camiyiseviyorum/baskanin-mesaji.html).

Another issue that was hotly debated in 2011 was the 'Mele Project'
of the Diyanet, which can be summarized as the employment of Kurdish
*imam*s in Diyanet mosques and offices despite the fact that they have
not received official education in the public schools for the education
of *imam*s and preachers. This project has been criticized as part of
the state's assimilation politics for the Kurdish population. Mehmet
Görmez rejected the argument that this policy has a political or security
agenda, but claims that it has been a practice of the Diyanet since
1977 to employ men of religion who have received religious education
through private instruction (http://m.t24.com.tr/haber/gormez-mele-
siyaset-degil-diyanetin-projesi/187495).

It is self-evident that the Diyanet as a state institution for maintaining national unity and enlightening society in Islam is still fully embraced by the AKP. In June 2012 the deputy prime minister, Bekir Bozdağ, stated that in the new constitution being prepared by the government, the Diyanet would be exempt from the *laiklik* principle:

The *Diyanet*'s duty is to enlighten the society about Islam and administer the worship places. How will it do that? It will do that according to Quran and Sunna but not Laiklik. . . . There are different debates going on. Some say the Directorate of Religious Affairs should be closed down . . . some say different tariqas and sects should be represented in the *Diyanet*. . . . In my opinion, the *Diyanet* is the cement of this country . . . Article 136 is regulating the Directorate of Religious Affairs. This article has a point, which does not agree with the principle of Laiklik. . . . There is a structure which allows a religious expression and services to an extent that is allowed by Laiklik. . . . This is an interventionist conception of Laiklik. It is not acceptable. . . . The President of the *Diyanet* should do his job according to Quran and Sunna but not Laiklik. (*Zaman*, 4 June 2012, www.zaman.com.tr/haber.do? haberno=1298228&title=bozdag-diyanet-gorevini-laiklige-gore-degil-kuran-ve-sunnete-gore-yapacak)

The institutions and policies founded by the secular Kemalist state, which promoted a rationalized religion while simultaneously bureaucratizing religious services, are still active. Under the AKP administration the Turkish state still defines and promotes its 'correct' version of Islam and decides on the ways in which it will be promoted. The Diyanet remains an important institution for maintaining national unity and collective solidarity.

Conclusion

The case of the Turkish Diyanet is a clear illustration of Talal Asad's argument (Asad, 2003) that the secular, like religion, has a history and is mutually constitutive with religion, and cannot be separated either conceptually or historically. In other words, in the formation of the secular in Turkey we observe an entanglement of the religious and the political, and not a separate and independent history of Islam. The secular state in Turkey adopts a secular perspective that not only controls but also constructs and governs religion both within and outside its borders. Despite the fact that Alevis do not attend mosques but *cem* houses, the rapid increase in the number of mosques in the Alevi-majority city of

Tunceli since the 1980s through the involvement of the Diyanet is an example of how the Diyanet as a state institution not only represents but also becomes a tool in realizing state policies. Similarly, its increasing presence in European mosques and the institutions of an Islamic civil society is a different face of the Diyanet, which exports Turkish Islam while claiming to represent a neutral and moderate Islam.

The Republic was built on the assumption that 'Turkishness' would be sufficient to forge a national identity and create a unified society, but the state has gradually allowed Islam to play a greater part in social life. In our approach, we suggest that the Turkish state's relationship with Sunni Islam has not been merely one of control and oppression of religion, but that it has been a productive relationship, creating a form of nationalized and modern Islam in the very process of its establishment. Through people who went through the educational processes or employment in the Diyanet, it is possible to see how this modern nationalized perspective of Islam has been influential in the Islamic movements and communities in Turkey.

Management of religions has become a common tendency for the liberal state to achieve a peaceful coexistence of different religious groups, which have increasingly become 'public religions' during recent decades. In other words, multiculturalism as a condition of post-secular societies predominantly adopted a management of religion approach. However, in Turkey the experiments to shift to a multicultural approach as a part of the process of Turkey's integration into European Union have failed to a large extent. Although attempts were made to give more rights to religious minorities and to listen to the demands of Alevis, they have come to an end with little sign of success. Nevertheless, the secular state in Turkey represents and provides funds and services to the majority religion, Sunni Hanafi Islam. It promotes moral values of a certain interpretation of modern Turkish Islam and opens up more space for its representation. In this sense, we do not see a significant deviation from the practice of the secular state for the last ninety years in integrating religious services into the instruments of the state. However, since 2002, when the AKP came to power, the Diyanet has gained more influence through an increase in its budget and personnel. In parallel, it has been focusing on developing services that integrate Islamic practices into everyday lives, especially those of women, children and the elderly, on the one hand, and that increasingly reach to Europe and other areas outside Turkey, on the other.

Is this the retreat of Turkish secularism or a deepening of its paradox as the Diyanet takes an active role in the 'deprivatization' of religion? Alternatively, it has been seen as a transition to 'passive secularism' similar to the practice of secularism in the United States, where the secular state does not become aggressively involved with the field of religion (Kuru, 2009). By contrast, our analysis demonstrates that the Turkish state is far from pursuing a 'passive secularism'; on the contrary, it actively and extensively engages with the field of religion with increasing intensity. It remains the Turkish state (now governed by a pro-Islamic party) that defines what is religious and what is secular. However, this is not a deepening paradox, but a change in the approach of the state from an emphasis on religion as part of the private to the public domain. The state's support for 'religion' in the early Republic has become a policy to support an official Islam through the activities of the Diyanet.

PART IV

Conclusion

12 | *Popular religion and popular democracy*

Introduction: unpopular religion

Through most of the chapters so far I have concentrated on what we can regard as official, formal or institutionalized religions. I have concentrated on the literati in Confucianism, the Buddhist monks, and the priests and ministers of the Christian churches. In asking about the relationships between politics and religion I have examined the literate and formal dimensions of public religions. More specifically, my discussion of religion and politics has concentrated on the church and the state. However, religion in modern societies has become more informal, unofficial and post-institutional; in short, it has become popular. In order to round out our consideration of religion and politics we will have to attempt a definition of 'popular religion' and then to offer some examples. While it turns out that defining 'popular religion' is difficult, the thesis of this chapter is that in the modern world religion and politics have followed a similar trajectory. They have both become 'popular' in so far as they have become 'democratic'. As expressions of popular democratic culture the tension between religion and politics tends to disappear, and at the same time charisma is slowly converted into celebrity. There is one other equally important feature in modern society: popular religion is global.

In his contribution to *The religious significance of atheism* (Ricoeur and MacIntyre, 1969) Alasdair MacIntyre makes the point that atheism is only a serious option in a culture that has a dominant tradition of theism. It is for this reason that sociological conferences on unbelief or atheism in the contemporary world are not worth attending. A similar argument might be made about 'popular religion'. Taking popular religion seriously is probably only a real intellectual option in a society where a formal orthodoxy is still on the agenda. The idea of something being 'popular' in religious terms implies there is a hegemonic, comprehensive and commanding alternative to which the popular manifestations of religious life are subordinated, and probably oppositional. But in a modern society what is that alternative? To achieve some conceptual clarity we may have to invent the idea of an 'unpopular religion', otherwise the phrase 'popular religion' will cover everything from charismatic Catholicism to baseball to reggae. In this chapter I continue with an argument from *Religion in modern society* (Turner, 2011c), in which I proposed that in earlier times the Church dominated popular religion, because it enjoyed the benefit of an educated priesthood and a virtual monopoly over the means of grace. Before the Reformation its message was universal and Latin was the language of official public communication. The Church was also a land owner with important connections to the state, playing a significant role in the feudal economy. In the modern world, with the spread of literacy and the development of alternative sources of knowledge, the Church rarely has a monopoly over education and its priesthood has to compete with other intellectual elites for influence. Although churches, especially Catholic churches, play an important role in the provision of education and health services, their influence over national education systems is limited or is declining. Where there is an established church – such as the Anglican Church in the United Kingdom – organized religion enjoys certain benefits and privileges, as we saw in an earlier discussion of monarchy in Chapter 4. However, it no longer – or only on rare occasions – has the legal power to enforce its beliefs. The Witchcraft Act in the United Kingdom was abandoned, and since the 1950s neo-paganism has spread among younger generations. There are of course remnants of past religious hegemonies such as the blasphemy laws. The controversy surrounding *The Satanic Verses* was a dramatic reminder of the role of traditional values regarding religious authority, but that episode in British life was unusual, if not culturally unique.

Classical sociology and cultural anthropology

Defining 'popular religion' in the absence of hegemonic Christianity obviously presents problems, but to grapple with this issue we can start with a consideration of classical sociology. The notion of 'popular religion' did not play a large role in the classical sociology of religion, and only to some extent in anthropology. In *The sociology of religion* Max Weber (1966b) developed a model of virtuoso and mass religion that captures many of the issues relating to the tensions between popular and official religion. Weber was more interested in what we might call 'folk religion' such as Taoism rather than in 'popular religion'. However, as we have seen in earlier chapters, this model may in fact have been more relevant to Buddhism than to Christianity. In Buddhist countries the monastic tradition of Theravada Buddhism emphasized the difference between adepts, who followed the full range of disciplinary practices, and the laity, whose involvement in worldly activities prevented them from engaging in the virtuoso lifestyle. For Weber, then, the popular religion of the masses involved the quest for material rewards, which were best secured, not by personal discipline, but by the magical interventions of powerful charismatics. Although Weber did not address popular religion directly, his theory of charisma is nevertheless essential for understanding eruptions of unorthodox, oppositional and creative trends in religious life.

In Weber's comparative sociology, in the absence of a specific theory of popular religion we might say that outbreaks of popular religion among the disprivileged were associated with charismatic figures that stood outside the mainstream. In this sense, popular religions in the past were associated with unorthodox practices and beliefs. Charismatic figures have been prominent in the Abrahamic religions, especially around messianic figures. Charismatic movements in these prophetic religions are often disruptive problems for religious traditions. We might take as an example the life of Sabbatai Sevi (1626–76) as one obvious example. A Jewish messiah who converted to Islam in 1666, Rabbi Sabbatai Sevi had a significant impact across the Western world when it was widely believed that he was gathering the lost tribes of Israel. He demonstrated his authority by transgressions of Jewish ritual and belief, including pronouncing the Ineffable Name and declaring that the Law could be transgressed (Scholem, 1977). When he died, his death was kept secret by his inner circle of followers, but stories soon circulated to explain his death. It was claimed that he was buried in a cave, but that when his brother came to inspect the grave it was empty and the cave was full of light. A theology developed in which his death was merely an occultation and at an appointed time he would return to his followers, who thereby sustained the belief that Sabbatai Sevi was indeed the Messiah. What lessons for the study of popular religions might be revealed by the study of these religious figures? Sabbatai Sevi (or at least the Sabbatian movement) was a genuinely global phenomenon, with followers in the Middle East, Europe and North America.

This example suggests therefore that popular religions are not by definition local in contrast to the universal claims of official religions.

Weber's virtuoso–mass distinction found its parallel in the church–sect–mysticism typology of Ernest Troeltsch (1931) in *The social teaching of the Christian Churches*. When we think of popular religion within this tradition, sects, in appealing to a large audience of converts, are more open to popular idioms. Following the logic of the church–sect typology, some popular sectarian movements can become more mainstream and orthodox over time. This development is associated with the idea of 'denominationalization'. Perhaps the classic example of this process can be found in the history of Methodism. John Wesley (1703–91) in developing his preaching circuits and establishing independent chapels created a popular religious movement that had a strong appeal to the urban poor and the dispossessed. Wesley's field preaching was a challenge to the parish structure of Anglicanism and to the hierarchical authority of the local priesthood. At the same time Charles Wesley's hymns were popular alternatives to the formal worship of the Anglican liturgy. In *The making of the English working class* E. P. Thompson (1963) examined Methodism as an oppositional, working-class and dissenting tradition, which by the late nineteenth century had become a middle-class and mainstream denomination. One criticism raised by sociologists and historians against the idea that popular religions stand outside the mainstream is that the official religions of today are simply the popular religions of yesterday. In this respect the phrase 'popular religion' is often seen by contemporary sociologists as a pejorative and judgemental notion, rather like the concept of 'cults'. The inclination of contemporary sociological research is therefore to avoid the notion altogether as unsound if not ideological.

There is, however, a clear notion of popular and official religion in Judaism, Christianity and Islam, because all three are religions of the book, and historically there are religious intellectuals who have defended the written tradition against popular belief and practice. The official leadership roles of priests, rabbis and mullahs are traditionally assumed to impart authority to make statements about practice that carry some weight. However, there is an important organizational difference. Whereas Catholic Christianity developed a centralized system of institutions and offices, and an ecclesiastical bureaucracy in which ultimate power rested with the Bishop of Rome, Islam and Judaism have authority systems that are more local, devolved and focused on the teachings of the local rabbi or mullah. This observation suggests that the problem of popular religion has greater significance in the Christian tradition, where orthodoxy is concentrated in the hands of ecclesiastical officials such as bishops. Because Judaism and Islam are devolved, there is far less scope to create and impose orthodoxy. These traditions have nothing resembling the idea of papal infallibility or priesthood with a monopoly over the sacraments.

In terms of Islam, we can perhaps understand this oscillation between the official and unofficial forms of religion by reference to the work of Ernest Gellner (Hall, 2011). In the anthropology of Islam Gellner published two influential studies – *Saints of the Atlas* (1969) and *Muslim society* (1982) – that were based initially on a study of the Berber people of the Atlas Mountains. His thesis was that the popular saints of North African Sufism played an important role in creating the social solidarity that helped to contain tribal conflicts. In this political anthropology of the conflicts between urban Islam and its Sufi hinterland he studied the political oscillation of urban and rural elites. Because city life produced a weak foundation for social solidarity, the cities were periodically invaded and taken over by tribal elites who enjoyed a greater degree of solidarity. At the same time, this political cycle found its parallel structure in the relationships between puritan orthodox and literate Islam in the cities versus the unorthodox Sufi brotherhoods in the villages. Puritanical reformed Islam could survive and flourish in the context of urban modernity, and consequently he claimed that Islam, alone among the world religions, would be more able to resist secularization. The modernization of the Middle East would result in the dominance of the puritanical version of Islam over the mystical tradition of Sufism.

Popular religion in South Asia

The religious movement associated with the life of Sathya Sai Baba (1926–2011) offers an instructive example of popular religion and a dramatic illustration of Weber's theory of charisma, although within a modern global setting. This example from South Asia illustrates the evolution of popular religion drawing on a Hindu tradition of holy men in a culture where there is no centralized religious authority. Sai Baba claimed to be a reincarnation of the ascetic Sufi mystic Sai Baba of Shirdi, and by the end of his life he had become a global celebrity. His followers included figures such as Goldie Hawn, Sarah Ferguson and

Isaac Tigrett, the founder of Hard Rock Café. His death sparked off an unseemly squabble over the control of assets and created a problem about the status of his body as an avatar. Sai Baba was an Indian guru deeply embedded in Hindu culture and spirituality, and a messiah who later identified himself with Christianity. He functioned in a competitive religious environment within Indian culture, but his charismatic gifts won him a global following.

Sathyanarayana Raju was born to a peasant family in the remote Indian village of Puttaparthi in Andhra Pradesh on 23 November 1926, but the subsequent declaration of his divinity was drawn out and complex. On 8 November 1940, in the village of Uravakonda, the young Sai Baba was apparently stung by a scorpion and, after sleeping for several days, awoke completely transformed, singing songs in Sanskrit. On returning to his village, he began to materialize luxury goods such as sugar and flowers, which he gave to the poor villagers. After performing *leela* (play or miracles), he declared to his father 'I am Sai, I belong to *Apasthamba Suthra* [the Brahma Sutras]: I am of the *Bharadwaja gothra* [lineal descent from the Hindu sage Bharadwaja]; I am Sai Baba and I have come to ward off all your troubles and to keep your houses clean and pure.' In a second episode he revealed himself as the reincarnation of a southern Indian saint, the Maharashtrian Muslim *faqir* Shirdi Sai Baba, who died in 1918. Demanding that people address him as Sathya Sai, he connected himself to the Sufi tradition of Shirdi Sai Baba, who had both Hindu and Muslim disciples. In a further episode in his transformation Sai Baba left home, announcing that *maya* (illusion) had gone and his *bhakta*s (devotees) were calling him. A divine halo appeared around his head, signifying the transition, and photographs from this period feature a handsome young man, seated in a tall wooden chair, wearing long garlands of flowers.

Over time Sai Baba became a cosmopolitan figure, combining a variety of religious traditions and with a multifaith following across the world, and yet he left India only once in his lifetime. Here we have an example of how an obscure village such as Puttaparthi could become the centre of a global religion, self-consciously combining Hinduism, Islam and Christianity to produce new hybrid spirituality. Having established himself as a divine avatar on earth to educate human beings, he began to connect himself with other divine beings. In the late 1960s he issued religious discourses on Christmas day, declaring that these events marked the beginning of the Christian era, and in 1972 he claimed to be the

'Cosmic Christ'. By the mid-1970s the official newsletter *Sanathana Sarathi* carried an international logo depicting the cross of Christianity, the crescent of Islam, the fire of Zoroastrianism and the wheel of Buddhism.

In the famous account of charismatic authority in *The sociology of religion* Weber dwelt on two crucial issues: first, on the authorization and legitimacy of charisma; and second, on its institutionalization. The performance of miracles was a decisive aspect of Sai Baba's authentication, starting with his materialization of sweets in his youthful revelation. These distinctive practices remained important, becoming integral to his healing activities. Famous as a guru for sprinkling *vibhuti* (sacred ash) from his head over his followers, this act is regarded as an important feature of his mercy (*daya*) and his kindness (*karuna*). Other gifts such as watches and rings conferred blessings of happiness, freedom from want and protection from danger. Having established his personal authority, the Sathya Sai movement became institutionalized through a cluster of organizations: the Sri Sathya Sai Seva Organization, the Sri Sathya Sai Institute of Higher Learning, the Sri Sathya Sai Institute of Higher Medical Sciences, and the Sri Sathya Sai Urban Development Authority. Within each country there is often an organization to oversee the national movement, such as the Sri Sathya Sai Central Council of Malaysia.

In what sense was Sai Baba a charismatic figure? The first issue is the question of agency. I have argued in Chapter 2 that typically a genuine charismatic cannot choose to be a religious leader, but that rather they are chosen by some higher power against their will. In short, a charismatic can exercise no agency with respect to a personal calling. This is true of Sai Baba. Nevertheless, charismatics must position themselves within the religious field if they are ever to be recognized by disciples, and thereby to become successful charismatics. To take one example from Sai Baba's life, in July 1957 he travelled to various sacred sites in the Himalayas to receive religious legitimacy and to confirm his status as a rising guru. Proclaiming that there is only one genuine religion, a religion of love, he declared himself to be a guru–avatar – an avatar for all ages and a human guru. There is an interesting cultural disjuncture here. While true charisma is compulsive, to become authenticated a charismatic leader exercises agency in presenting credible claims to a legacy such as that of Shirdi Sai Baba.

The idea of charismatic compulsion does not sit easily with the culture of modernity, which is saturated with accounts of self-help, self-care and self-development, namely a dominant discourse of individualism, choice and identity. Unsurprisingly, the modern literature in the anthropology and sociology of religion is also about how religious movements are important in empowering individuals and how spirituality is transformative in providing techniques for improving self-management. The Sathya Sai movement offers members of the urban middle classes a set of techniques for self-transformation. The language of the postmodern self, like the language of consumerism, is primarily about agency and self-production, but these notions are not easily reconciled with the ancient religious belief that humans are called by divine powers to fulfil certain roles in this world. The pristine notion of charismatic purity and grace is a language regarding the fateful – indeed, unwelcome – calling to a life of service rather than an invitation to fashion a new self.

The second issue is the problem of charismatic authentication. Weber implied that pure charisma offers no necessary reward or benefit to disciples. Christ issued a command, 'Follow me', and thus the promise of salvation by Christ cannot be reduced simply to an offer of personal happiness or earthly rewards. Yet followers, desiring tangible proof of charismatic powers, demand material signs and actual rewards, thereby threatening to transform pure charisma into magic. Sai Baba showered his disciples with gifts: honey, sweets, milk, currency, visiting cards, diamond rings, marriage necklaces, talismans, silver and gold rings, and gold necklaces allegedly flowed from his mouth, and were consequently condemned as mere gimmickry by his critics. He was also accused of leading a luxurious lifestyle and accumulating a personal fortune out of keeping with his divine status. In short, his numerous critics saw his personal lifestyle as consistent with global consumerism rather than with holiness.

To test Sai Baba H. Narasimhaiah, the vice-chancellor of Bangalore University, chaired a committee in 1976 to conduct a scientific study of the alleged miracles, and challenged Sai Baba to materialize objects under controlled conditions. Similar attempts by the Indian rationalist Basava Premanand to prove that Sai Baba's activities were simply a hoax were inconclusive, and Sai Baba simply ignored these demands for scientific testing and verification. Was Sai Baba simply a clever magician who by trickery created a modern movement with millions of followers, or was he an example of pure charisma?

The third is the problem of the death of religious charismatics who claim to be divine and immortal. The death of Sai Baba raised critical questions about his authenticity, about spiritual succession and about the ontological status of his body. Weber identified this problem clearly, but he was probably more interested in the institutionalization of charisma than its authentication. Sai Baba had predicted that he would die at the age of ninety-six, and would remain healthy until his ultimate demise. In fact, he died in 2011 at the age of eighty-five, and had been in poor health since 2006, when he had fractured his hip. The faithful may expect Sai Baba as an avatar to be reincarnated in a new body, and will await his return; the disillusioned will continue searching elsewhere for personal identity and self-creation.

Gender and popular religion

Gender appears to play an important part in popular religions, both now and in the past. Women have for centuries been associated with witchcraft, and in Christianity the figure of Eve has been connected with betrayal, sensuality and deviance. Women have also been associated with popular dissent against institutionalized Christian authorities. In seventeenth-century New England, in the Massachusetts Bay Colony, Puritan elders would often call upon magistrates to inflict punishment on dissenters, especially notoriously disobedient Quaker women who periodically 'invaded' the colony. Laws were specifically created to chastise female Friends who arrived in New England to trouble the community. Women such as the antinomian Anne Hutchinson, who was tried in 1638, and the Quaker Mary Dyer, who was hanged in 1660, were treated as criminal, unnatural and disruptive. The religious and legal authorities colluded to suppress women who stepped outside their traditional roles as wives and mothers to presume to prophesy and to preach to men (Tartar, 2001). Their dissent was 'popular' in the sense that it existed outside the official power structure of the churches and the law.

Contemporary research shows that religion – in terms of belief and participation – plays a much larger role in the lives of women than of men, and yet the dominant roles in religious organizations are typically occupied by men (Roberts and Yamane, 2012: 262–91). Feminist religious studies have also drawn attention to the fact that official religions are not only dominated by men in terms of ecclesiastical roles (essentially the sacerdotal priesthood) but their theologies are patriarchal. The prophets of the Old Testament and the philosophers of the axial age were, generally speaking, all men. Obviously there are many examples of female saints and influential pious women, but religious organizations tend to reserve key roles and spaces for men. Women struggle to become 'ordained' as nuns in Buddhist institutions in Thailand, and in Islam women do not routinely attend mosques and are separated from men during prayers. In Roman Catholicism women have historically been barred from the priesthood. In the Episcopal tradition the ordination of women into the priesthood led to a schism and the establishment of the Anglican Church in America. In the Nation of Islam, Elijah Muhammad and Malcolm X affirmed the need to control women, who were regarded as weak and inferior. The role of women was to reproduce, and hence the leadership of the Nation opposed contraception (Marable, 2011: 142–3). Consequently official religions are in general accused of misogyny by feminist scholarship (Ruether, 1974).

Women struggle for recognition and representation in official religious institutions – in Roman Catholicism, in the Anglican tradition, in Thai Buddhism, in Islam in the United States, and so on. However, women have also become attracted to popular religions that combine sensitivity to women's issues alongside care for the environment that are in turn buttressed with religious ideas about Nature and mother goddesses. Nature worship, environmentalism, aboriginality and feminism have become important components of oppositional popular religion. For example, in Australia there has been in recent years an interaction between Christian and Aboriginal beliefs specifically combining New Age religions and Aboriginal spirituality (Sutton, 2010). These combinations – Aboriginal religious traditions relating to the Dreaming with New Age 'spirituality' – are often inappropriate and artificial. New Age authors often borrow shamelessly from Aboriginal traditions to create a synthetic urban religiosity that is well suited to modern notions of self-help, therapy, expressivity, experimentation and ecological conservationism. However, anthropologists claim that Aboriginal ideas about 'fertility mothers' always referred to local and specific sacred sites rather than to some abstract and general idea of earth and motherhood (Berndt and Berndt, 1989). Before the early 1980s there was no credible evidence that Aboriginals had any notion of 'Mother Earth'. These borrowings and adaptations are doubly problematic when some Aboriginal authors themselves consciously adopt New Age ideologies, asserting that the basis of traditional Aboriginal belief was the idea that 'the Earth is our Mother' (Hiatt, 1997). In an urban setting, when Aboriginals are far removed from their tribal past and their ancestral homes, a postmodern *mélange* of diverse beliefs is probably inevitable. These developments are not confined to Australia, and similar religious movements integrating and merging aboriginal myths and cosmologies with eco-feminism and New Age spirituality have been observed in North America (Bellah, 2011: 154–9).

Feminist ideas about fertility and earth mothers are obviously not confined to aboriginal religions and post-colonialism; they bear directly on the history of Christianity. The history of the Virgin Mary and the growth of an orthodox theology of Mary provide important lessons about the complex relationship between popular and orthodox religious traditions. Mary plays a relatively small role in the New Testament narrative of the birth and death of Jesus, but she became a central figure in the landscape of Catholic Christianity. The Virgin evolved both as an orthodox figure in Catholic theology and a figure in popular practice and belief. Her historical and sociological role has indeed been to link the sternly orthodox and the wildly popular.

In this discussion so far I have considered examples of the conflict between popular and official, but the evolution of the Mary 'cult' and its impact in Latin America and many Mediterranean cultures suggest that the Church can tolerate, if not promote, a popular tradition that can act as a vehicle for missionary activity, and as a mechanism for imposing its authority on otherwise divergent traditions. As we will see, Mary in the Roman Catholic and Orthodox traditions, and among some Anglo-Catholics, has become a central figure in orthodox teaching and practice, serving often to mark the boundaries between orthodoxy and the outside world. In medieval times she served to distinguish Christians from Jews, and after the Reformation to separate Catholics from Protestants. While Mary became an object of pious devotion in the Catholic tradition, her worship was dismissed by Protestants as an idolatrous practice that they labelled as 'Mariolatry'. However, theological conflicts within the Catholic Church regarding her status have at times been equally violent and vitriolic. For example, conflicts over the correct mode of address regarding Mary had become problematic by the 420s CE when different parties within the Church supported divergent ideas of Mary as *Theotokos* (Bearer of God), *Christotokos* (Bearer of Christ) or *Anthropotokos* (Bearer of Man). The perennial problem was how to recognize Christ's divinity and humanity in one person, and hence the role played by Mary in the life of Jesus. Was she simply a passive channel for Christ's entry into the world? How could she be fully human without compromising Christ's divinity? During the Easter celebrations of 431 CE bishops with contending views assembled in Ephesus to decide on her theological status, and after considerable verbal and physical combat they decided to support belief in her as *Theotokos*. From that moment her cult spread through much of the Roman Empire, and she was embraced by women from influential imperial families including Pulcheria, the eldest sister of Theodosius II, who took a vow of virginity and devoted her life to promoting the Church. From Constantinople, the city that had enthusiastically welcomed the doctrine of the Virgin as *Theotokos*, her imperial image was carried throughout the Mediterranean world on coins and celebrated in liturgies. Her image, through the art of religious panel painting, became a powerful devotional icon. As a consequence of this process, Mary became an imperial person and part of the court ceremonial, and at the same time a powerful figure in defining Christian orthodoxy and the Christian identity of the empire, and her imperial elevation had the effect of further defining Jews as a dangerous minority, responsible for the death of Jesus.

Through subsequent centuries Mary remained identified with power. In medieval Europe she became associated with powerful feudal patrons of the Church, and Marian devotion became a foundation of familial worship and female piety. Mary continued to be associated with campaigns against heretics, and most specifically against Jews and Muslims. We can recognize this development most clearly in the Christianization of Spain, which was finally concluded with the fall of Granada in 1492. This 'Iberian enterprise also aimed at traversing the Atlantic, and that is how the momentous encounter between the Iberian politics of religious aggression and the adventures motivated by the desire for trade and prosperity brought Christianity to the Caribbean Islands and America' (Rubin, 2009: 385). Mary came to the New World on the backs of soldiers, priests and merchants, and she played a critical role in this state enterprise of colonialism and conversion.

In the New Spain the official image of the Virgin was soon adapted to local cultures, languages and traditions. Mary merged easily with the local religious cultures of fertility that were associated with native goddesses, and hence Mary once more found a nurturing place in the hearts and homes of her new devotees. She was indigenized by friars who were sympathetic to the themes of Passion and compassion that had been woven into the story of Mary and her child Jesus. Although the missionaries could control the practice of Christianity in the towns, in the rural parishes in the hinterland Mary was more thoroughly localized, becoming herself a goddess of fertility, good fortune, solace and hope for the illiterate and disprivileged. Christianity in Latin America as elsewhere had a special attraction for women as a fertility cult, but local cultures resisted the piety associated with Mary's virginity.

However, Mary's identification with an emergent nationalist culture in Mexico occurred famously when Juan Diego, an illiterate peasant, had a vision of a beautiful woman on a hillside in Tepeyac in 1531. The site was in fact already a sacred place of indigenous religious practice, and Juan Diego was a Christian convert. At first this vision was rejected by the Church, but Mary instructed Juan Diego to gather roses in the unseasonable month of December, to wrap them in his cloak and take them to the bishop. On presentation of the cloak to the authorities, the image of Mary was found imprinted on the cloth. From this miraculous event there emerged the worship of Our Lady of Guadalupe. However, in Latin America Mary assumed various guises according to the different needs of local cultures. For the indigenous she became a symbol of resistance to white invasions, but for the settlers she could protect them from the revenge of the conquered. From a comparative perspective we can see a parallel in terms of national symbolism between the Lady of Guadalupe in Mexico and the Lady of Czestochowa in Poland in representing the suffering of the people (Warner, 1983). In other parts of the world Mary and her son Jesus were absorbed into the local and popular cultures of the Philippines and through French colonial influence into the local cultures of Vietnam.

However, despite the multiplicity of these Marian images and beliefs, she is inextricably connected with underprivileged and downtrodden women. This role has historically given Catholicism an important missionary advantage over Protestantism, which expunged female saints and regarded Mary as only a minor figure in the New Testament narrative. The attachment of women to the figure of Mary is especially strong for example in Brazilian *favela*s. Lisa Brown (2011) in *Body parts on Planet Slum* provides a rich account of how popular culture in the shape of *telenovela*s combines with Catholic teaching to create a theodicy at the everyday level. The *bairro*s of Santa Cruz have many Catholic churches, but in addition there is a large but unknown number of Candomble temples – a popular religion of West African origin involving spirit possession. Poor women typically belong to both

Catholicism and Candomble. Furthermore, while there has been a decline in Catholicism in Brazil as a whole, in Bahia, the early slave capital of Brazil, Pentecostalism has increased to some 12 per cent of the population. Its principal appeal is the prosperity gospel, and its message is one of personal discipline and abstinence from alcohol and illicit sexual relationships. While the women find meaning in the popular themes of the *telenovela*s and companionship in watching TV in social groups, Marian Catholicism and charismatic Pentecostalism offer competing religious responses to urban poverty (Lehmann, 1996).

Commercialization and religion in the United States

In modern European societies the official churches are often in decline, but at the same time there has been a significant growth in popular religions, which are typically individualistic, post-institutional and heterodox in belief and practice. Contemporary sociologists are therefore more likely to think in terms of a range of new concepts such as 'invisible religion' (Luckmann, 1967), 'implicit religion' (Bailey, 1997), 'spirituality' (Hunt, 2005) and hyper-religion (Possamai, 2012) to describe these new phenomena. However, do these developments represent an actual growth of religion, or rather the emergence of privatized therapeutic practices that simultaneously address problems about personal identity and connect spirituality to modern consumerism? Religion in a consumer society and an information-driven economy is transformed into a lifestyle that is ironically compatible with secularization. In a consumer society, religion, both popular and serious, gets caught up in the endless cycle of individual consumption. Religion becomes essential to the manufacture of urban lifestyles and to the branding of identities. Sai Baba and his global organization, whatever his claims to an ascetic religious legacy, merged effortlessly into the global circuit of commodities, and his materializations might be regarded as manifestations of what Karl Marx had called the fetish of commodities. One aspect of my argument in *Religion and modern society* (Turner, 2011c) was that religions, especially in the West, have become democratized, with the result that there is no hierarchy of authority as such. With a weak and fragmented orthodoxy, the ineffable character of the sacred comes to an end. In a democracy everything has to be popular and effable.

As evidence of this trend towards the merger of consumerism and popular religion I would include the growth of evangelical conservatism, the prosperity gospel and the rise of mega-churches. In the United States there is a strong and continuing relationship between wealth and religious membership. Looking at income and assets, there is a striking relationship between denominational affiliation, education, marriage, occupation and wealth. The idea that Protestantism and economic success are connected was the starting point of Max Weber's famous argument in *The Protestant Ethic and the spirit of capitalism* (2002). At the time the overrepresentation of Protestants in capitalist enterprise was well known in Germany, and could be taken for granted. Weber made reference to the statistical information provided in Martin Offenbacher's *Konfession und soziale Schichtung* (1900), where a comparison between Protestants and Catholics had demonstrated the social advancement of Protestants into key areas of industry by the end of the nineteenth century. In contemporary America, whereas white Catholics have enjoyed considerable social mobility, Hispanic Catholics, black American Protestants and conservative Protestants are relatively unsuccessful when compared to liberal Protestants, Mormons and Jews (Keister, 2011). One can understand why it is that religious groups on the margins of American society in terms of wealth and prestige are drawn to a prosperity gospel, and why mega-churches often find a following among African Americans who live below the poverty line.

One needs, however, to be careful about making this common-sense assumption. There is a tension between the commitment of active churchgoers who acknowledge the legitimate needs of the poor and downtrodden, and the potential for a radical criticism of capitalism in which there are systematic forms of inequality. Outreach in the form of charity and social service does not necessarily lead to any sustained criticism of American capitalism, and on the other hand charity can result in 'moral hazard'. Does charitable support for the poor merely reinforce a life of dependency on social institutions without moral reform? Conservative evangelical Christianity has struggled to develop a consistent theology of capitalism, and has instead found in attacks on abortion and gay marriage a far more congenial political platform (Omri, 2011). William F. Connolly (2008) argues that the moral doctrine of the Christian Right, in focusing its political campaigns on individual responsibility for sexual conduct and abandoning the idea of Social Gospel, found a comfortable alliance with the neo-conservatism of the Reagan era.

The religious origins of political conservatism in the early 1970s came from diverse sources such as Catholics who were opposed to the Vatican

242   Conclusion

II reforms and conservative Southern Protestants who were exercised by what they saw as the moral decline of the United States (Wilentz, 2008). Reagan was successful in embracing anti-feminist Catholics, blue-collar workers who feared for their jobs and Southern anti-civil rights campaigners. While Margaret Thatcher and Ronald Reagan are often identified with a common economic and political strategy, their relationship to religion was entirely different. By the end of the 1970s there was no significant connection between political conservatism and religion in Great Britain. Throughout the Troubles in Northern Ireland various British governments had been drawn into the sectarian conflict, and Conservative politicians found themselves in an alliance with Protestant Unionists, but in general the connection between politics and religion in Britain was a thing of the past. What Reagan and Thatcher had in common was a clever use of the media to promote their political objectives. Here again there is an important difference between the religious scenes in America and in Britain. It was the Reverend Jerry Falwell of Lynchburg, Virginia, who most successfully combined TV evangelism and politics, and in his political message on taxation, foreign policy and sexual rights found a natural alliance with the politics of the secular new right. By the end of the century the Moral Majority had lost the battle over gay rights and same-sex marriage, but the conflict over abortion, evolution and immigration continues.

Conclusion: we are all popular now

In *The elementary forms of religious life* Émile Durkheim (2001) defined religion as 'the serious life', pointing out that it typically involved discipline and training, and participation in public rituals that defined the life cycle and identity of the participants. Religion was not about personal therapy, and even less about lifestyle and leisure. In this chapter I have argued, by contrast, that religions, at least those that wish to survive secular consumerism, have to become popular, because the official, institutionalized and hierarchical forms of religion are weak, if not disappearing. The growth of popular religion in modernity is closely connected to the democratization of politics. As the franchise became universal, politicians had to formulate a message which had to be sold to the electorate. In order to understand what the electorate wants, it is important to use surveys and focus groups, and to employ the services of public relations experts. There are two main consequences. The first is that extreme political attitudes and personalities are rarely successful in democratic elections, because there is an inevitable drift towards the centre. The political agendas of parties begin to look very similar. Politicians with extreme views who win elections generally speaking have to moderate their views when in office. Second, there is the rise of celebrity politics as politicians have to embrace the media in order to compete as part of a star system. This process of mass democratization has accelerated with the growth of the mass media and the increasing role of investment in politicians and parties by corporations and rich individuals. In this democratic populist culture the churches are also under pressure to democratize – to accept women into the priesthood, to accept gay bishops, to celebrate same-sex marriages, to weaken the authority of the ecclesiastical hierarchy, to experiment with new liturgies, to promote the use of vernacular languages, to appoint growth-management teams to increase membership numbers, and to simplify the theological message of tradition. It also means, as rational choice theory suggests, greater competition between denominations and sects. The rise and vibrancy of popular religion is a function of cultural democratization. In popular democracies the religious and the political share the same historical trajectory.

13 | *The state and freedom of religion*

Introduction: Erastian constitutions

Secularization can be defined in many different ways. Perhaps the most basic definition is simply the separation of church and state. For the sake of simplicity, I start with this minimal position. This separation – or, in the language of American constitutionalism, 'the wall' – between church and state is often seen to be the very foundation of modernity. Yet in so many societies, and with respect to numerous political issues, they are not separate. In this volume I have been concerned to describe a somewhat different approach to secularization that involves 'Erastianism', namely the shaping and control of religion by the state. Thomas Erastus was a Swiss-German theologian who criticized ecclesiastical power, especially the power of excommunication, and his theological views promoted the control of religion by a secular state. In some respects this volume can be regarded as a comparative study of Erastianism, which can be simply called, with reference to modern societies, 'the management of religion' by the state (Barbalet, Possamai and Turner, 2011). In particular, these chapters have drawn attention to the enduring influence of the Treaty of Westphalia in so far as the modern system of nation-states in Europe had its origin in the religious settlement of 1648 which brought to an end the disastrous wars that had followed the Reformation. Its treaty arrangements worked towards an international system of sovereign states, each with its own prince, separate religions and legal sovereignty. It also assumed that religious membership was conventional and a consequence of baptism rather than conversion. Princes were necessarily nervous about the implications of conversion, because such activity threatened the balance of religious membership within civil society. Religious 'enthusiasm' was seen to be disruptive. The world in which we live is very different from the Europe of the seventeenth century, but many of these issues remain in the tensions between state and church, problems of membership with respect to citizenship and religious identity, the unsettling effects of evangelical conversion, and the extent of the authority of the state over religion. It has often been argued that globalization has brought about a very different post-Westphalian system in which nation-states no longer enjoy autonomy and sovereignty, and religions have become global rather than local and national. These claims are exaggerated. As the financial and economic meltdown has demonstrated only too well, nation-states have to intervene in the functioning of a capitalist society to resolve crises that are taking place in the market. While we live in a world that is very different from that of 1648, many of our contemporary problems can be understood with ideas that we have inherited from the past.

In this study I have gone against the trend of much modern anthropology and sociology, which seek to deconstruct concepts in order to demonstrate their inescapable specificity to discrete cultures. By contrast I have treated the division between religion and politics (or more specifically church and state) as a generic division relevant to both Western and non-Western societies. Clearly the notion of 'church' cannot be easily and unambiguously applied to all religious institutions, and it may have little relevance in many Asian societies, but I have used the term generically to refer to any institutional arrangement of religious belief and practice. In a similar fashion I have used 'state' to refer to any assemblage of power existing over time and enjoying some degree of sovereignty in a territorial space. Whether a society has a 'state' is nevertheless an empirical question. Nevertheless, with the globalization of religions, these terms can be used with more confidence to describe the institutional arrangements between religion and politics outside the West. One could accept the argument that 'religion' is a product of nineteenth-century Western colonialism and still argue that 'religion' (and many adjacent concepts) is widely and commonly understood in the contemporary world. However, in this conclusion I am primarily concerned with the West, and specifically with the United States.

I have argued that the separation of church and state in the Westphalian system, while in many ways unrealistic, nevertheless created an early institutional framework for a peaceful settlement between a number of churches with incommensurable beliefs. We can call this peaceful settlement a minimal arrangement for 'tolerance'. This ecclesiastical settlement was in part a consequence of the decline of populations following the wars of religion in Europe, where princes were reluctant to lose any more citizens through continuing religious violence. Another aspect of seventeenth-century tolerance was the growing openness of societies that were engaged in long-term trade and colonization. It is often argued that the notorious tolerance of diversity in sea-ports such as Amsterdam was a consequence of international trade and exposure to other cultures. Trade relations and the quest for profits encouraged acceptance of religious differences. The drive for profit through the exploitation of the new colonies in the Americas often led to a willingness to tolerate difference. The fundamental assumptions of the Enlightenment – the primacy of the individual, contract, rationalism and tolerance – were consistent with exchange relations between strangers in the common search for profit, and the result was an indifference to cultural and religious distinctiveness (Goldmann, 1973).

A theory of tolerance appeared eventually in John Locke's 'A letter on tolerance' in 1667, giving early expression to a limited acceptance of religious differences within the British Isles, but its influence spread much further. However, it was in Massachusetts and Rhode Island that 'genuine religious liberty [was] obtained by all' (Nussbaum, 2012: 149). Roger Williams, who sailed from England for Massachusetts in 1630, was remarkable for his open approach towards religious diversity and for his respect for the dignity of the Native Americans of New England. Williams embraced a much wider and more generous understanding of religious liberty than Locke, extending tolerance to Jews, Turks and Native Americans. His publications showed an unmatched sensitivity to difference and sympathy towards indigenous peoples. He learnt the language of the Narragansett Indians, and, despite the fact that the Narragansett were a semi-nomadic people, he recognized their property rights over the land. For Nussbaum's theory of tolerance, Williams's life is an important example of the role of imagination to respect the dignity of the Other.

In the nineteenth century the publication of John Stuart Mill's essay 'On liberty' in 1859 offered a more elaborate and sophisticated defence of religious tolerance. Yet Mill (1989: 11) had to admit that, while the 'great writers' agreed that freedom of conscience was an 'indefeasible right', it was an unavoidable fact that 'religious freedom has hardly anywhere been practically realised'. In this study I have explored the various cases and places where, with reference to other values such as equality and social stability, the state intervenes to regulate religions in societies that are divided by different cultures and religious traditions. Mill (1989: 92) recognized the difficulty of reconciling freedom of religion with gender equality in his complaints about the practice of polygamy among 'Mahomedans, and Hindoos, and Chinese', and he went on, with reference to 'this Mormon institution', to assert that 'far from being countenanced by the principle of liberty, it is a direct infraction of that principle, being a mere rivetting of the chains of one half of the community, and an emancipation of the other from reciprocity of obligation towards them'. He speculated that the only reason a woman might willingly commit herself to a polygamous relationship was that she would 'prefer being one of several wives, to not being a wife at all' (Mill, 1989: 92).

In the West the same dilemmas persist, namely how to respect the demands of different cultures with different religious and legal traditions, and at the same time to recognize equality as a foundational principle of liberal democracies. Post-Enlightenment demands for respect of cultural differences appear to be too willing to give up the idea that in a secular democracy people have a right to be treated equally, and a corresponding obligation to promote egalitarianism. Secular intellectuals in demanding equality of condition may have difficulty understanding why a woman for religious reasons might willingly choose polygamy. Here is the rub – how to shore up secular equality and recognize the right of an individual to follow their conscience. The point of my sociological comparisons has been to suggest that, regardless of the philosophical issues surrounding freedom and equality, states as a matter of fact intervene to regulate religious choices in ways that do not necessarily respect the idea of a 'level playing field'; they do so in the interests of the political over the religious.

The American constitution and the management of religion

In this study I have adopted a comparative sociological approach to religion and religions. Although there are common patterns, there are also clear and important differences between the United States and the United Kingdom in terms of their institutional and constitutional arrangements. In Chapter 12 I explored differences in terms of popular religion. In this conclusion I return to the theme of liberalism and secularism by looking at significant differences in terms of freedom of conscience and state intervention into the religious arena.

What I have called 'the management of religions' creates special problems in the United States, where state involvement in religious belief and practice appears to contradict a basic principle of the constitution, namely the clear separation of church and state. This basic principle of secularization – the so-called wall between church and state – has been compromised in the United States and in many other Western societies as a consequence of the need for increased security with the growth of both international and domestic terrorism. Throughout my examples in Part II I have noted that, in problems relating to marriage, divorce and legal pluralism, questions about religious differences are in fact about the problem of Islam in Western liberal societies. Questions about tolerance, equality and women's rights inevitably involve debates about Islam rather than any other religious tradition, and so for example the crisis around multiculturalism has been in practice a crisis around Islam. In the United States the Jews as a minority were often in the past regarded with suspicion over the question of their divided loyalties, and in the twentieth century Roman Catholics were the target of public discrimination, but in the late twentieth and early twenty-first centuries it is uniformly Islam that is the topic and target of public suspicion and hostility. Thus, following the 9/11 attack most Western governments adopted more rigorous and extensive counter-radicalization programmes that were designed to address potential causes of terrorism before they could develop. These measures were often aimed at radical religious ideologies and groups. They generally sought to persuade young people not to adopt radical ideas, and set out to present a positive image of the West. The target of these programmes has typically been Muslim communities. Because these measures involved the state in managing religion, they raised difficult legal issues, especially in the United States where they ran the risk of colliding with the principles of freedom of religion in the First Amendment's Religion Clauses. It has been argued that in the United States these developments are contributing to the establishment of an 'Official Islam', namely a version of Islam compatible with the administration's view of the Good Muslim (Rascoff, 2012). The involvement of the state in shaping Islam to match American values and institutions appears to contradict the Establishment Clause. The founding legal traditions were anti-Erastian – that is, the constitution set its face sternly against the English tradition in which the monarchy has authority over the Church. Apart from the legal implications of these policy developments, what we may call 'the securitization of religion' raises important practical questions: does the state have the capacity, let alone the legitimacy, to attempt to regulate religious belief and practice, and will these interventions into private lives have a 'blow-back effect' in deepening suspicion of the intentions of secular governments?

Counter-radicalization strategies can have many different arms. They can involve foreign policy objectives, as for instance when the American government contributes foreign aid to unstable societies such as Pakistan and the Yemen with the aim of reducing youth unemployment and alleviating poverty. Of more interest to the sociology of religion are those policies that attempt to change beliefs and attitudes. These measures include: calls for the retraining of Islamic *imam*s; sending modern *imam*s from the West to inform Muslims in developing countries that the West is not hostile to 'moderate Islam'; and targeting young people thought to be at risk of radicalization with the intention of providing them with alternative ideologies that are favourable to the West. These policies are now embraced by the United States, but they are common elsewhere. In the case of Singapore, the creation of MUIS (the Muslim Council) as a government agency provides educational opportunities for Muslim leaders to study in the United States, exercises oversight of the Friday sermon, and attempts to improve the educational standards of the *madrasa*s (religious schools). In the United Kingdom early official indifference to cultural identities has, after the attacks in July 2005 on the London Underground transport system, been replaced by a more determined security strategy of surveillance and intervention. A bundle of policies known as 'Prevent' has similar aims to de-radicalize youth, to counter the radical message of Hizb ut-Tahrir and Tablighi Jamaat, and in general to identify sources of discontent that can evolve into religious radicalism. In Europe attempts to regulate the headscarf in public in France, or to control minaret building in Switzerland, or pronouncements about *shari'a* in the United Kingdom, constitute procedures by which to define the nature of citizenship and the place of Muslims in that system of rights and duties. These efforts to regulate Islam have also involved building institutions such as the French Council of Muslims and in Germany recruiting moderate Muslims to train instructors in the public schools. However, what these policies shared is what can be described as an 'upgrading' of Islam, namely achieving security and social harmony through training young Muslims to make them rational and law-abiding citizens (Kamaludeen, Periera and Turner, 2010).

One can detect similar patterns across Europe, but there are important differences between Europe and the United States. In the United

Kingdom the majority of Muslims entering Britain as a migrant labour force came from India, Pakistan and Bangladesh, and their modest educational qualifications did not provide them with skills that would give them opportunities for social mobility or high incomes in the labour market. In France Muslims came predominantly from what had been French colonies in Africa, and the presence of these North African Muslims cannot be easily detached from the history of colonial conflict in Algeria. French republicanism has required a definite commitment to secularism, which has been absent in Britain. In the United States the history of Islam cannot be separated from the history of slavery (Dannin, 2002), and in the twentieth century Islam became associated with black radicalism through the Nation of Islam and with the career of Malcolm X. Despite the historical connection with slavery and protest, Muslim communities in the United States were better educated than Muslim migrants to Europe, and they moved relatively easily into the middle class. Their assimilation was obviously challenged by the aftermath of the attack on the Twin Towers, and subsequently the demand for domestic security has brought into play a wide range of counter-terrorist strategies. Samuel Rascoff (2012) categorizes these measures as engagement, bureaucratic entrenchment and expression. The first strategy involves outreach to Muslim communities with the intention of engaging cooperatively with Muslims. The second concerns the ways in which government itself has been transformed by these counter-radicalization strategies, and the final strategy involves the processes by which the government communicates its view of Official Islam, including apparently authoritative 'pronouncements by the president's top counterterrorism adviser about what *jihad* does and does not mean in Islam' (Rascoff, 2012: 147).

These measures in the United States conflict with the Establishment Clause in several important respects. The American government has been put in the position of being (as it were) the 'official theologian' in judging what is good and bad Islamic belief, especially over such issues as *jihad*, *shari'a* and the apostasy rules. These anti-radicalization strategies also run counter to the 'endorsement test'. By endorsing a particular version of Islam, the government unintentionally and implicitly generates a perceived inequality between citizens as a consequence of their particular beliefs and practices. Rascoff argues that the critical issue is the so-called *Lemon* test, which seeks to avoid excessive government involvement or 'entanglement' with religion. The anti-Erastian views of the framers of the constitution such as Madison in colonial America and Locke in seventeenth-century England established the principle that a magistrate had no capacity to make binding pronouncements on religion, because belief was ultimately a matter of the private understanding and conscience of the citizen. The Establishment Clause was designed to prevent the government from making authoritative statements about theology that would impinge on freedom of religion. However, by attempting to transform Islam into a 'normal' religious denomination in a system of religious pluralism, the American government has become involved in the 'management of religion'. There is a more practical and pragmatic reason for believing that state intervention in the conduct of religion is problematic, namely that these interventions will be at best ineffective and at worst counter-productive. The problem is that both reformed and radicalized versions of Islam have emerged precisely in order to reject the compromises that are entailed in Official Islam.

From a sociological perspective we can interpret the management of religion as an attempt to control any eruption of charismatic leadership, and by contrast to extend the sway of legal rationality over the public conduct of religion. In Weber's terminology these regulations and interventions constitute an official wall against the eruption of any vibrant religious movement, and they have the effect of absorbing charisma into the institutions of government through the creation of official ecclesiastical institutions such as religious councils and tribunals. There is as a result an inevitable tension between religious and secular life.

Privacy and morality

Western notions of religious freedom owe a great deal to the First Amendment in American constitutional history, which famously defines the rights of the individual to believe and practise religion without let, and to enjoy freedom of association without hindrance. However, what we might call the general rights of privacy have never been absolute (Allen, 2004). Legislators and religious reformers have always been somewhat nervous about what individuals, especially morally corrupt or sinful individuals, might do in private. The moral corruption of individuals in private had always been an issue in Christian culture, but by the end of the nineteenth century new technologies such as photography were beginning to change public attitudes, which demanded more regulation. In 1890 Louis Brandeis and Samuel Warren published a famous article, 'The right to privacy', in the *Harvard Law Review* (Brandeis and Warren, 1890), in which they raised fears about how photography might invade privacy by allowing individuals to be photographed without consent and how gossip circulating in mass-produced newspapers could corrupt morality. The new technology had, they claimed, already invaded 'the sacred precincts of private and domestic life'. In the twenty-first century Facebook and Twitter have intensified such fears, and the hacking scandals around the *News of the World* in 2011–12 have led to demands for greater protection of privacy. Modern informational surveillance may be compared to a form of panoptic control in which there is a generalized overview that is neither obvious nor transparent. Modern technology has thus transformed the relationship between the private and the public, because, with modern forms of surveillance, everything is in the public domain. For example, in the scandal surrounding Dominique Strauss-Kahn's encounter with a hotel maid in New York in 2011, modern technology – electric door keys in hotels, mobile phone messages, CCT camera surveillance, Blackberry, DNA testing and other gadgetry – made it possible for detectives to calculate that the sexual encounter with the maid within the privacy of his hotel room took exactly six minutes. In a modern society almost no private action takes place outside the public domain, or at least outside the public gaze. Conducting one's religion in private has become a legal fiction.

In the United States, however, there are instances where the emphasis on individual rights in relation to freedom of speech often appears to undermine the 'wall' between church and state that was created by the founding fathers. For example, the controversial decision by the Supreme Court in the case of *Good News Club* v. *Milford Central School* 533 U.S. 98 (2001) raised controversial and troublesome issues about freedom of speech, the protection of children from indoctrination, and the separation of church and state. The Good News Club is an evangelical Christian movement that has focused much of its attention on the conversion of young schoolchildren by presenting their message in public schools. They argued that when public school principals and their boards, representing a 'limit public forum', denied them access to public schools to present their ideas, their exclusion from school premises represented a denial of freedom of speech. Their claim was upheld by Justice William Rehnquist and a majority of the Supreme Court.

Critics of this legal decision argue that the Good News Club can, as a result of the legal decision, use public school facilities to proselytize children, thereby eroding the separation of state and religion (Stewart, 2012). It is also claimed that the introduction of the Good News Club into public schools with children from diverse religious and ethnic backgrounds divides children against children and parents against parents, because the message of the Club is exclusive: only those children who strictly subscribe to the teachings of the Good News Club about salvation can go to heaven; for the rest – liberal Protestants, Roman Catholics, Jews, Buddhists, Muslims and those with no religion – there is no hope.

Conclusion: post-secularization or the breakdown of secularization?

Why is the secularization of society that was implicit in the settlement in the Treaty of Westphalia breaking down? In the West it is believed that this system is crumbling under the impact of migration, the creation of diasporic minorities, the rise of fundamentalism, the intensity of religious competition, the growth of legal pluralism and identity politics – in short, globalization. Westphalian and Protestant assumptions about private conscience and the constitutional separation of church and state no longer easily apply in a world of religious revivalism, when Hindu nationalism, Islamic *da'wa/dakwah* (renewal, return), the Christian Right, engaged Buddhism, Liberation Theology, charismatic Christianity and Pentecostal evangelism in the Third World compete for a place in the global civil society.

With the spread of various forms of radical religion, the state management of religion has become more routine and more extensive. From a historical point of view these strategies can be construed as a secularization of society, because the state regulates where and how religion can operate. However, if we take the separation of church and state as one simple (if minimal) definition of a secular society, then of course this 'entanglement' cannot be seen exactly as secularization. Entanglement is obviously not separation, but it cannot be seen as 're-sacralization' either. It is in fact compatible with Erastianism, namely the control of religion by the state in the name of civil peace and individual security. These examples support neither Jürgen Habermas's idea of a post-secular dialogue between religious and secular citizens nor John Rawls's idea of an overlapping consensus of fundamental doctrines. The notion of rational dialogue fails to address the problem that charismatic leaders may see no reason to engage in such debates, and Western societies appear to be deeply divided over 'fundamental doctrines' in which there are no solutions or agreements on the horizon.

As we saw in Chapter 3, political philosophers such as Seyla Benhabib have argued that modern citizenship needs to be disaggregated, and in the same chapter I suggested that the modern citizen is merely a denizen. The ties that bind citizens together and the bonds that hold congregations together have been eroded, and with a general sense of insecurity individuals have turned towards gated communities, privatized security and the construction of enclave societies. Societies have become less cohesive and sticky, and more fractured and elastic. Many of these changes have their origins in the conservative revolution of the 1970s with its emphasis on individual responsibility, the market, small government and so forth. Although in many ways the Reagan era was one of optimism and confidence, the current period is one of uncertainty and pessimism. The state's regulation of religion, especially of Islam, is a function of this sense of insecurity. Without common citizenship there can be little hope for consensus or security.

References

Akay, Hale 2011. 'Uygulamada Laiklik: Devlet-Din Ekseninde Özgürlükler, Hizmetler ve Finansman', *Toplum ve Bilim* **120**: 10–47.

Akbarzadeh, Shahram (ed.) 2010. *Challenging identities: Muslim women in Australia*. Melbourne: Melbourne University Press.

Allen, Anita L. 2004. 'Privacy in American law', in Beate Rossler (ed.), *Privacies: philosophical evaluations*. Stanford: Stanford University Press, pp. 40–51.

Amstutz, Galen 1997. *Interpreting Amida: history and Orientalism in the study of Pure Land Buddhism*. Albany: State University of New York Press.

An-Na'im, Abdullahi A. 2008. *Islam and the secular state: negotiating the future of Shari'a*. Cambridge, MA: Harvard University Press.

Anderson, Perry 1964. 'Origins of the present crisis', *New Left Review* **23**: 27–53.

Arkoun, Mohammed 2002. *The unthought in contemporary Islamic thought*. London: Saqi.

Asad, Talal 1993. *Genealogies of religion: disciplines and reasons of power in Christianity and Islam*. Baltimore: Johns Hopkins University Press.

1996. 'Comments on conversion', in Peter van der Veer (ed.), *Conversion to modernities: the globalization of Christianity*. New York and London: Routledge, pp. 263–74.

2003. *Formations of the secular: Christianity, Islam, modernity*. Stanford: Stanford University Press.

Ashiwa, Yoshiko and Wank, David L. (eds.) 2009. *Making religion, making the state: the politics of religion in modern China*. Stanford: Stanford University Press.

Badiou, Alain 1982. *Theorie du suject*. Paris: Seuil.

2003. *Saint Paul: the foundation of universalism*. Trans. Ray Brassier. Stanford: Stanford University Press.

Baer, Marc David 2010. *The Donme: Jewish converts, Muslim revolutionaries and secular Turks*. Stanford: Stanford University Press.

Bagehot, Walter 2009. *The English constitution*. Project Gutenberg Ebook. Online: www.gutenberg.org/files/4351/4351-h/4351-h.htm, accessed 11 May 2011.

Bailey, Edward 1997. *Implicit religion in contemporary society.* Leiden: Kok Pharos Publishing House.

Balakrishnan, Gopal 2000. *The enemy: an intellectual portrait of Carl Schmitt.* London: Verso.

Barbalet, Jack, Possamai, Adam and Turner, Bryan S. (eds.) 2011. *Religion and the state: a comparative sociology.* London: Anthem.

Bardakoğlu, Ali 2004. '"Moderate perception of Islam" and the Turkish model of the Diyanet: the president's statement', *Journal of Muslim Minority Affairs* **24** (2): 367–74.

Barnett, Correlli 2001. *The audit of war.* London: Pan.

Barry, Brian M. 2001. *Culture and equality: an egalitarian critique of multiculturalism.* Cambridge, MA: Harvard University Press.

Bauman, Zygmunt 2000. *Liquid modernity.* Cambridge: Polity Press.

Beasley, W. G. 1973. *The Meiji Restoration.* Stanford: Stanford University Press.

Beck, Ulrich 2000. 'The cosmopolitan perspective: sociology in the second age of modernity', *British Journal of Sociology* **51** (1): 79–105.

Bell, Daniel 1976. *The cultural contradictions of capitalism.* New York: Basic Books.

Bell, Daniel A. 2008. *China's new Confucianism: politics and everyday life in a changing society.* Princeton: Princeton University Press.

Bell, Daniel A. and Chaibong, H. (eds.) 2003. *Confucianism for the modern world.* Cambridge: Cambridge University Press.

Bellah, Robert N. 1957. *Tokugawa religion: the values of pre-industrial Japan.* Glencoe, IL: Free Press.

  1963. 'Reflections on the Protestant Ethic analogy in Asia', *Journal of Social Issues* **19**: 52–60.

  1967. 'Civil religion in America', *Daedalus* **96** (Winter): 1–27.

  1978. 'Religion and legitimation in the American republic', *Society* **15**: 16–23.

  1999. 'Max Weber and world-denying love', *Journal of the Academy of Religion* **67** (2): 277–304 (reprinted in Robert N. Bellah and Steven M. Tipton (eds.), *The Robert Bellah reader.* Durham, NC, and London: Duke University Press, pp. 123–49).

  2003. *Imagining Japan: the Japanese tradition and its modern interpretation.* Berkeley: University of California Press.

  2006. 'God and king', in Robert N. Bellah and Steven M. Tipton (eds.), *The Robert Bellah reader.* Durham, NC, and London: Duke University Press, pp. 357–79.

  2011. *Religion in human evolution: from the paleolithic to the axial age.* Cambridge, MA: Belknap Press of Harvard University Press.

Bellah, Robert N. and Tipton, Steven M. (eds.) 2006. *The Robert Bellah reader.* Durham, NC, and London: Duke University Press.

Benhabib, Seyla 2004. *The rights of others: aliens, residents and citizens.* Cambridge: Cambridge University Press.

Berkes, Niyazi 1998. *The development of secularism in Turkey.* London: Hurst.

Berndt, R. M. and Berndt, C. H. 1989. *The speaking land: myth and story in Aboriginal Australia.* Ringwood: Penguin.

Berwick, Andrew [Anders Behring Breivik] 2011. *2083: a European declaration of independence.* London: n.p.

Beveridge, William 1942. *Social insurance and allied services.* London: His Majesty's Stationery Office.

Bix, Herbert P. 2000. *Hirohito and the making of modern Japan.* New York: HarperCollins.

Blackburn, Susan 2000. *Women and the state in modern Indonesia.* Cambridge: Cambridge University Press.

Bostrom, Nick 2005. 'In defence of posthuman dignity', *Bioethics* **19** (3): 202–14.

Bourdieu, Pierre 1987. 'Legitimation and structured interest in Weber's sociology of religion', in Scott Lash and Sam Whimster (eds.), *Max Weber, rationality and modernity.* Trans. Chris Turner. London: Allen & Unwin, pp. 119–36.

  1990. *The logic of practice.* Cambridge: Polity Press.

  2000. 'Mit Weber gegen Weber: Pierre Bourdieu im Gespräch', in Franz Schultheis, Andreas Pfeuffer and Stephan Egger (eds.), *Pierre Bourdieu, Das religiöse Feld: Texte zur Ökonomie des Heilsgeschehens.* Trans. Stephan Egger. Konstanz: Universitätsverlag Konstanz, pp. 111–29.

Bourdieu, Pierre and Wacquant, Loic J. D. 1992. *An invitation to reflexive sociology.* Chicago: University of Chicago Press.

Brandeis, Louis and Warren, Samuel 1890. 'The right to privacy', *Harvard Law Review* **4** (5): n.p.

Bronkhorst, Johannes 2011. *Buddhism in the shadow of Brahmanism.* Leiden: Brill.

Brown, Lisa Beljuli 2011. *Body parts on Planet Slum: women and telenovelas in Brazil.* London: Anthem.

Brown, Peter 1964. 'St. Augustine's attitude to religious coercion', *Journal of Roman Studies* **54**: 107–16.

  1989. *The body and society: men, women and sexual renunciation in early Christianity.* London: Faber & Faber.

  2000. *Augustine of Hippo: a biography.* Berkeley and Los Angeles: University of California Press.

Browning, Don S. and Clairmont, David A. (eds.) 2006. *American religions and the family: how faith traditions cope with modernization and democracy.* New York: Columbia University Press.

Burke, Edmund 1955. *Reflections on the Revolution in France*. New York: Liberal Arts Press.

Burns, John F. 2011. 'This tarnished crown', *New York Times*, 24 April, pp. 1, 5.

Caldwell, John C. and Caldwell, Pat 1986. *Limiting population growth, and the Ford Foundation contribution*. London: Frances Pinter.

Carroll, Michael 1989. *Catholic cults and devotions: a psychological inquiry*. Montreal: McGill-Queen's University Press.

Chang, Kyung-Sup 2010. *South Korea under compressed modernity: familial political economy in transition*. London and New York: Routledge.

Çıtak, Zana 2010. 'Between "Turkish Islam" and "French Islam": the role of the Diyanet in the Conseil Francais du Culte Musulman', *Journal of Ethnic and Migration Studies* 36 (4): 619–34.

Clammer, John 2000. 'Received dreams: consumer capitalism, social process and the management of emotions in Japan', in J. S. Eades, Tom Gill and Harumi Befu (eds.), *Globalization and social change in contemporary Japan*. Melbourne: Trans Pacific Press, pp. 203–23.

Connolly, William E. 2008. *Capitalism and Christianity, American style*. Durham, NC, and London: Duke University Press.

Conrad, Dieter 1986. 'Max Weber's conception of Hindu dharma as a paradigm', in Detlef Kantowsky (ed.), *Recent research on Max Weber's studies of Hinduism*. Munich: Weltforum, pp. 169–92.

Crapanzano, Vincent 1973. *The Hamadsha: a study of Moroccan ethnopsychiatry*. Berkeley: University of California Press.

Crick, Bernard 1962. *In defence of politics*. Chicago: University of Chicago Press.

Dahlgren, Susanne 2012. '"She brings up healthy children for the homeland": morality discourses in Yemeni legal debates', in Maaike Voorhoeve (ed.), *Family law in Islam: divorce, marriage and women in the Muslim world*. London: I. B. Tauris, pp. 13–30.

Dale, Peter N. 1986. *The myth of Japanese uniqueness*. London: Croom Helm.

Dannin, Robert 2002. *Black pilgrimage to Islam*. Oxford: Oxford University Press.

Davidoff, Leonore 1973. *The best circles*. London: Cresset Library.

Davie, Grace 1994. *Religion in Britain since 1945: believing without belonging*. Oxford: Blackwell.

Davis, Winston 1989. 'Buddhism and the modernization of Japan', *History of Religions* 28 (4): 304–39.

de Grey, Aubrey (with Michael Rae) 2008. *Ending aging: the rejuvenation breakthroughs that could reverse human aging in our lifetime*. London: St Martin's Press.

de Sousa Santos, B. 1995. *Toward a new common sense: law, science and politics in paradigmatic transition.* New York: Routledge.

de Tocqueville, Alexis 2004 [1834 and 1840]. *Democracy in America.* New York: Library of America.

Delanty, Gerard 2009. *The cosmopolitan imagination: the renewal of critical theory.* Cambridge: Cambridge University Press.

Derrida, Jacques 2000. 'Foreigner question', in *Of hospitality.* Stanford: Stanford University Press, pp. 3–73.

Diessenbacher, Hartmut 1998. *Kriege der Zukunft: die Bevolkerungsexplosion gefahrdet den Frieden.* Munich: Hanser.

Drexler, Eric 1986. *Engines of creation: the coming era of nanotechnology.* New York: Doubleday.

Durkheim, Émile 2001. *The elementary forms of religious life.* Oxford: Oxford University Press.

Duus, Peter 1998. *Modern Japan* (2nd edn). Boston: Houghton Mifflin.

Einstein, Mara 2008. *Brands of faith: marketing religion in a commercial age.* London: Routledge.

Eisenstadt, Shmuel N. (ed.) 1986. *The origins and diversity of axial age civilizations.* Albany: State University of New York Press.

　1996. *Japanese civilization: a comparative view.* Chicago: University of Chicago Press.

Eliade, Mircea 1964. *Shamanism: archaic techniques of ecstasy.* New York: Ballingen Foundation.

Elias, Norbert 2000. *The civilizing process.* Oxford: Blackwell.

Elliott, Anthony and Turner, Bryan S. 2012. *On society.* Cambridge: Polity Press.

Engel, Matthew 2011. 'Kate expectations', *Financial Times*, 22 April, pp. 1–2.

Estin, Ann Laquer 2004. 'Embracing tradition: pluralism in American family law', *Maryland Law Review* 63: 540–604.

Ferguson, Niall 2012. *Civilization: the West and the rest.* New York: Penguin Press.

Fingarette, Herbert 1972. *Confucius: the secular as sacred.* Prospect Heights, IL: Waveland Press.

Finley, Moses I. 1983. *Politics in the ancient world.* Cambridge: Cambridge University Press.

Foucault, Michel 1977. *Discipline and punish: the birth of the prison.* London: Tavistock.

Fowler, Bridget 2011. 'Pierre Bourdieu: unorthodox Marxist?', in Simon Susen and Bryan S. Turner (eds.), *The legacy of Pierre Bourdieu: critical essays.* London: Anthem Press, pp. 33–58.

Frank, Andre Gunder 1998. *ReOrient: global economy in the Asian age.* Berkeley: University of California Press.

Fredriksen, Paula 2008. *Augustine and the Jews*. New York: Doubleday.

Friedlander, Saul 1997. *Nazi Germany and the Jews*. New York: HarperCollins.

Fujita, Yuiko 2009. *Cultural migrants from Japan: youth, media and migration in New York and Tokyo*. Lanham, MD: Lexington Books.

Fulsom, Don 2012. *Nixon's darkest secrets: the inside story of America's most troubled president*. New York: St. Martin's Press.

Gager, John G. 2000. *Reinventing Paul*. Oxford: Oxford University Press.

Gellner, Ernest 1969. *Saints of the Atlas*. London: Weidenfeld & Nicolson.
   1982. *Muslim society*. Cambridge: Cambridge University Press.

Gerth, Hans and Mills, C. Wright (eds.) 2009. *From Max Weber: essays in sociology*. London: Routledge.

Gibbon, Edward 2005. *The decline and fall of the Roman Empire*. New York: The Modern Library.

Gokhale, Balkrishna 1966. 'Early Buddhist kingship', *Journal of Asian Studies* **26**: 23–36.

Goldmann, Lucien 1973. *The philosophy of the Enlightenment*. London: Routledge.

Gombrich, Richard 1996. *How Buddhism began: the conditioned genesis of the early teachings*. London: Athlone.

Goodman, Roger, Peach, Ceri, Takenaka, Ayumi and White, Paul (eds.) 2003. *Global Japan: the experience of Japan's new immigrants and overseas communities*. London: Routledge/Curzon.

Gözaydın, İştar 2008. 'Diyanet and politics', *Muslim World* **98**, 2(3): 216–27.
   2009. *Diyanet: Türkiye Cumhuriyeti'nde Dinin Tanzimi*. Istanbul: İletişim Yayınları.

Grubb, Judith Evans 1995. *Law and family in late antiquity*. Oxford: Oxford University Press.

Gutman, David 1973. 'The subjective politics of power: The dilemma of the post-superego man', *Social Research* **40**: 570–616.

Habermas, Jürgen 1996. *Between facts and norms: contributions to a discourse theory of law and democracy*. Cambridge: Polity Press.
   2006. 'Religion in the public sphere', *European Journal of Philosophy* **14** (1): 1–25.
   2008. *Between naturalism and religion*. Cambridge: Polity Press.

Haddad, Yvonne Yazbeck and Smith, Jane I. (eds.) 2002. *Muslim minorities in the West*. Walnut Creek, CA: AltaMira.

Hafez, Sherine 2011. *An Islam of her own: reconsidering religion and secularism in women's Islamic movements*. New York and London: New York University Press.

Hall, John A. 2011. *Ernest Gellner: an intellectual biography*. London and New York: Verso.

Hart, H. L. A. 1961. *The concept of law*. Oxford: Clarendon Press.

Hassan, Mona 2011. 'Women preaching for the secular state: official female preachers (bayan vaizler) in contemporary Turkey', *International Journal of Middle East Studies* **43**: 451–73.

Hastings, Max 2012. 'Long may she reign – with dignity and endearing dullness', *Financial Times*, 2 June, p. 9.

Hayden, Ilse 1987. *Symbol and privilege: the ritual context of British royalty*. Tucson: University of Arizona Press.

Hefner, Robert (ed.) 1993. *Conversion to Christianity: historical and anthropological perspectives on a great transformation*. Berkeley: University of California Press.

Hegel, Georg Wilhelm Friedrich 1956. *The philosophy of history*. New York: Dover.

Hennis, Wilhelm 1988. *Max Weber: essays in reconstruction*. London: Allen & Unwin.

Hervieu-Léger, Danièle 2000. *Religion as a chain of memory*. Cambridge: Polity Press.

Hiatt, L. R. 1997. 'A new age for old people', *Quadrant*, June: 35–40.

Hildburgh, W. L. 1955. 'Images of the human hand as amulets in Spain', *Journal of the Cortauld and Warburg Institute* 18 (1/2): 67–89.

Hirschman, Albert O. 1970. *Exit, voice and loyalty: responses to decline in firms, organizations and states*. Cambridge, MA: Harvard University Press.

Holton, Robert J. 2009. *Cosmopolitans: new thinking and new directions*. Basingstoke: Palgrave Macmillan.

Howard, Thomas Albert 2011. *God and the Atlantic: America, Europe and the religious divide*. Oxford: Oxford University Press.

Hunt, Stephen 2005. *Religion and everyday life*. London: Routledge.

Huntington, Samuel P. 1993. 'The clash of civilizations', *Foreign Affairs* **72** (3): 22–48.

   1997. *The clash of civilizations: remaking of world order*. New York: Touchstone.

Itoh, Mayumi 1995. *Globalization of Japan: Japanese sakoku mentality and US efforts to open Japan*. New York: St. Martin's Press.

Jacobson, Cardell K. and Burton, Lara (eds.) 2011. *Modern polygamy in the United States: historical, cultural and legal issues*. Oxford: Oxford University Press.

Jacques, Martin 2009. *When China rules the world: the end of the Western world and the birth of a new global order*. New York: Penguin Press.

James, William 1929 [1902]. *The varieties of religious experience: a study of human nature* (37th impression). London: Longmans, Green & Company.

Jansen, Marius B. 2000. *The making of modern Japan*. Cambridge, MA: Belknap Press of Harvard University Press.

Jaspers, Karl 1953. *The origin and goal of history*. London: Routledge & Kegan Paul.

Jellinek, Georg 2009 [1904]. *The declaration of the rights of man and of citizens*. Lexington: World Library Classics.

Jones, Henry Ford 1898. *The rise and growth of American politics*. New York: The Macmillan Company.

Joppke, Christian 2004. 'The retreat from multiculturalism in the liberal state: theory and practice', *British Journal of Sociology* 55 (2): 237–57.

Joseph, Suad (ed.) 2000. *Gender and citizenship in the Middle East*. Syracuse, NY: Syracuse University Press.

Judt, Tony 2005. *Postwar: a history of Europe since 1945*. New York: Penguin.
2010. *Ill fares the land*. New York: Penguin.

Juvin, Herve 2010. *The coming of the body*. London: Verso.

Kadıoğlu, Ayşe 2010. 'The pathologies of Turkish republican laicism', *Philosophy and Social Criticism* 36 (3–4): 489–504.

Kamaludeen, Mohamed Nasir, Pereira, Alexius A. and Turner, Bryan S. 2010. *Muslims in Singapore: piety, politics and policies*. New York: Routledge.

Kantorowitz, Ernst H. 1957. *The king's two bodies: a study in mediaeval political theology*. Princeton: Princeton University Press.

Keane, Webb 2007. *Christian moderns: freedom and fetish in the mission encounter*. Berkeley: University of California Press.

Keister, Lisa A. 2011. *Faith and money: how religion contributes to wealth and poverty*. Cambridge: Cambridge University Press.

Keith, Ronald C. and Lin, Zhiqiu 2006. *New crime in China: public order and human rights*. Routledge Contemporary China Series. London and New York: Routledge.

Keyes, Charles F. 1971. 'Buddhism and national integration in Thailand', *Journal of Asian Studies* 30: 551–68.
1976. 'Millenialism, Theravada Buddhism and Thai society', *Journal of Asian Studies* 36: 283–303.

Kissinger, Henry 2011. *On China*. New York: Penguin.

Kruger, Steven F. 2006. *The spectral Jew: conversion and embodiment in medieval Europe*. Minneapolis: University of Minnesota Press.

Kuru, Ahmet 2009. *Secularism and state policies toward religion: the United States, France, and Turkey*. Cambridge: Cambridge University Press.

Kymlicka, Will 1995. *Multicultural citizenship: a liberal theory of minority rights*. Oxford: Oxford University Press.
2009. 'The multicultural welfare state?', in Peter Hall and Michele Lamont (eds.), *Successful societies: how institutions and culture affect health*. Cambridge: Cambridge University Press, pp. 226–53.

Lammy, David 2012. *Out of the ashes: Britain after the riots*. London: Guardian Books.

Larsson, G. 2009. *Islam in the Nordic and Baltic countries*. London: Routledge.

Lassman, Paul and Velody, Irving (with Herminio Martins) (eds.) 1989. *Max Weber's 'science as a vocation'*. London: Unwin Hyman.

Lassman, Peter 2000. 'The rule of man over man: politics, power and legitimation', in Stephen Turner (ed.), *The Cambridge companion to Weber*. Cambridge: Cambridge University Press, pp. 83–98.

Lehmann, David 1996. *The struggle for the spirit: religious transformation and popular culture in Brazil and Latin America*. Cambridge: Polity Press.

Letki, Natalia 2008. 'Does diversity erode social cohesion? Social capital and race in British neighbourhoods', *Political Studies* 56: 99–126.

Levy, Jacob 2000. *The multiculturalism of fear*. Oxford: Oxford University Press.

Lindholm, Charles 1990. *Charisma*. Oxford: Basil Blackwell.

Locke, John 1946. *The second treatise of government and a letter concerning toleration*. Oxford: Basil Blackwell.

Love, John 2000. 'Max Weber's Orient', in Stephen Turner (ed.), *The Cambridge companion to Weber*. Cambridge: Cambridge University Press, pp. 172–99.

Luce, Henry R. 1941. 'The American century', *Life*, 17 February.

Luckmann, Thomas 1967. *The invisible religion: the problem of religion in modern society*. London: Macmillan.

Luzzatto, Sergio 2005. *The body of Il Duce: Mussolini's corpse and the fortunes of Italy*. New York: Metropolitan Books/Henry Holt & Company.

2010. *Padre Pio: miracles and politics in a secular age*. New York: Metropolitan Books/Henry Holt & Company.

MacInnes, John and Diaz, Julio Perez 2009. 'The reproductive revolution', *The Sociological Review* 57 (2): 262–84.

Manby, Bronwen 2009. *Struggles for citizenship in Africa*. London and New York: Zed Books.

Marable, Manning 2011. *Malcolm X: a life of reinvention*. New York: Viking.

Mardin, Şerif 2006. *Religion, society, and modernity in Turkey*. New York: Syracuse University Press.

2011. *Türkiye, İslam ve Sekülarizm*. Istanbul: İletişim Yayınları.

Maritain, Jacques 1958. *Reflections on America*. New York: Charles Scribner's Sons.

1968. *Integral humanism: temporal and spiritual problems of a new Christendom*. New York: Charles Scribner's Sons.

1986a. *Christianity and democracy*. San Francisco: Ignatius Press.

1986b. *Rights of man and natural law*. San Francisco: Ignatius Press.

Marsden, Richard 2003. 'Catholic revival during the reform era', *China Quarterly* 174 (2): 471.

Marshall, Thomas H. 1950. *Citizenship and social class and other essays*. Cambridge: Cambridge University Press.

Marzouki, Nadia 2012. 'Conversion as statelessness: a study of contemporary Algerian conversions to evangelical Christianity', *Middle East Law and Governance* 4: 69–105.

Maung Maung, U. 1991. *Burmese nationalist movements 1940–1948*. Honolulu: University of Hawaii Press.

Mauss, Marcel 1976 [1924]. *The gift*. New York: Norton.

Mayer, Jacob Peter 1998 [1944]. *Max Weber and German politics: a study in political sociology*. London: Faber & Faber.

McLain, Linda C. 2010. 'Marriage pluralism in the United States: on civil and religious jurisdiction and the demands of equal citizenship', *Boston University School of Law Working Paper* No. 10–14.

Mead, Kullada Kesboonchoo 2004. *The rise and decline of Thai absolutism*. New York: RoutledgeCurzon.

Meier, Heinrich 1995. *Carl Schmitt and Leo Strauss*. Chicago and London: University of Chicago Press.

Meyer, Eduard 1912. *Ursprung und Geschichte der Mormonen: mit Exkursen über die Anfange des Islams und Christentums*. Darmstadt: Wissenschaftliche Buchgesellschaft.
 1978 [1884]. *Geschichte des Altertums* (8th edn). Darmstadt: Wissenschaftliche Buchgesellschaft.

Michels, Robert 1962 [1911]. *Political parties: a sociological study of oligarchical tendencies in modern democracy*. New York: Free Press.

Mill, John Stuart 1989. *On liberty and other writings*. Cambridge: Cambridge University Press.

Mills, C. Wright 1959. *The sociological imagination*. New York: Oxford University Press.

Molesworth, William 1839. *The English works of Thomas Hobbes, vol. III (Leviathan)*. London: Longman, Brown, Green & Longmans.

Mommsen, Wolfgang 1984. *Max Weber and German politics 1890–1920*. Chicago: University of Chicago Press.

Moyn, Samuel 2010. *The last utopia: human rights in history*. Cambridge, MA: Belknap Press of Harvard University Press.

Münkler, Herfried 2005. *The new wars*. Cambridge: Polity.

Nairn, Tom 1977. *The break-up of Britain: crisis and neonationalism*. London: Radius.
 1994. *The enchanted glass: Britain and its monarchy* (2nd edn). London: Vintage.
 2000a. *After Britain: New Labour and the return of Scotland*. London: Granta Books.
 2000b. 'Ukania under Blair', *New Left Review* January–February: 69–103 (new series).

2002. *Pariah: misfortunes of the British kingdom*. London and New York: Verso.

Narayanan, Vasudha 2005. 'Hinduism', in Michel H. Coogan (ed.), *Eastern religions*. London: Duncan Baird Publishers, pp. 15–109.

Nedostup, Rebecca 2010. *Superstitious regimes and the politics of Chinese modernity*. Cambridge, MA: Harvard University Press.

Neustadt, Richard E. 1990. *Presidential power and the modern presidents*. New York: The Free Press.

Nichols, Joel A. 2007. 'Multi-tiered marriage: ideas and influences from New York and Louisiana to the international community', *Vanderbilt Journal of Transnational Law* 40 (January): 135–96.

Nisbet, Robert 1975. *Twilight of authority*. New York: Oxford University Press.

1986. *The making of modern society*. New York: New York University Press.

1990 [1953]. *The quest for community: a study in the ethics of order and freedom*. San Francisco: ICS Press.

Nussbaum, Martha C. 2012. *The new religious intolerance: overcoming the politics of fear in an anxious age*. Cambridge, MA: Belknap Press of Harvard University Press.

O'Connell, Robert 1969. *St. Augustine's confessions: the odyssey of a soul*. Cambridge, MA: Belknap Press of Harvard University Press.

O'Donnell, James J. 2001. 'Augustine: his time and lives', in Eleonore Stump and Norman Kretzmann (eds.), *The Cambridge companion to Augustine*. Cambridge: Cambridge University Press, pp. 8–25.

Offe, Claus 2005. *Reflections on America: Tocqueville, Weber and Adorno in the United States*. Cambridge: Polity Press.

Offenbacher, Martin 1900. *Konfession und soziale Schichtung: eine Studie uber die wirtschaftliche Lage der Katholiken und Protestanten in Baden*. Tübingen and Leipzig: Verlag von J. C. B. Mohr (Paul Siebeck).

Ogawa, Akihiro 2009. *The failure of civil society? The third sector and the state in contemporary Japan*. Albany: State University of New York Press.

Omri, Elisha 2011. *Moral ambition: mobilization and social outreach in evangelical megachurches*. Berkeley: University of California Press.

Ong, Aihwa 1999. *Flexible citizenship: the cultural logics of transnationality*. Durham, NC: Duke University Press.

2008. 'Please stay: pied a terre subjects in the megacity', in Engin Isin, Pedter Nyers and Bryan S. Turner (eds.), *Citizenship between past and future*. London: Routledge, pp. 81–91.

Orwell, George 1989 [1937]. *The road to Wigan Pier*. London: Penguin Books.

Özcan, Yusuf Ziya 1990. 'Ülkemizdeki Cami Sayıları Üzerine Sayısal Bir İnceleme', *İslami Araştırmalar Dergisi* 4 (1): 5–20.

Pak, Katherine Tegtmeyer 2000. 'Foreigners are local citizens too: local governments respond to international migration in Japan', in Mike Douglass and Glenda Susan Roberts (eds.), *Japan and global migration: foreign workers and the advent of a multicultural society*. London and New York: Routledge, pp. 243–74.

Parla, Taha and Davison, Andrew 2008. 'Secularism and laicism in Turkey', in Andrew Davison, Janet R. Jacobsen and Ann Pellegrini (eds.), *Secularisms (a social textbook)*. Durham, NC: Duke University Press.

Parsons, Talcott 1951. *The social system*. New York: The Free Press.

 1974. 'Religion in postindustrial America: the problem of secularization', *Social Research* **51** (1–2): 193–225.

Parsons, Talcott and Shils, Edward (eds.) 1951. *Toward a general theory of action*. Cambridge, MA: Harvard University Press.

Pateman, Carol 1988. *The sexual contract*. Stanford: Stanford University Press.

Perkins, Franklin 2004. *Leibniz and China: a commerce of light*. Cambridge: Cambridge University Press.

Pimlott, Ben 2001. *The Queen: Elizabeth II and the monarchy*. London: HarperCollins.

Pinker, Stephen 2011. *The better angels of our nature: why violence has declined*. New York: Viking.

Possamai, Adam (ed.) 2012. *Handbook of hyper-real religions*. Leiden: Brill.

Pound, Roscoe 1966. *An introduction to the philosophy of law*. New Haven and London: Yale University Press.

Pufendorf, Samuel 2002. *Of the nature and qualification of religion in reference to civil society*. Indianapolis: Liberty Fund.

Radkau, Joachim 2009. *Max Weber: a biography*. Cambridge: Polity Press.

Rascoff, Samuel J. 2012. 'Establishing official Islam? The law and strategy of counter-radicalization', *Stanford Law Review* **64** (1): 125–89.

Rawls, John 1933. *Political liberalism*. New York: Columbia University Press.

 1999. *The law of peoples*. Cambridge, MA: Harvard University Press.

Reitan, Richard M. 2010. *Making a moral society: ethics and the state in Meiji Japan*. Honolulu: University of Hawaii Press.

Rex, John 1961. *Key problems of sociological theory*. London: Routledge & Kegan Paul.

Rey, Terry 2007. *Bourdieu on religion: imposing faith and legitimacy*. London: Equinox.

Ricoeur, Paul and MacIntyre, Alasdair 1969. *The religious significance of atheism*. New York: Columbia University Press.

Roberts, Keith A. and Yamane, D. 2012. *Religion in sociological perspective* (5th edn). Los Angeles: Sage.

Robertson, Roland 1982. 'Societies, individuals and sociology: intra-civilizational themes', *Theory, Culture and Society* **1** (2): 6–17.

1992. *Globalization: social theory and global culture*. London: Sage.

Robertson, Roland (with J. Chirico) 1985. 'Humanity, globalization and worldwide religious resurgence', *Sociological Analysis* **46** (3): 219–42.

Robinson, Kathryn 2009. *Gender, Islam and democracy in Indonesia*. London and New York: Routledge.

Roth, Günther 1975. 'Socio-historical model and developmental theory: charismatic community, charisma of reason, and the counter culture', *American Sociological Review* **40** (2): 148–57.

Roth, Joshua Hotaka 2002. *Brokered homeland: Japanese Brazilian migrants in Japan*. Ithaca: Cornell University Press.

Rousseau, Jean-Jacques 1956. *The creed of a priest of Savoy*. New York: Frederick Ungar Publishing Company.

1973. *The social contract and discourses*. London: Dent.

Rubin, Miri 2009. *Mother of God: a history of the Virgin Mary*. New Haven and London: Yale University Press.

Ruether, Rosemary Radford (ed.) 1974. *Religion and sexism*. New York: Simon & Schuster.

Sadiq, Kamal 2009. *Paper citizens: how illegal immigrants acquire citizenship in developing countries*. New York: Oxford University Press.

Said, Edward W. 1978. *Orientalism*. New York: Pantheon.

Sawada, Janine 2004. *Practical pursuits: religion, politics and personal cultivation in nineteenth-century Japan*. Honolulu: University of Hawaii Press.

Saxonhouse, Arlene W. 1992. *Fear of diversity: the birth of political science in ancient Greek thought*. Chicago and London: University of Chicago Press.

Schama, Simon 2011. 'Dynastic lessons from the familiar Windsor flourish', *Financial Times*, 30 April/1 May, p. 7.

Schluchter, Wolfgang (ed.) 1984. *Max Webers Studie uber Konfuzianismus und Taoismus*. Frankfurt am Main: Suhrkamp.

Schmitt, Carl 1985 [1922]. *Political theology: four chapters on the concept of sovereignty*. Cambridge, MA: MIT Press.

1996. *The concept of the political*. Chicago and London: University of Chicago Press.

2004 [1932]. *Legality and legitimacy*. Durham, NC: Duke University Press.

Scholem, Gershom 1977. *Sabbatai Sevi: the mystical messiah*. Princeton: Princeton University Press.

Schwarz, Carolyn and Dussart, Françoise 2010. 'Christianity in Aboriginal Australia revisited', *The Australian Journal of Anthropology* **21**: 1–13.

Shankland, David 2003. *The Alevis in Turkey: the emergence of a secular Islamic tradition*. London and New York: RoutledgeCurzon.

Shils, Edward 1987. 'Max Weber and the world since 1920', in Wolfgang J. Mommsen and Jurgen Osterhammel (eds.), *Max Weber and his contemporaries*. London: Unwin Hyman, pp. 547–73.

   2006. *A fragment of a sociological autobiography: the history of my pursuit of a few ideas*. New Brunswick: Transaction Books.

Shils, Edward A. and Young, Michael 1953. 'The meaning of the Coronation', *The Sociological Review* 3: 63–81 (reprinted in Edward A. Shils 1975. *Center and periphery*. Chicago: University of Chicago Press).

Silber, Ilana Friedrich 1995. *Virtuosity, charisma and social order: a comparative sociological study of monasticism in Theravada Buddhism and medieval Catholicism*. Cambridge: Cambridge University Press.

Smith, Brian K. 1994. *Classifying the universe: the ancient Indian varna system and the origins of caste*. New York: Oxford University Press.

Smith, William Robertson 1997. *Lectures on the religion of the Semites*. London: Routledge.

Spaht, Katherine Shaw 1998. 'Louisiana's covenant marriage: social analysis and legal implications', *Louisiana Law Review* 59 (Fall): 63–160.

Spinner-Halevy, Jeff 2005. 'Hinduism, Christianity and liberal religious tolerance', *Political Theory* 33 (1): 28–57.

Srinivas, Mysore Narasimhachar 1989. *The cohesive role of Sanskritization*. Delhi: Oxford University Press.

Stark, Rodney and Finke, Roger 2000. *Acts of faith: explaining the human side of religion*. Berkeley and Los Angeles: University of California Press.

Stauth, Georg and Turner, Bryan S. 1986. 'Nietzsche in Weber oder die Geburt des modernen Genius im professionellen Menschen', *Zeitschrift für Soziologie* 15 (2): 81–94.

Stephens, Philip 2011. 'Confessions of a lapsed Republican', *Financial Times*, 29 April, p. 9.

Sternheimer, Karen 2011. *Celebrity culture and the American dream: stardom and social mobility*. New York: Routledge.

Stewart, Katherine 2012. *The Good News Club: the Christian right's assault on America's children*. Philadelphia: Public Affairs.

Strabac, Zan and Listhaug, Ola 2008. 'Anti-Muslim prejudice in Europe: a multilevel analysis of survey data from 30 countries', *Social Science Research* 37 (1): 268–86.

Strauss, Leo 1952. *The political philosophy of Hobbes: its basis and its genesis*. Chicago: University of Chicago Press.

   1965. *Spinoza's critique of religion*. New York: Schocken.

Sugimoto, Yoshio 2010. *Introduction to Japanese culture*. Cambridge: Cambridge University Press.

Sutton, Peter 2010. 'Aboriginal spirituality in a new age', *The Australian Journal of Anthropology* 21: 71–89.

Tabuchi, Hiroko 2012. 'Educated, but not fitting in', *New York Times Business Day*, 30 May, pp. B1–B2.

Tamanaha, Brian Z. 1997. *Realistic socio-legal theory: pragmatism and a social theory of law*. Oxford: Clarendon Press.

2008. 'Understanding legal pluralism: past to present, local to global', *Sydney Law Review* 30: 375–411.

Tambiah, Stanley J. 1976. *World conqueror and world renouncer: a study of Buddhism and polity in Thailand against a historical background*. Cambridge: Cambridge University Press.

Tanguay, Daniel 2007. *Leo Strauss: an intellectual biography*. New Haven and London: Yale University Press.

Tartar, Michele Lise 2001. 'Quaking in the light', in Janet More and Michele Lise Tartar (eds.), *A center of wonders: the body in early America*. Ithaca and London: Cornell University Press, pp. 145–62.

Taubes, Jacob 2004. *The political theology of Paul*. Stanford: Stanford University Press.

Temple, William 1942. *Christianity and the social order*. New York: Penguin Books.

Tenbruck, Friedrich H. 1987. 'Max Weber and Eduard Meyer', in Wolfgang J. Mommsen and Jurgen Osterhammel (eds.), *Max Weber and his contemporaries*. London: Allen & Unwin, pp. 234–67.

Teubner, Gunther (ed.) 1997. *Global law without a state*. Dartmouth: Aldershot.

Thomas, James 2002. *Diana's mourning: a people's history*. Cardiff: University of Wales Press.

Thompson, Edward P. 1963. *The making of the English working class* (2nd edn). London: Gollancz.

Thompson, Laurence G. 1996. *Chinese religion: an introduction*. Belmont: Wadsworth Publishing Company.

Troeltsch, Ernst 1931. *The social teaching of the Christian Churches*. London: George Allen & Unwin.

Turner, Bryan S. 1974. *Weber and Islam: a critical study*. London: Routledge & Kegan Paul.

1986. *Citizenship and capitalism: the debate over reformism*. London: Allen & Unwin.

1991. *Religion and social theory* (2nd edn). London: Sage.

2001. 'The erosion of citizenship', *British Journal of Sociology* 52 (2): 189–209.

2005. 'Leibniz, Islam and cosmopolitan virtue', *Theory, Culture & Society* 22 (6): 139–47.

2007. 'The enclave society: towards a sociology of immobility', *European Journal of Social Theory* 10 (2): 287–303.

2008. *Rights and virtues: political essays on citizenship and social justice.* Oxford: Bardwell Press.

2009. 'Goods not gods: new spiritualities, consumerism and religious markets', in Ian Rees Jones, Paul Higgs and David J. Erkerdt (eds.), *Consumption and generational change: the rise of consumer lifestyles.* New Brunswick: Transaction Publishers, pp. 37–62.

2011a. 'Legal pluralism, state sovereignty and citizenship', *Democracy and Security* 7 (4): 317–37.

2011b. 'Pierre Bourdieu and the sociology of religion', in Simon Susen and Bryan S. Turner (eds.), *The legacy of Pierre Bourdieu: critical essays.* London: Anthem Press, pp. 233–45.

2011c. *Religion and modern society: citizenship, secularisation and society.* Cambridge: Cambridge University Press.

(ed.) 2012. *The Routledge handbook of body studies.* London: Routledge.

Turner, Bryan S. and Khondker, Habibul Haque 2010. *Globalization East and West.* London: Sage.

Turner, Bryan S. and Zengin Arslan, Berna 2011. 'Shari'a and legal pluralism in the West', *European Journal of Social Theory* 14 (1): 139–59.

Twining, William 2000. *Globalisation and legal theory.* London: Butterworth.

Urry, John 2000. *Sociology beyond societies: mobilities for the twenty-first century.* London: Routledge.

van der Veer, Peter (ed.) 1996. *Conversion to modernities: the globalization of Christianity.* New York and London: Routledge.

Viswanathan, Gauri 1996. 'Religious conversion and the politics of dissent', in Peter van der Veer (ed.), *Conversion to modernities: the globalization of Christianity.* New York and London: Routledge, pp. 89–114.

Voorhoeve, Maaike (ed.) 2012. *Family law in Islam: divorce, marriage and women in the Muslim world.* London: I. B. Taurus.

Waghorne, Joanne Punzo 2004. *Diaspora of the Gods: modern Hindu temples in an urban middle-class world.* New York: Oxford University Press.

Warner, Marina 1983. *Alone of all her kind: the myth and cult of the Virgin Mary.* New York: Vintage Books.

Watt, Lori 2009. *When empire comes home: repatriation and reintegration in postwar Japan.* Cambridge, MA: Harvard University Asia Center.

Weber, Max 1951. *The religion of China: Confucianism and Taoism.* New York: The Free Press.

1958. *The religion of India: the sociology of Hinduism and Buddhism.* New York: The Free Press.

1966a. *The city.* New York: The Free Press.

1966b. *The sociology of religion.* Trans. Ephraim Fischoff, with an introduction by Talcott Parsons. London: Methuen.

1978 [1928]. *Economy and society: an outline of interpretive sociology*, 2 vols. Berkeley: University of California Press.

2002. *The Protestant Ethic and the 'spirit' of capitalism and other writings*. New York: Penguin.

2009a. 'Politics as a vocation', in Hans Gerth and C. Wright Mills (eds.), *From Max Weber: essays in sociology*. London: Routledge, pp. 77–128.

2009b. 'Religious rejections of the world and their directions', in Hans Gerth and C. Wright Mills (eds.), *From Max Weber: essays in sociology*. London: Routledge, pp. 323–59.

2009c. 'The social psychology of the world religions', in Hans Gerth and C. Wright Mills (eds.), *From Max Weber: essays in sociology*. London: Routledge, pp. 267–301.

Weiner, M. 1997. *Japan's minorities: the illusion of homogeneity*. London: Routledge.

Weithman, Paul 2001. 'Augustine's political philosophy', in Eleonore Stump and Norman Kretzmann (eds.), *The Cambridge companion to Augustine*. Cambridge: Cambridge University Press, pp. 234–52.

Whimster, Sam 1987. 'The secular ethic and the culture of modernism', in Sam Whimster and Scott Lash (eds.), *Max Weber, rationality and modernity*. London: Allen & Unwin, pp. 259–90.

Wilentz, Sean 2008. *The age of Reagan: a history 1974–2008*. New York: Harper.

Wills, Garry 2007. *Head and heart: a history of Christianity in America*. New York: Penguin.

Wittfogel, Karl A. 1957. *Oriental despotism: a comparative study of total power*. New Haven: Yale University Press.

Wolin, Sheldon 1961. *Politics and vision*. London: Allen & Unwin.

Woodbridge, Frederick J. E. (ed.) 1930. *Hobbes selections*. New York: Charles Scribner's Sons.

Xi, Lian 2010. *Redeemed by fire: the rise of popular Christianity in modern China*. New Haven: Yale University Press.

Yang, Fenggang 2012. *Religion in China: survival and revival under communist rule*. Oxford: Oxford University Press.

Yeğenoğlu, Meyda. 2011. 'Clash of secularity and religiosity: the staging of secularism and Islam through the icons of Atatürk and the veil in Turkey', in Jack Barbalet, Adam Possamai and Bryan S. Turner (eds.), *Religion and the state: a comparative sociology*. London: Anthem Press.

Yıldız, Ahmet. 2001. *Ne Mutlu Türküm Diyebilene Türk Ulusal Kimliğinin Etno-Seküler Sınırları (1919–1938)*. Istanbul: İletişim Yayınları.

Yurdakul, Gökçe and Yükleyen, Ahmet 2009. 'Islam, conflict, and integration: Turkish religious associations in Germany', *Turkish Studies* 10 (2): 217–231.

Zakaria, Fareed 2008. *The post-American world*. New York: W. W. Norton.

Index